MW00344909

中文百宝箱
Chinese Treasure Chest

(Simplifed Character Edition)

January – August

Volume
2

林宛芊
Marisa Fang

马慕贞
Helen Jung

傅爱玫
Rosemary Firestein

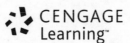
CENGAGE
Learning™

Andover • Melbourne • Mexico City • Stamford, CT • Toronto • Hong Kong • New Delhi • Seoul • Singapore • Tokyo

Chinese Treasure Chest (Volume 2)
(Simplified Character Edition)

Marisa Fang, Helen Jung, Rosemary Firestein

Publishing Director, CLT Product Director:
Paul K. H. Tan

Editorial Manager:
Zhao Lan

Editor:
Titus Teo

Associate Development Editor:
Coco Koh

Senior Graphic Designer:
Melvin Chong

Senior Product Manager (Asia):
Joyce Tan

Product Manager (Outside Asia):
Mei Yun Loh

Assistant Publishing Manager:
Pauline Lim

Production Executive:
Cindy Chai

Country Manager (China):
Caroline Ma

Account Manager (China):
Arthur Sun

ISBN-13: 978-981-4246-62-0
ISBN-10: 981-4246-62-X

Cengage Learning Asia Pte Ltd
5 Shenton Way
#01-01 UIC Building
Singapore 068808

Cengage Learning is a leading provider of customized learning solutions with office locations around the globe, including Andover, Melbourne, Mexico City, Stamford (CT), Toronto, Hong Kong, New Delhi, Seoul, Singapore and Tokyo. Locate your local office at: **www.cengage.com/global**

Cengage Learning products are represented in Canada by Nelson Education, Ltd.

For product information, visit **www.cengageasia.com**

Printed in Singapore
3 4 5 6 14 13 12 11

Message from the Authors

Chinese Treasure Chest is a comprehensive resource for anyone who wants to introduce Mandarin Chinese to young learners. It is divided into two volumes, and contains hundreds of ready-to-use games, songs, craft projects, delightfully illustrated worksheets, and teacher-directed activities designed to help children in kindergarten through eighth grade learn the Chinese language and culture. These activities could also supplement any textbook material to liven up your Chinese lessons.

Over the past ten years, we have had the unique opportunity to experiment and adapt different teaching methods in our school district's successful Chinese FLES (Foreign Language for Elementary Schools) program. This has enabled us to assemble a "treasure chest" of fun, meaningful, content-area related lessons through which our students, mostly from non-Chinese speaking families, learn Chinese and develop an appreciation for the Chinese culture.

Our teaching approach is largely influenced by Stephen Krashen's Language Acquisition Theory[1], which asserts that with natural communication and meaningful interaction in the second language, children can acquire a second language as naturally and effortlessly as they learn their first language. We strongly believe that children learn best when they are actively engaged in activities that are enjoyable to them as well as educational.

We also subscribe to Dr. Howard Gardner's Theory of Multiple Intelligences[2], which suggests that children and adults learn by means of eight different intelligences: Linguistic (word smart), Logical-mathematical (number/reasoning smart), Spatial (picture smart), Bodily-Kinesthetic (body smart), Musical (music smart), Interpersonal (people smart), Intrapersonal (self smart) and Naturalist (nature smart). Lessons and activities provided in *Chinese Treasure Chest* facilitate differentiated instruction to accommodate students with different learning styles and intelligences. In this resource, you will find a broad range of activities including:

---

[1] Krashen, Stephen. *Principles and Practice in Second Language Acquisition*, Oxford; New York: Pergamon Press (1982).

[2] Gardner, Howard. *Frames of Mind: The Theory of Multiple Intelligences*, New York: Basic Books (1983). The second edition was published in Britain by Fontana Press in 1993.

- Songs, rhymes, and Chinese dances
- Role play
- TPR (Total Physical Response)
- Storytelling
- Arts & crafts
- Riddles
- Games
- Visualizations
- Cultural activities
- Puppet shows
- Poems
- Charts and graphs
- Creating mini-books
- Cooking recipes
- Projects that foster students' critical thinking skills
- Integrated technology; online research, PowerPoint presentations, online dictionary

In addition, we have carefully integrated the "5Cs" principles of ACTFL[3]'s National Standards for Foreign Language Education — Communication, Cultures, Comparisons, Connections, and Communities, into the activities of this resource book.

Chinese Treasure Chest is organized into 12 monthly sections and incorporates themes that directly correspond to the content areas in the elementary school curriculum. Each activity is clearly defined by its type (e.g. Coloring, Song, etc.) and its level of difficulty (Beginner, Intermediate or Advanced). This format enables teachers to pick and choose the activities that are best suited to their students' needs and abilities.

The Cultural Link section provided for each month features holidays, seasonal events and various topics about culture to celebrate and discuss. Notes for teachers are provided to explain each activity, the learning objectives and suggested strategies to achieve the desired outcomes. This information allows educators to choose the activities best suited to their student population, time constraints and classroom settings. Reproducible materials such as song sheets, coloring pages, puzzles, cut-outs and flash cards are included in *Chinese Treasure Chest* to support each lesson. The *hanyu pinyin* used in this book is referenced from the Contemporary Chinese Dictionary (5th edition, Commercial Press, China, 2005).

---

[3] ACTFL: American Council on the Teaching of Foreign Languages (www.actfl.org).

How to use this resource book?

1. Browse the Table of Contents to choose the activity based on the desired lesson theme, activity type and level of difficulty.

Beginner ☆
Learners who are at the early stage of learning Chinese. They use a limited number of isolated words, two or three-word phrases, and/or longer memorized expressions in familiar topic areas. They rely on pinyin most of the time.

Intermediate ☾
Learners who can interpret new information and messages in new contexts when supported with contextual clues. They are able to handle a limited number of everyday social interactions. They are able to read and write Chinese characters with some help of pinyin.

Advanced ○
Learners who have a broad enough vocabulary for discussing social and academic topics, and understand speech at a normal rate. They are able to read and write short passages with minimal assistance.

2. Follow the page reference to the teachers' notes to check for any special instructions for that activity.
3. Follow the page reference to reproducible worksheet(s) needed to complete the activity.

Chinese language is spoken by one-fifth of the world's population. China's world influence continues to grow, and it is increasingly important for us to prepare the next generation of young people with the language skills and expanded world view to compete and be successful in today's global market. We find great joy and satisfaction in putting together *Chinese Treasure Chest*, and we sincerely hope that this resource will help you and your students succeed in the learning of Chinese and Chinese culture.

Marisa Fang (林宛芊)
Helen Jung (马慕贞)
Rosemary Firestein (傅爱玫)

New York, USA

January
一月

☆ Beginner ☾ Intermediate ☆☾ Beginner-Intermediate ☾◯ Intermediate-Advanced ◯ Advanced ☺ All

February
二月

☆ Beginner   ☾ Intermediate   ☆☾ Beginner-Intermediate   ☾○ Intermediate-Advanced   ○ Advanced   ☺ All

T A B L E   O F   C O N T E N T S

March
三月

☆ Beginner ◖ Intermediate ☆◖ Beginner-Intermediate ◖○ Intermediate-Advanced ○ Advanced ☺ All

☆ Beginner   ☾ Intermediate   ☆☾ Beginner-Intermediate   ☾○ Intermediate-Advanced   ○ Advanced   ☺ All

April
四月

☆ Beginner ☾ Intermediate ☆☾ Beginner-Intermediate ☾○ Intermediate-Advanced ○ Advanced ☺ All

T A B L E   O F   C O N T E N T S

May
五月

☆ Beginner   ☾ Intermediate   ☆☾ Beginner-Intermediate   ☾○ Intermediate-Advanced   ○ Advanced   ☺ All

T A B L E   O F   C O N T E N T S

June
六月

☆ Beginner   ☾ Intermediate   ☆☾ Beginner-Intermediate   ☾◯ Intermediate-Advanced   ◯ Advanced   ☺ All

July
七月

☆ Beginner   ☾ Intermediate   ☆☾ Beginner-Intermediate   ☾○ Intermediate-Advanced   ○ Advanced   ☺ All

August
八月

☆ Beginner ☾ Intermediate ☆☾ Beginner-Intermediate ☾○ Intermediate-Advanced ○ Advanced ☺ All

Appendices
附录

T
A
B
L
E

O
F

C
O
N
T
E
N
T
S

Notes for Teachers
教学重点

January 一月

January Calendar 一月月历

☺ **1. Coloring Activity: Zodiac Animals 涂颜色：十二生肖** 74

Students will enjoy coloring the zodiac animals as a follow-up activity after hearing the story about the zodiac animal race. These pictures can also be enlarged, colored and laminated for use in lessons about the Chinese zodiac.

听了十二生肖的故事以后，学生会更喜欢这个涂色活动。教师可以把图片放大，塑封作为教具。

2. My January Calendar 我的一月月历 75

The calendar provided for each month can be used in a variety of ways. To begin with, the picture on the calendar page can be used as a springboard for discussion about the month's cultural theme. It can also be used to review numbers, days of the week, and special days that occur in each month. It may be necessary to provide copies of the calendar with numbers for new learners; more advanced learners can be directed to write the numbers themselves.

This month's calendar can also be used to count down the number of days until the first day of the Lunar New Year or, if you are planning one, the day of your school's Lunar New Year celebration.

月历可供多种用途。
一、主题讨论：用月历上的图片谈论当月的文化主题；
二、教数学：初学中文时，由教师在月历填上数字。教过数字后，让学生们在月历上描数字、读数字；程度较好的学生可以组成小组或全班一起在月历上写数字；
三、学星期：可让孩子用月历来练习说星期一至星期日；
四、说节日：可用月历来说明和谈论当月的特殊日子，如节日、生日等。

本月月历也可以用来倒数农历新年或学校的春节庆祝日。

3. What's Happening in January? 一月知多少? 76

This fill-in-the-blank worksheet, which is included with each month, allows advanced learners to review numbers, dates, important holidays and events of that month in a familiar and consistent way.

高年级的学生可以在月历的基础上，通过这样的填空题复习数字和星期，熟悉每月重要的日子。

☆ Beginner ☾ Intermediate ☆☾ Beginner-Intermediate ☾○ Intermediate-Advanced ○ Advanced ☺ All

Zodiac Animals 十二生肖

☺ **1. Story-Telling: Zodiac Animal Story 讲故事：十二生肖的故事**

Bring the Zodiac Animal story to life by using a set of large, brightly colored zodiac animals and strip of blue cloth to represent the river when telling the story.

Arrange the animals in the correct order away from students' view. When it is time to name each of the animals that finishes the race, provide students with a clue, such as the animal's first letter, and invite them to guess. After students guess "ox" as the second animal, use the props to demonstrate how the clever rat rode on the ox's back when he swam across the river.

教师放大十二生肖图片（彩色图片为佳），并用蓝色布条作河景来讲述生肖的故事。依十二生肖的顺序先后介绍动物图片。教师可以偶尔停顿卖关子，制造悬念，激发脑力，提升学习兴趣。可强调聪明的老鼠如何骑在牛背上过河，赢得比赛。讲故事的时候，声音和表情可以夸张些。

☺ **2. Role Play: The Cat and the Rat 角色扮演：花猫与老鼠的故事**

"The Cat and the Rat" is a popular version of the zodiac animal story that can easily be made into a drama in which students participate by pretending to be the animal that they are assigned to represent.

You will need a pre-made cut-out of each of the zodiac animals plus one for the cat and a prop for the river. You may wish to tape a stick onto the back side of each animal to make it into a zodiac animal "lollipop". Start by assigning a zodiac animal for each student to represent and asking them to line up on one side of the classroom. If there are more than 13 students in the class you can ask some students to be in pairs or repeat the story again with a second set of students and let the others observe. Place the prop for the River of Heaven in front of the students and indicate where the finish line to the race is. Now you are ready to act as narrator and begin telling the story, "The Cat and the Rat". As students listen to the lively description of the zodiac animal they are portraying, they should be encouraged to act out how the animal crosses the river and races to the finish line. Most students will love to use their imagination to figure out the best possible way to act out their animal's character. It is especially fun to see how the other animals interact with the cat that was tricked!

You may wish to do a follow-up activity to see how well the students remember the story. Students who participate in this little drama usually remember the story very well.

《花猫与老鼠的故事》是一个很流行的生肖故事版本。可让学生搬演其中的故事情节，借以引介十二生肖。

预先剪出各生肖动物以及花猫和河流的图片作为道具。在动物图片背面贴上小棒子，制成"动物棒棒糖"。给学生分配动物角色，让他们在教室的一边排成一线。若班上有超过13位学生，可分成两组轮流进行角色扮演。将天河布景摆在学生面前，并指明赛跑终点线的位置。一切准备就绪，便可充当叙述者讲述《花猫与老鼠的故事》。当学生听着有关他们所扮演的动物角色的生动描述时，鼓励他们搬演动物游过天河抵达终点的情节。多数学生会喜欢运用想象力想出体现动物个性的最好方法，尤其是众生肖动物和受骗花猫之间的互动。

表演完毕，教师可适时复习动物名称及故事内容。通常戏剧表演的体验能帮助学生加深印象。

☆ **3. Vocabulary Flash Cards: Zodiac Animals 词卡：十二生肖**

After students become familiar with the Zodiac Animal story, they can use the worksheet on

☆ Beginner ☾ Intermediate ☆☾ Beginner-Intermediate ☾〇 Intermediate-Advanced 〇 Advanced ☺ All page 77 to make zodiac animal flash cards. Making constant reference to the story will enhance the learning of these vocabulary words and help make this activity more interesting.

学生熟悉十二生肖的故事后，便可用本页图片制作词卡。教师可联系本页词汇和生肖故事以促进学习，增添本活动的趣味性。

☆ **4. Find and Color: Who Are the Winners? 找一找，涂一涂：谁赢了?** 78

Begin with a brief review of the zodiac animal story and the animal names in Chinese. Students can then work alone or in small groups to complete this activity in which they must find and color the zodiac animals.

先复习十二生肖的故事和动物名称，然后让学生独立或组成小组找出赢得赛跑前十二名的动物，然后给它们涂上颜色。

☾◯ **5. Group Activities: Zodiac Animal Challenge 集体游戏：生肖挑战**

1. Activity 1: This is a fun group activity to review the 12 zodiac animals. Divide the class into teams of four or five students. Give each team a sheet of paper and a pencil and ask them to brainstorm to list as many of the 12 animals they can remember. The team that recalls the most animals in the allotted time wins. To take this challenge to a higher degree of difficulty, ask teams to list the animals in the correct order.

   活动一：复习十二生肖名称。将全班分成4至5人一组，分别给纸和笔。要求学生尽可能依顺序写出生肖名称。（依学生程度可写英文、拼音或汉字。）在指定时间内写出最多动物的小组获胜。

2. Activity 2: Distribute a set of 12 zodiac animal cards to each team. Teams will first race to put the animal cards in the correct order. When this task is completed, team members will work together to remember the names of all 12 animals in Chinese. The first team to do this wins the "race".

   活动二：每组分一套十二生肖图卡或字卡。每组比赛将十二生肖依顺序排好。最先完成的小组为赢家。（依学生程度，教师可以使用有动物图片或没动物图片的字卡。以汉字或拼音注明为宜。最好不要有英文。）

3. Activity 3: Sing a song of the 12 zodiac animals using the same melody as "Twinkle, Twinkle, Little Star". The lyrics are as follows:

   活动三：用《一闪一闪亮晶晶》的旋律来唱《生肖歌》。

   鼠牛虎兔，龙蛇马羊，
   (Twinkle, twinkle, little star,)

   猴鸡狗猪，十二生肖。
   (How I wonder what you are.)

   老鼠第一，猪在最后。
   (Up above the world so high,)

   老鼠第一，猪在最后。
   (Like a diamond in the sky.)

   鼠牛虎兔，龙蛇马羊，
   (Twinkle, twinkle little star,)

   猴鸡狗猪，十二生肖。
   (How I wonder what you are!)

☆ **6. Cut and Paste: What Is the Next Zodiac Animal?**
剪一剪，贴一贴：下一个生肖是什么? 79

This cut and paste activity provides a challenge for students to recall the correct order of the zodiac animals in the race. The three pictures at the bottom provide a hint to assist the beginner learners.

这个剪贴活动让学生练习排列生肖的正确顺序。本页下方的三张图是答案提示。

答案：2001—蛇；2005—鸡；2010—老虎

☆ Beginner ☾ Intermediate ☆☾ Beginner-Intermediate ☾◯ Intermediate-Advanced ◯ Advanced ☺ All

Review the names of the 12 zodiac animals in pinyin and Chinese character so that students will be able to do this activity. Students can then cut out the pictures and work with a partner to play a matching game or a memory game.

进行这个活动前先复习十二生肖的名称（汉字和拼音）。学生可以把图和字分别剪开，然后和伙伴进行图卡配对和记忆游戏。

Using the Venn Diagram provided on page 390, students will compare two zodiac animals. Describe their color, size, body parts, and what they can do (run, climb, swim, etc).

Depending on the students' level, the teacher may require students to write the names of the zodiac animals in Chinese character, pinyin, or English. For the bonus question, the teacher may ask the students to search online to find Chinese idioms that use one or two animals.

用第390页的异同比较表来比较两种动物的异同。描述它们的颜色、大小、四肢，以及能做的事（例如跑、爬、游泳、飞等）。

教师可视学生程度，要求他们用中文、拼音或英文写下十二生肖的名字。至于后面的加分题，教师可引导学生上网搜索含有一或两个动物名称的成语。

If possible, pre-record animal sounds for this activity. Otherwise, mimic the animal sounds for students to guess the name of the animals in Chinese.

可能的话，预录一些动物的叫声，让学生猜是哪一种动物。（玩具店可能有此类玩具。）否则，模仿动物叫声也可以。

> **答案**：1. 鸡；2. 老鼠；3. 龙；4. 老虎；5. 马；6. 猪；
> 7. 蛇；8. 兔子；9. 羊；10. 狗；11. 牛；12. 猴子

A quick TPR activity to review action words will be helpful in preparing for this mini book activity. Next, review the animals' names in Chinese and ask students to name the actions that each animal can do. Students can then follow directions to make a mini-book, color the pictures and practice reading the sentences on each page. Upon completion, students can read their mini-books to each other in small groups or volunteer to read them in front of the class.

先用 TPR 肢体反应教学法复习动作词汇。然后复习动物名称，问学生动物能做什么（例如：牛会做什么？答案：牛会拉车）。学生依步骤制作小书，涂色后随教师练习阅读小书。最后，可让学生和伙伴互相朗读，或者请一小组同学自愿到台上朗读给全班同学听。

> **答案**：图五：吃；　图六：拉；　图七：爬；　图八：跳；　图九：飞；　图十：游泳；
> 图十一：跑；　图十二：吃；　图十三：爬；　图十五：吠；　图十六：睡觉

Invite students to take turns reading the personality traits of each zodiac animal, and then follow with a class discussion. Encourage students to bring the chart home and share it with their family.

教师请学生轮流念每个生肖的个性，随后引导全班讨论。学生可把生肖个性图表带回家，与家人分享中国生肖的趣味性。

☺ **12. Writing Activity: What Zodiac Animal Sign Do They Have?**

To complete this activity, students need to know the year that each member of their family was born. Next, refer to the chart on page 87 and conduct a class discussion about the personality traits. Then direct students to fill in the blanks of the wheel with appropriate words (either in English or Chinese). More advanced students can extend each sentence by adding adjectives listed in the chart (p. 87) to describe their family members.

事先请学生问明家人的出生年，然后参考前页生肖个性，和全班一起讨论生肖与个性的关系。接着，教师视学生程度，指导学生完成生肖轮盘和下方的问题。程度好的学生可以从第87页的生肖个性图表中选出更多形容词加入句中，拓展句子。

◖○ **13. Draw and Write: My Favorite Zodiac Animal**
画一画，写一写：我最喜欢的生肖

For further practice, ask students which of the animals they are able to draw or if they keep any of the animals as pets. More advanced students should be encouraged to share as much information as possible in Chinese.

作为延伸活动，可让学生画出十二生肖中他们最喜爱或者最想饲养的动物。程度较好的学生可用中文分享。

☆◖ **14. Word Search: Zodiac Animals ❶ 找一找：生肖 ●**

This word search activity provides students with more practice to learn the names of the zodiac animals in Chinese thoroughly. First, students must write the English translation for each of the animal names, then they must find all of the words in the puzzle in pinyin.

首先，学生必须把生肖的中文名称翻译成英文，然后在字谜中找出动物的拼音字。答案可向右、向下、逆向或斜行。

☆◖ **15. Word Search: Zodiac Animals ❷ 找一找：生肖 ●**

This activity will help students identify Chinese words for animals.

这个字谜活动能加强学生对动物的中文名称的辨识。

☺ **16. Art Project: Zodiac Animal Projects 创意手工：十二生肖手工艺**

Making a special project about the zodiac animal that represents the coming new year is a terrific way to generate excitement for and decorate your school during the Lunar New Year holiday. You can easily find templates and ideas for zodiac animal projects appropriate for your class on the Internet. Many of the projects can be done using recycled materials such as plastic containers or empty paper towel rolls. It is especially attractive if you have a large number of students making the same project and display them together in one area of the school. (See project sample on p. 399)

指导学生制作新年的生肖手工艺品不仅可以提升学习兴趣，也可增添学校的新年气氛。教师可以很容易地在网络上找到合适的资料。鼓励学生使用再循环的材料制作手工，既环保又经济。（作品展示见第399页）

☆ **17. Art Project: Chinese Zodiac Lantern 创意手工：生肖灯笼**

Firstly, ask students to draw the missing zodiac animals. Then, color the zodiac animals and cut out the lantern shape. (See project sample on p. 399)

指示学生补上三个空白的生肖，然后涂色，并剪下灯笼形状。（作品展示见第399页）

☆ Beginner   ◖ Intermediate   ☆◖ Beginner-Intermediate   ◖○ Intermediate-Advanced   ○ Advanced   ☺ All

18. Art Project: Zodiac Fortune Wheel 创意手工：生肖轮盘

Cut out the two circles to make the two parts of the zodiac wheel. Then cut out the two windows on wheel A. Place wheel A on top of wheel B and attach the center with a brass paper fastener. Students enjoy using this to look up friends and family member's Chinese zodiac signs and personality traits.

剪下两个圆形，并按虚线剪下轮盘 A 的两个框。将轮盘 A 放在轮盘 B 上面，用大圆钉钉牢。学生喜欢用这个作品来找出朋友或家人的生肖和个性。

☆☾ 19. Art Project: Zodiac Animal Necklace, Headband, or Banner
创意手工：生肖项链、头环和条幅

The zodiac animals found on page 77 can be used to make any of these projects. First, students should color and cut out the 12 zodiac animals.

1. To make a necklace, students can arrange the animals in the correct order in a circle and paste onto a 18" strip of construction paper, then staple the two ends together to form a necklace. (See project sample on p. 400)

2. To make a headband, provide each student with two 18"x 3" strips of construction paper stapled together. Students can then arrange and paste the animals onto the strips beginning about 4" from the left side. Cross the two ends of the strips and staple them together so that the headband fits nicely on the student's head.

3. To make the banner, follow the directions for the headband, but arrange and paste the pictures vertically.

学生可以将词卡（第77页）上的图片剪下做以下手工：

一、项链：把十二生肖涂色后依顺序排成圆圈，贴在18"图画纸条上。将纸条两端钉起来，即成项链。（作品展示见第400页）

二、头环：将两条 18"x3" 纸条钉成一条，分发给每一个学生。学生把生肖词卡按顺序贴好，开端留出 4"。然后依学生头围将两端钉拢。

三、条幅：将两条 18"x3" 纸条钉成一条，把十二生肖涂色后按顺序纵向排列。在纸条上端贴一小棍儿即成。

☾○ 20. Reading: Story of the 12 Zodiac Animals 读一读：十二生肖的故事

Provide each student with a copy of the story to follow along while it is read to them. Using the pinyin translation provided will be helpful to beginner students. Be sure to explain the highlighted vocabulary words.

教师在念故事给学生听的时侯，可为每位学生提供本页短文，让他们边听边读。

借由拼音辅助，学生可以大声朗读十二生肖的故事。然后教师解说重要生词（粗体标示的词汇）。

☾○ 21. Vocabulary Review: Story of the 12 Zodiac Animals
词汇练习：十二生肖的故事

This exercise requires students to match Chinese vocabulary words from the story with their meanings in English.

此练习要求学生将故事里的中文词汇及其英文意思正确连线。

> **Answer key:** 十二生肖 – 12 zodiac animals; 请求 – asked; 召集 – summoned (called); 聪明的 – wise; 最先 – first; 结束 – ended; 开始 – began; 最后 – at last; 忘记 – forgot; 动物 – animals; 赛跑 – race; 重复 – repeated.

☆ Beginner ☾ Intermediate ☆☾ Beginner-Intermediate ☾○ Intermediate-Advanced ○ Advanced ☺ All

☾○ **22. Quiz: Story of the 12 Zodiac Animals** 考考你：十二生肖的故事 96

This quiz can be used to assess how well students know the story of the 12 zodiac animals. For additional practice students can also be asked to fill in pinyin for each word.

这个活动可以用来测试学生对十二生肖故事的理解程度。作为额外练习，可让学生为每个汉字填上拼音。

答案：1. 聪明；2. 忘记；3. 动物；4. 赛跑、最先；5. 召集；6. 重复；7. 开始；8. 请求；
9. 最后、结束、十二生肖；10. 鼠、牛、虎、兔、龙、蛇、马、羊、猴、鸡、狗、猪

○ **23. Math Fun: Chinese Zodiac Animals** 算一算，数一数：十二生肖 97

Students may need to refer to the story of the 12 zodiac animals on page 93 and the personality trait chart on page 87 to complete this math activity about zodiac animals.

请学生参考第93页和87页来做这个练习。必要时教师提供协助。

挑战题答案：五

Chinese New Year (Spring Festival) 农历新年（春节）

Chinese New Year provides us with scores of opportunities to teach our students about Chinese culture. Children love learning about the customs and traditions associated with this wonderful holiday. You can create an exciting environment in your school by having your students make bright red and gold decorations to hang. There are many to choose from in this unit. Students will gain a deeper appreciation for Chinese culture through enjoying the numerous activities introduced this month.

庆祝农历新年是介绍中国文化的好机会。学生喜欢了解春节的传统习俗。教师可以设计一些喜庆贺岁的手工进行教学，用学生作品来布置学校，增添春节气氛。书中提供许多材料供选择。经由这些手工制作，学生可以深入体验春节的传统文化。

☆☾ **1. Vocabulary Flash Cards: Chinese New Year** 词卡：农历新年 98

This set of flash cards introduces nine new words that are associated with Chinese New Year. Students should cut out and color their own sets of cards for review and practice.

这套词卡介绍和农历新年相关的九个新词语。学生可以把词卡剪出来并涂色，作为练习与复习之用。

☆☾ **2. Word Search: Chinese New Year** 找一找：农历新年 99

This word search activity allows students to review the newly learned vocabulary about Chinese New Year in a fun way.

此活动让学生通过有趣的方式复习刚学到的农历新年词语。

☾○ **3. Vocabulary Review: Chinese New Year** 词汇练习：农历新年 100

To complete this review worksheet students must read clues about the new vocabulary words and fill in the correct word using characters or pinyin.

要完成这个练习，学生必须先看提示，然后用汉字或拼音填写答案。答案如下。

Answer key: 1. 生肖 2. 鱼 3. 饺子 4. 红包 5. 舞龙／舞狮 6. 桔子
7. 鞭炮 8. 守岁 9. 恭喜发财 10. 春节

☆ Beginner ☾ Intermediate ☆☾ Beginner-Intermediate ☾○ Intermediate-Advanced ○ Advanced ☺ All

Many children are not familiar with many of the traditional foods eaten to celebrate Chinese New Year. If possible, bring in some of the foods to show students. After checking for food allergies, you may wish to let students who are willing to sample some of them.

很多学生对中国春节的传统食品不熟悉。教师可以设法准备一些传统的新年食品在课堂上展示并让自愿的学生试吃。教师务必事先查询学生是否对某些食品过敏（如花生、瓜子等）。

Distribute this survey worksheet to use as a follow-up activity after introducing the Chinese New Year foods. Students can conduct a survey with their classmates using the question "你喜欢吃_____吗？"

首先和学生复习第101页的词汇，接着分发第102页的问卷。教师指导学生用"你喜欢吃_____吗？"进行问卷调查。

In the first line of this rhyme, "Dong, dong, qiang" represents the sound of gongs and drums. Students can simulate this sound by clapping and tapping their legs or by using percussion instruments such as castanets, bells, and tambourines. Participation that includes making some noise while reciting this rhyme makes it much more fun for children to learn and remember.

这是一个顺口好记的数来宝。第一行是锣鼓的声音。念数来宝时，教师可以指导学生用拍手、拍腿、或用打击乐器如响板或铃鼓来制造音效，增添趣味性，加深印象。

After a class discussion about Chinese New Year customs, students can make their own little book as a review and to take home to their families. To make this book, students need to cut out the pages, put them in order, staple the book together and color the pictures. Upon completion, students can practice reading their mini-book in small groups or in front of the class.

全班讨论农历新年的传统习俗后，便可以制作自己的小书。先将图片剪下，依顺序排好，让教师打钉，然后涂色。最后教师带领全班朗读课文，并让学生彼此分享成果。可请一组学生上台朗读。必要时教师给予协助。答案见下文。

> **Answer key:** Picture 1: clean, sweep, new; Picture 2: couplets, paper, cuts; Picture 3: clothes, haircuts; Picture 4: reunion; Picture 5: chicken, duck, fish, dumplings; Picture 6: Gong Xi Fa Cai, envelopes; Picture 7: firecrackers

To complete this activity, students need to identify each of the characters, find its corresponding letter in the code box and write that letter above the character. After cracking the code students will reveal the secret phrase connected with Chinese New Year.

辨识每一个汉字，将它相应的英文字母逐一填入空格里以组成一串密语。答案见下文。

> **Answer Key:** We wear red for good luck and to scare away evil spirits.

☆ Beginner　☾ Intermediate　☆☾ Beginner-Intermediate　☾○ Intermediate-Advanced　○ Advanced　☺ All

9. Character Code Challange: Chinese New Year Message ❷
解码游戏：新年密语 ⬤ 109

Same as above. See answer key below.

方法同上。答案见下文。

> **Answer Key:** Whole fish are served with the heads and tails on to represent happy beginnings and endings.

10. Art Project: Lucky Messages for New Year 创意手工：新年吉祥话 110

Read and discuss the meaning of these popular New Year phrases with students. Each student should then choose their favorite one and write it on a sheet of red construction paper with a calligraphy brush or black marker.

向学生解说每一句吉祥话的意义并带领朗读。然后让学生选择一句吉祥话，用黑色马克笔或毛笔写在红纸上。

11. Art Project: Chinese New Year Couplets 创意手工：对联 111

Teachers may enlarge and copy these two templates on red papers for students to practice writing the lucky messages learned on page 110. Ask students to choose their favorite ones and practice writing them. When they are ready to make their good copy, provide each student with the project sheet found on page 111 which they will need to cut out. Students can then write the couplets on the project papers with a calligraphy brush, gold paint pen, or marker. Their completed couplets project can be hung on both sides of a door frame at school or at home to bring good luck. (See project sample on p. 400)

教师可将本页放大，印在红纸上，让学生练习书写在第110页所学过的吉祥话。学生可以选择他们最喜欢的吉祥话来练习书写。熟练后，可为学生提供第111页的图案，让他们剪出来，然后用毛笔或马克笔在上面写出吉祥话，制作对联。可将他们的成品挂在门框两边以图好运。（作品展示见第400页）

12. Art Project: Chinese New Year Ornament – Paper-cut Fish
创意手工：新年挂饰 112

This paper-cut fish art project looks even more colorful if the picture is copied on bright colored paper. Fold the sheet in half vertically with the illustration facing out. Cut along the lines to make the symmetrical fish ornament. Color the picture and paste it onto a sheet of construction paper. Hang it up for display. (See project sample on p. 400)

将本页图案用红纸复印。从中间对折，图形向外。依虚线剪出左右对称的双鱼和"吉"字。涂色后贴在红色或金色纸板上，做成挂饰。（作品展示见第400页）

13. Art Project: Dragon Puppet 创意手工：龙头纸偶 113

Color and cut out the dragon picture. Paste the dragon's head onto the base flap of a folded brown paper bag. Provide students with four 3"x2" pieces of colorful tissue or crepe paper to attach to the sides of the bag. Demonstrate how to write the character for dragon for students to copy on the front of the paper bag. (See project sample on p. 400)

学生在龙的图画上涂色，并剪下图案，贴在折平的牛皮纸袋底部的四方形处。另外准备一些小彩条让学生粘贴在龙面四周，作为龙须。最后指导学生在做好的成品上写上"龙"字，并在龙身上彩绘。可展示一些龙的图片或样本让学生参考模仿。（作品展示见第400页）

This art project has a special significance because the fish is a good luck symbol in Chinese culture. Explain to students that the words for "fish" and "surplus" have the same sound in Chinese and, because of this, fish are considered lucky. (See project sample on p. 400)

制作前，教师先解说"鱼"在中国文化里代表的意义（"鱼"和"余"同音，象征年年有余）。然后分发图画和材料，依纸上的步骤完成作品。（作品展示见第400页）

Make copies of these templates on yellow or red paper if possible. Fold in half along the dotted line and cut along the black lines. Open up and paste diagonally onto a 9" square of red construction paper (use the reverse side to hide the dotted line). These decorations look particularly nice when displayed horizontally and/or vertically. Another option is to trace the patterns on bright origami paper and cut them out. (See project sample on p. 401)

把第115页的模板剪下并复印在黄纸或是红纸上。沿虚线对折，依黑线剪下，张开即成左右对称的吉祥字。将字贴在四方形的对角线上（背面朝上以遮盖虚线），做成挂饰。（作品展示见第401页）

You can use the hand-made red envelope project or store-bought ones to teach your students about the custom of giving red envelopes filled with lucky money as a gift for the New Year. Fill the envelopes with paper money or a "lucky" penny and when it is time to give them out, use this occasion to explain the polite way of giving and receiving gifts in Chinese culture: with two hands. It is also a great opportunity to teach the popular New Year greeting, "Gōng Xǐ Fā Cái". When giving out the red envelopes say "Gōng Xǐ Fā Cái" to each child and ask them to say it back to you because you would like to have happiness and good fortune in the New Year, too! "Sam and the Lucky Money" is a good book to read and discuss with the class in conjunction with the red envelope activity.

As character education (such as sharing, caring, respectful, honest, etc) is greatly reinforced in elementary curriculum, through reading and discussing the story with your class, it is appropriate to integrate the character education curriculum into this project. (See project sample on p. 401)

用第116页的模板制成红包，或用从商店买来的红包来介绍农历新年时小孩向大人拜年拿红包的习俗。教师可以用玩具纸钞或象征性的"幸运铜板"放在红包中，让学生实际体验拿红包的乐趣。教师也可借此机会向学生示范用双手送红包和接受红包的礼仪，并教导学生说"恭喜发财"的吉祥话。《Sam and the Lucky Money》是适合用来讨论农历新年和拿红包习俗的故事书。在一般小学教育阶段，培养儿童分享、关爱、尊敬、诚实等品德是很重要且必须强化的。因此，教师可以借由这本故事书延展讨论关于尊敬、爱心等相关的品德。（作品展示见第401页）

Setting off firecrackers to scare away evil spirits is an important part of the Chinese New Year celebration. Students will enjoy making their own paper firecrackers by following the directions on page 117. (See project sample on p. 401)

燃放鞭炮是庆祝农历新年不可少的传统习俗。学生会喜欢动手制作鞭炮挂饰。依照第117页的制作步骤便可完成。（作品展示见第401页）

Make the Dragon Game board with the template on page 118. It can be enlarged, mounted on oak tag and laminated to last longer. The object of the game is for players to advance their marker

☆ Beginner   ☾ Intermediate   ☆☾ Beginner-Intermediate   ☾○ Intermediate-Advanced   ○ Advanced   ☺ All

toward the dragon's head each time they answer a question correctly. The player who reaches the dragon's head first is the winner.

Different ways to play:

1. To make game cards about Chinese New Year trivia, use page 119.

2. To play the game with questions about zodiac animals, students who can translate the animals from Chinese to English or vice versa can move toward the Dragon's head.

3. To play the game with questions about Chinese numbers, prepare index cards with numbers 1-30 written in Chinese or English.

4. To play the game with solving math problems, the teacher can write a math problem on each dragon section.

5. This dragon design can also be used as a coloring activity. The teacher can use a color code such as color sections 1, 3, 5, 12 in red; color sections 2, 9, 20, 23 in green and so on, preferably in Chinese. Students can also be given the option of making their own color code.

将第118页的图放大，塑封，制成纸板游戏。学生每答对一题，便可向龙头靠近一步。先到达龙头的是赢家。

几种玩法：

1. 用第119页的题目来进行游戏。

2. 用十二生肖做题目。能说出动物中英文名称者即可晋级。

3. 用中文数字做题目。准备1-30的中文或英文数字卡。

4. 用算术应用题做题目。老师可以在龙身上的空格里加一道数学题。
（如：3 + 8 = ？，23 - 6 = ？；视学生程度调整题目难度）

5. 涂色游戏。教师可以在每一空格里指定颜色（以中文标示为宜），亦可由学生自行涂色。

☽◯ 19. Game: Chinese New Year Qs and As 问答游戏：农历新年知多少 119

The questions about the customs and traditions surrounding Chinese New Year provided on page 119 are to be used with the Chinese New Year Dragon Game. Teachers can substitute their own questions or ask students to make up some questions to use for this game, too.

本页关于农历新年的风俗习惯可以配合龙形棋一起玩。教师也可改用自己的题目或让学生自己设题。

☺ 20. Song: Happy New Year! 新年歌：恭喜！恭喜！ 120

Let students become familiar with the song by playing a recording of it, if possible. Hand out the song sheet on page 120 and go over the English translation. Practice reading the Chinese version together, with emphasis on pronunciation and tones. Challenge students to identify and circle the following Chinese characters in the song (大, 小, 每个人, 嘴, 恭喜). Students can volunteer to sing the song together in small groups in front of the class.

播放录音带让学生熟悉这首新年歌的曲调。然后把歌词发给学生，讲解英文翻译。等学生更熟悉歌曲以后，再领唱中文歌词，特别注意学生的咬字发音。教师也可以让学生找出歌词中的一些字（大、小、每个人、嘴、恭喜），增加趣味性。接着，可以请学生上台表演。

☺ 21. Recipe: Dumplings 下厨乐：包饺子 121

Making dumplings together is a tradition for many families in China. Dumplings are often served as part of the Chinese New Year meal. Share this recipe for dumplings on page 121 with your students to make in class or at home.

很多中国家庭在除夕夜有吃饺子的习俗。第121页是包饺子的食谱。教师可以在课堂上和学生讨论并示范。学生可以把食谱带回家给父母做参考。

Other Group Activities for Chinese New Year 其它的农历新年庆祝活动

Below are some other ideas for Chinese New Year celebration:

以下提供三个额外的庆祝新年的活动点子供教师参考：

☺ **22. Group Activity 1: Let's Celebrate Chinese New Year!**
集体活动一：我们一起欢庆农历新年！

Suggested activities:

1. Do an online research on the dates of the next 5-10 years of Chinese New Year. Let students draw the conclusion that Chinese New Year alternates between January and February each year.

2. Cooperate with the classroom teachers to clean the classroom to get ready for Chinese New Year.

3. Compare the similarities and the differences between Chinese New Year and New Year Day on January 1st, and the other cultures in the world that celebrate their New Year at a different time in the year.

4. Decorate the Chinese classroom with spring couplets, lanterns, ornaments, and of course, students' projects.

5. Bring samples of symbolic Chinese New Year foods for students to see.

一些活动建议：

1. 学生上网查询未来五至十年里农历新年的确切日期。让学生由此得出农历新年是在每年一或二月的结论。

2. 和学生一起打扫教室、清理桌柜，象征除旧布新。

3. 比较农历新年和阳历新年的异同；比较农历新年和世界其他文化中的新年。

4. 用学生制作的春联、灯笼、手工艺品来装点教室。

5. 展示一些农历新年的传统食品。

☺ **23. Group Activity 2: Let's Have a Parade! 集体活动二：农历新年游行**

The Lion/Dragon parade is the most exciting event during the Chinese New Year celebration. Check with your school administrators to see if you can make a parade throughout your school on one day of the New Year period. If this is not possible, you can improvise by making a smaller parade in the classroom. If your school has a budget, you can order a Lion costume for your school's annual parade. If not or if you prefer to make a dragon for your parade, you can make one out of a large box attached with a long red length of cloth. Decorate it with paint, sequins, and pompoms.

You may assign one grade or several classes to participate in the parade, while the other students can also participate by wearing red and line up against the walls in the hallway outside their classrooms as bystanders. Student projects such as fans, ribbons (for ribbon dances), lanterns, zodiac hats, etc. can be carried in the parade. Some students can also be asked to carry musical instruments such as gongs and drums. It is important to include lively Chinese New Year music with your Dragon Parade. This can be done by carrying an electronic music player run on batteries or by having the music played over the school's PA system.

舞龙舞狮是农历新年重要的庆祝活动之一。教师向校方请示是否可以在春节当天在校内举行游行。如果不能，老师可自行在教室内举办小型游行。如果学校有预算，可为校内游行订购一套狮服。如果没有，或如果你喜欢亲手制作，也可以系着长红布条的大纸箱作为狮服，然后用颜料、珠片和彩球装饰。

☆ Beginner ᶜ Intermediate ☆☆ Beginner-Intermediate ᶜ☺ Intermediate-Advanced ○ Advanced ☺ All

教师可视学生人数多寡指定一个年级或几班参加游行。其他学生可以穿着红衣，在教室外观看游行。学生可以在游行队伍中展示手工作品，如折扇、飘带、灯笼和生肖帽子等。中国乐器如锣鼓、笙、萧等都可展示。游行时最好有热闹的农历新年配乐，如果能用学校扩音设备播放喜庆歌曲就更理想了。

☺ **24. Group Activity 3: Chinese New Year Feast 集体活动三：农历新年大餐**

Work with parents to hold a Chinese New Year feast in class or school wide. Students can use this opportunity to use chopsticks. After the feast, the teacher can conduct a survey on the board by instructing students to say "我爱（最爱）吃＿＿＿＿。" Note to teachers: always check for food allergies.

建议教师请家长协助举办全校农历新年大餐。教师务必事先查询学生是否对某些食品过敏。学生也可以借此机会学习使用筷子。之后，教师可以做问卷调查，请学生说：我爱（最爱）吃＿＿＿＿。

Lantern Festival 元宵节

☺ **1. Mini-Book: The Lantern Festival 我的小书：元宵节** 122

This mini-book explains the most important parts of the Lantern Festival. To make it, students need to cut out the book pages found on pages 122-124, put them in order, staple the book together, and color the pictures. Upon completion students can practice reading their books in small groups or volunteer to perform the story in front of the class.

学生把第122-124页的图片剪开，依顺序排好，让教师打钉，制成小书后让学生涂色。最后教师带领全班学生一起朗读。可以让学生和伙伴配对互相练习。教师可请学生们自愿上台表演。答案见下文。

> **Answer key:** Picture 1: fifteenth, Lantern; Picture 2: full, moon; Picture 3: yuan, xiao; Picture 4: lanterns, dance, fireworks; Picture 5: riddles.

☆ **2. Art Project: Chinese Lantern Paper Cut 创意手工：灯笼剪纸** 125

Copy the worksheet on yellow or red paper. Cut out the template and follow the diagrams on the worksheet to make the paper cut. Fold the dotted lines back and forth (accordion style) to the end, and then cut along the black lines to make the lantern pattern. (See project sample on p. 402)

教师先用黄色纸或是红色纸复印第125页，然后让学生把模板剪下来。接着指导学生按照图表所示，像折扇子的方式一上一下折纸。沿黑线剪出灯笼形状，打开即成。（作品展示见第402页）

☺ **3. Art Project: Chinese New Year Lantern 创意手工：新年灯笼** 126

Students will enjoy making and decorating their own Chinese New Year lantern to display for the Lantern Festival. Provide each student with a sheet of construction paper and follow the directions on the activity page to make this fun and colorful project with your students. (See project sample on p. 402)

为每个学生提供一张图画纸，按照活动纸上的指示，带领学生制作一个漂亮的新年灯笼。（作品展示见第402页）

☺ **4. Riddle Game: Riddles for Lantern Festival 猜一猜：趣味灯谜** 127

Hang 20 Chinese New Year lanterns with one riddle hanging from the bottom of each lantern. (The riddles must be numbered 1-20). Place 20 plastic cups each with a number from 1-20 on a table in the classroom and provide students with 3" x 3" squares of paper on which to write their name and the answer to the riddle. Challenge students to go from lantern to lantern and solve the riddles after reading them. Students then write the answer on the paper square and place it in the corresponding numbered cup. When time is up, announce "Lucky Draw Time". Read each riddle out loud, give the answer and take out one paper from the cup for each riddle. If the answer is correct, the student wins a prize such as a hongbao with a lucky penny inside.

准备20个新年灯笼，并为20个灯谜标上编号1-20，然后挂在灯笼下方。将20个已经编号的塑料杯（1-20号）置放在桌子上。提供每个学生几张 3" x 3" 的白纸写名字和灯谜的答案。指示学生在规定时间内去猜灯谜，然后把写上答案和名字的白纸投入对应的塑料杯里。解答灯谜时，教师大声朗读灯谜并给予正确答案，同时在对应纸杯抽出一张纸。如果答案正确，该名学生就能获得奖品。

答案：	1. 雨伞 (umbrella)	2. 扇子 (fan)	3. 筷子 (chopsticks)
	4. 毽子 (shuttlecock)	5. 茶壶 (teapot)	6. 对联 (couplets)
	7. 竹子 (bamboo)	8. 自行车 (bicycle)	9. 灯笼 (lantern)
	10. 寿桃 (peach)	11. 乌龟 (turtle)	12. 蚕 (silkworm)
	13. 鞭炮 (firecrackers)	14. 熊猫 (panda)	15. 鼓 (drum)
	16. 月亮 (moon)	17. 耳朵 (ears)	18. 香蕉 (banana)
	19. 年龄 (age)	20. 桌子 (table)	

Try It Out! 每月一练

☆(**a. Let's Talk! 说一说**

1. What's Your Zodiac Sign? 你属什么？ 129

Practice reading the lines in this dialogue with the entire class. Then ask students to read it in pairs.

可以全班朗读，也可以让学生配对练习。

☆(**2. What's Your Favorite Zodiac Animal? 你最喜欢的生肖是哪一个？** 129

Students can then take turns telling their favorite zodiac animal and explain why by referring to the personality traits on page 87.

学生可以和伙伴配对练习，说说自己最喜欢的生肖以及原因。（如有必要，可以参照第87页的生肖个性图表。）

☆(**3. Happy New Year! 新年快乐！** 129

Students will practice saying these popular Chinese New Year greetings found on page 129, and describe at least two celebration activities for Chinese New Year.

学生可以配对练习这两句普遍的新年吉祥话，同时说一说至少两个新年的庆祝活动。

☆(**b. Let's Write! 写一写** 130

天、米 、早、土、多、少

(For Character Writing Sheets, see pp. 391, 392. 写字练习纸见本书附录 pp. 391, 392。)

☆ Beginner (Intermediate ☆(Beginner-Intermediate (○ Intermediate-Advanced ○ Advanced ☺ All

Notes for Teachers
教学重点

February 二月

February Calendar 二月月历

☺ **1. Coloring Activity: Valentine's Day** 涂颜色：情人节 132

The Valentine's Day on February 14th provides us with a wide array of opportunities to introduce new vocabulary and at the same time, to incorporate much of the vocabulary learned in previous months. Valentine's Day was traditionally a romantic occasion for two people in love to celebrate their love for each other. Over time it has become more generalized and children exchange valentines with their friends, teachers and family members. Cards decorated with hearts, chocolate candies and flowers are popular Valentine's Day gifts. The traditional theme of love is further extended in the connection made between Valentine's Day and the Chinese festival, Qī Xī (七夕), which is based on the love story about the Cowherd (牛郎 Niú Láng) and the Weaving Maiden (织女 Zhī Nǚ).

教师可以借着二月十四日情人节的机会介绍生字，同时也可以复习很多以前学过的词语。情人节最早是由两人之间的爱情故事慢慢演变成今天这种泛爱式的对朋友、家人和师长的祝福。爱心卡片、巧克力糖和鲜花都是常见的情人节礼物。教师们也可借此机会介绍中国七夕牛郎织女的情人节，并让学生把东西方的情人节做个比较。

☾○ **2. My February Calendar** 我的二月月历 133

The calendar provided for each month can be used in a variety of ways. To begin with, the picture on the calendar page can be used as a springboard for discussion about the month's cultural theme. It can also be used to review numbers, days of the week, and special days that occur in each month. It may be necessary to provide copies of the calendar with numbers for new learners; more advanced learners can be directed to write the numbers themselves.

Teachers can also use the February calendar page to mark the number of days since the school year began, beginning on the first Monday of the month. This activity will support learning higher numbers as well as generate excitement about the 100th day of school.

月历可供多种用途。

一、主题讨论：用月历上的图片谈论当月的文化主题；

二、学数字：初学中文时，由教师在月历填上数字。教过数字后，让学生们在月历上描数字、读数字；程度较好的学生可以组成小组或全班一起在月历上写数字；

三、学星期：可让孩子用月历来练习说星期一至星期日；

四、说节日：可用月历记录来说明和谈论当月的特殊日子，如节日、生日等。

教师也可以利用二月月历记录开学至今的天数，可从本月的第一个星期一开始。这能辅助有关数字的学习，并且为上学一百天增添趣味。

☆ Beginner ☾ Intermediate ☆☾ Beginner-Intermediate ☾○ Intermediate-Advanced ○ Advanced ☺ All

This fill-in-the-blank worksheet, which is included with each month, allows advanced learners to review numbers, dates, important holidays and events of that month in a familiar and consistent way.

高年级的学生可以在月历的基础上，通过这样的填空题复习数字和星期，熟悉每月重要的日子。

100 Days of School 上学一百天

The 100th day of school is an important day in elementary schools across the United States. Following are some ideas for planning lessons and projects for this special day. These ideas integrate the learning of Chinese with relevant concepts taught in the disciplines of math, language arts, art and even music!

上学百日在美国小学课程中是一个重要的日子。以下提供几项相关的教学活动，当中结合了数学、语言和音乐等方面的学习。

Use the chart to teach or review the Chinese numbers from 1 to 100.

这张 "1-100" 数字表能帮助学生复习中文数字的规则性，并加强两位数的加法计算技能。

Students can work in small groups to create this banner that celebrates the 100th day of school. Each banner should have the Chinese characters, "一百" displayed in a large size in the center.

To decorate the banner students should color Chinese characters and add 100 images that the group agrees on. These images can include hand-drawn or cut-out pictures or lightweight objects glued onto the banner. If possible, hang students' banners in a prominent area in your school building for everyone to see. (See project sample on p. 402)

学生可分组制作这面百日旗，庆祝上学一百天。每面旗中心位置应有放大的 "一百" 二字。让学生将二字涂色，并加上小组所同意的一百个图样。这些图样可以是手画的，也可以是从别处剪出来的图画或轻巧的物件。学生作品可以展示在教室内或校园其他显眼处。（作品展示见第402页）

Teachers lead the class to review numbers 1-100 using the number chart on page 135. Then students can work independently or in small groups to complete this assignment.

教师用第135页的数字表带领全班复习中文数字。然后学生可以独立或分小组一起完成这个作业。

This challenging activity requires students to make up combinations of numbers that equal 100. Teachers may wish to review the numbers from 1-100 using the number chart provided and drill students using flash cards with random numbers to make sure students recognize the higher numbers necessary to complete this activity.

这个活动很有挑战性，要求学生练习两位数的加法，找出和均为一百的数字组合。教师可用数字表先让学生复习1-100的数字，并用数字卡来锻练学生认读两位数，然后再做这个练习。

☆ Beginner   ☾ Intermediate   ☆☾ Beginner-Intermediate   ☾◯ Intermediate-Advanced   ◯ Advanced   ☺ All

5. Writing Activity: 100 Words in Chinese 写一写：中文100字

Challenge students to work on their own or in a team to create a list of 100 words or phrases in Chinese. Students can use the initials and finals listed in the worksheet, as well as books, dictionaries, online resources and their Chinese folders to look up words. Upon completion, students can share and compare their lists with each other.

对程度较好的学生，这个活动具有高度挑战性。学生可以借声母韵母表的提示想出100个中文字，也可以从书本、词典、网络或笔记找字来完成这项作业。

Valentine's Day 情人节

Valentine's Day, which is very popular in America, is gaining popularity in China.

In this section we introduce new vocabulary associated with Valentine's Day and provide the opportunity to review family member vocabulary. We have included activities and projects which will support learning about this special festival and at the same time, enhance students' learning about Chinese language and culture. Finally we make a cultural comparison between Valentine's Day and the Chinese Festival Qī Xī (七夕) in relating the legend about the Cowherd (牛郎) and the Weaving Maiden (织女).

情人节在美国非常普遍，在中国也渐渐流行。本单元介绍很多和情人节相关的新词语并扩展和家人相关的形容词。 通过介绍牛郎织女的故事，学生能够认识东方情人节——七夕，借此作为一种文化比较。为了达到 "5C" 外语教学目标，我们建议学生用异同比较表 (见附录) 来比较东西方情人节的异同。

1. Sign Language: Three Important Words 手语：三个重要的字

Try introducing the words "I love you" in Chinese to beginner students for the first time accompanied by the following hand motions:

1. Point to the nose while saying 我 (wǒ).
2. Cross your arms across the chest while saying 爱 (ài).
3. Point to the person to whom you are speaking while saying 你 (nǐ).

Assign students to use this method to tell two family members these three important words as a simple homework assignment.

首先介绍三个最重要的字"我爱你"。建议用如下手语：

1. 我：食指指着自己鼻子
2. 爱：双臂环抱于胸前
3. 你：食指指着对方

鼓励学生回家用手语教家人说"我爱你"。

2. Story-telling: A Little Love Story 讲故事：小小爱情故事

While telling the story on page 141, you can demonstrate to students how to write the simplified character for love (爱). Students can follow by writing out the strokes in the empty heart at the bottom of the worksheet as you demonstrate them.

You may wish to use the reverse side to teach the traditional character (愛).

让学生在本页下端的心形内照着教师描述的故事情节描画出"爱"字。可用背面描画出其繁体字形。

☆ Beginner ☾ Intermediate ☆☾ Beginner-Intermediate ☾○ Intermediate-Advanced ○ Advanced ☺ All

☺ **3. Song: A Little Love Song 儿歌：我爱你** 142

Use the worksheet on page 142 to teach your students the Chinese words in this simple Valentine's song. After learning the words, practice singing the song to the melody of "Twinkle, Twinkle, Little Star" with the class. Students can then color their worksheet and give it to someone special as a Valentine gift.

用《一闪一闪亮晶晶》的曲调来教学生唱情人节的歌。初学的幼童只需教他们家庭成员的称谓和"我爱你"。然后学生可以涂色并剪下心形，将它送给朋友或家人作为情人节礼物。 此时如果教师认为合适的话，可以把歌词第二句改成"这个心我送给你"。

◖◯ **4. Art Project: My Little Heart for You 创意手工：我的心送给你** 143

More advanced students can take one more step by filling in the empty hearts in this valentine with the suggested words in Chinese. (See project sample on p. 402)

程度较好的学生可以在这个心形情人卡的空白处填上中文字，然后送给朋友或教师。（作品展示见第402页）

◯ **5. Word Chart: Heart to Heart 配一配：心心相印** 144

Begin by asking students to recall phrases that contain the word "心". Distribute the worksheet and discuss the meaning of each of the phrases. Use the worksheet to assess your students' understanding of the new phrases.

首先教师请学生脑力激荡想一想，"心"有哪些词语？然后解释本页所列的词语意思。下面的连一连和填空题可以测试学生的理解能力，并加强印象。

> 答案：连一连： 1. careful —— 小心 2. not worried —— 放心 3. happy —— 开心
> 4. patient —— 耐心 5. sad —— 伤心 6. attentive —— 细心
>
> 填空题： 1. 小心 2. 伤心 3. 开心 4. 耐心 5. 放心 6. 细心

◖◯ **6. Vocabulary Flash Cards: Valentine's Day 词卡：情人节** 145

The vocabulary flash cards for Valentine's Day can be used to introduce the new words necessary for the activities in this unit. An enlarged set of cards can be made to use for group activities. Copies of the cards can be made for students to review and use for games such as Memory game or Go Fish.

这个词卡是介绍情人节的相关词语。放大版的词卡可以用来进行集体活动。学生也可以用这词卡来复习，或玩记忆游戏、钓鱼游戏等。

☆ **7. Match and Write: Valentine Words 连一连，写一写：情人节词语** 146

To complete this activity students must first find the hearts with the same patterns. Then, translate the words written inside the hearts in Chinese characters or pinyin and write the answers in the matching hearts.

找出图案相同的心形。把英文字翻译成中文字或拼音，然后填入相同的心形图案中。

◖◯ **8. Word Puzzle: Valentine's Day 填字谜：情人节** 147

This activity is designed to help students become more familiar with the new Valentine vocabulary words. First, students must fill in the missing letters to form the pinyin vocabulary words. Then, they need to write each word in Chinese characters and English. At the bottom of the page students are to put all the missing letters together to form a secret phrase related to Valentine's Day.

☆ Beginner   ◖ Intermediate   ☆◖ Beginner-Intermediate   ◖◯ Intermediate-Advanced   ◯ Advanced   ☺ All

每个拼音字都少一个字母。学生填好后把中文字和英文字写在右边的横线上。最后用写在横线上的拼音字母组成有意义的语词破解下端的两个问题。

> **Answer key for the surprise 3-word phrase:** qíng rén jié; 情人节; Valentine's Day.

9. Pattern Challenge: Valentine Words 找规律：情人节词语 148

This activity provides students with another opportunity to practice reading and writing the new Valentine vocabulary words. Students need to find the pattern, fill in the missing word to complete the pattern, and demonstrate that they understand each word by drawing a picture of it in the space provided.

这个活动让学生练习认读和书写新学的情人节词语。找出中文语词的规律再填入正确中文字。然后在右边的空格里画图说明。

> 答案：2. 花；3. 心；4. 花；5. 情人卡；6. 爱；7. 巧克力；8. 二月

10. Mini-Book: My Valentine's Day 我的小书：我的情人节 149

Use the worksheets to make this mini-book. Students can assemble their books and practice reading them in pairs or small groups. Children should be encouraged to take their books home and read them to someone special.

学生可以自己制作小书，配对或分小组练习阅读。鼓励学生到台上念给同学听或把小书带回家念给特别值得分享情人节的人听。

11. Vocabulary List: Good Luck Words 词表：吉祥字 151

The good luck words presented in this unit are very popular ones in Chinese culture. Many home goods and jewelry sold in America display these words, too. If possible, bring in some objects with the characters introduced here to show students or ask students to bring in some objects to show the class. Make a set of large flash cards for group activities and individual sets of cards for students to review and practice with.

本页所列的词语是中华文化里常用的吉祥字。在北美地区，许多家庭用品或首饰盒上都常见这些字。可能的话，教师带一些印有吉祥字的物品来给学生看，或是让学生带来给同学们看。把这些吉祥字放大制成闪示卡，可分组进行游戏。

12. Art Project: Valentine Gift Box 创意手工：情人节礼盒 153

If possible, make copies of the template for this Valentine Gift Box project on colored card stock paper. Review the good luck words on pages 151-152. Students should first consider who they would like to give their gift box to and then choose the two characters they would like to write for that person on their gift box. After writing the characters with a pencil, they can trace over them with markers and add some designs before cutting and folding the box.

可能的话用彩色纸复印此情人节礼盒。学生先想好礼物要送给谁，然后从第151-152页的吉祥字表中选出合适的字写在盒面上。先用铅笔描写，然后用彩色笔加粗字，再将盒子图形剪下做成礼盒。

13. Reading: The Love Story of the Cowherd and the Weaving Maiden
读一读：牛郎织女的故事 154

Qī Xī, the Chinese festival that celebrates love can be compared to the Valentine's Day. Tell and discuss the love story about the Cowherd and the Weaving Maiden with students. Afterwards,

☆ Beginner 〖 Intermediate ☆〖 Beginner-Intermediate 〖○ Intermediate-Advanced ○ Advanced ☺ All

make a Venn diagram and ask students to provide information to reflect the similarities and differences between these two festivals. A literature book "Legend of the Milky Way" is recommended to introduce the Chinese Qī Xī Festival.

和学生讨论中国七夕牛郎和织女的故事，并和西方情人节作个比较。用附录的异同比较表列出相同和不同的地方（包括日期、节日的意义、庆祝的方式和交换礼物等习俗）。

Adjectives to Describe People 描写人物的形容词

1. Vocabulary Flash Cards: Adjectives to Describe People
词卡：描写人物的形容词 156

Make a large set of adjective flash cards to introduce the new vocabulary to the class. For each adjective presented ask students to name three classmates who have that attribute. Students can use their own set of flash cards to write down the names of three classmates for each.

用本页介绍的形容词制作一套放大的词卡。每一个形容词都请学生提名符合条件的三位同学。学生也可以在自己的词卡上写上三位同学的名字。

2. Game: Bumble Bee 游戏：小蜜蜂 157

This game is a good one for students to use the vocabulary in this unit to describe themselves and for students to interact with and learn about each other. Begin by directing students to fill out the Bumble Bee worksheet using adjectives from the vocabulary flash cards. Next, students can use their descriptions of themselves to play this game for further practice.

Divide the class into two teams. Invite one student from each team to come to the front of the class with their paper and take turns asking the question: "谁很_____?" (fill in the blank with one of the 12 adjectives) Students on the opposite team who have that answer raise their hands and respond saying, "我很_____." The student who asks the question gets one point for each player from the other team who has that adjective on their worksheet for his/her team.

After completing this activity, students' work can be put up to make a nice bulletin board display.

这个游戏让学生使用本单元的词汇来形容自己，并提供机会让他们相互交流，认识彼此。先让学生用词卡上的形容词完成本页作业。之后，学生便可将本页用来玩小蜜蜂的游戏，作为额外练习。

把全班分成两队。每队轮流由一个同学拿着作业上前问"谁很_____?"（可用12个形容词的其中一个回答）。另一队中若有同学的作业里有该形容词，便可举手回答"我很……"。如果另一队中有一人的作业里有该形容词，问话那一队的学生便可得一分，若有两人回答有，问话那一队便可得两分，依此类推。

完成活动后，可将学生的作品展示在布告栏上。

3. Writing Activity: Describe My Family Members 写一写：形容我的家人 158

This is a good writing activity that enables students to practice using new adjective vocabulary items with more familiar family member vocabulary. Encourage students to share their completed work with family members as a homework assignment for further practice.

这个写作练习可以帮助学生使用新学习的形容词来形容自己熟悉的家人。鼓励学生把作业带回家与家人分享并复习。

☆ Beginner   ⅏ Intermediate   ☆⅏ Beginner-Intermediate   ⅏○ Intermediate-Advanced   ○ Advanced   ☺ All

◐ **4. Word Search: Adjectives 找一找：人物形容词**

Students will write English meaning for each adjective word listed at the bottom. Then they will find pinyin words in the word search.

学生先把每一个拼音字翻译成英文填入空格。然后在字谜中找出这些拼音字。

◐ **5. Crossword Challenge: Adjectives 填字谜：人物形容词**

This crossword puzzle provides opportunity for students to practice translating adjectives from English to Chinese.

这个作业可让学生练习把英文形容词翻译成中文。

Telling Time 现在几点（钟）？

Telling time is an essential life skill. The following activities will reinforce students' existing time telling skills and help them practice telling time in Chinese.

具有时间观念是日常生活必须具备的技能。本活动可以强化学生既有的时间观念，进而学习用中文报时。

◐ **1. Vocabulary List: What Time Is It Now? 词表：现在几点(钟)？**

Students will cut out the clock hands and use a brass paper fastener to attach them to the clock. Now students can practice telling time in Chinese.

Teachers will first review numbers 1-12 in Chinese for the hours. After some practice, teachers will review numbers 1-60 in Chinese for the minutes. After students are familiar with the patterns, encourage them to tell time with the terms "in the morning", "at noon" and "in the evening".

学生把时针和分针剪下用铜扣钉在背面夹紧。完成后学生可以使用小钟来学习报时。首先教师带领复习1-12正点报时，接下来可以学习分钟报时（先学半小时的说法，然后15分钟，最后每分钟）。等学生熟练以后，再学习加上上午、中午和晚上的报时方法。

☺ **2. Art Project: The Clock on the Great Wall 创意手工：长城上的大钟**

Each student can make their own Great Wall Clock. Teachers can use this Clock on the Great Wall to practice with the pattern, "现在是……点钟。"(It is_____o'clock now.) Students can manipulate the clock hands and time strips to show the correct time on their clocks. Beginner students will begin with telling time using only the hours; more advanced students can include the minutes.

You may wish to make an enlarged copy of the Great Wall Clock and mount it on oak tag to display in your classroom and use periodically throughout the year. (See project sample on p. 402)

每一个学生都制作一个长城钟。然后练习句型"现在是……点钟。"学生可以用手操作显示出正确的时间。初学者只需报整点时间。程度好的学生可以加上分针报时。先学半小时的报时（一点半，两点半……）。教师也可以制作一个大型的长城钟放在教室里展示。（作品展示见第402页）

☺ **3. Card Game: Wolf, Wolf, What Time Is It? 卡片游戏：老狼，老狼，几点钟？**

This card game is a modified version of a popular Chinese game called "老狼，老狼，几点钟？(Lǎo láng, lǎo láng jǐ diǎn zhōng?)" It can be played with cards from side A, side B or both. One way to

☆ Beginner   ◖ Intermediate   ☆◖ Beginner-Intermediate   ◖◯ Intermediate-Advanced   ◯ Advanced   ☺ All

play is a simple time-telling game. Invite one student to choose a card and call on classmates who volunteer to tell the time on the card in Chinese by asking, "老狼，老狼，几点钟？"The student who tells the time correctly will choose the next card and continue playing. Another way to play is to instruct students to make their own set of cards with their own initials on them to play together in small groups. The first player will ask, "老狼，老狼，几点钟？"The other players in the group will take turns telling the time on the card. The player who tells the time correctly keeps that card. At the end of the game the player with the most cards wins.

这个活动源自儿童游戏"老狼，老狼，几点钟？"。学生可以用 A 面，B 面或双面所列的时间来练习。最简单的玩法就是说出时间。先请一位同学抽出一张卡，然后从班上请一位自愿学生问"老狼，老狼，几点钟？"。第一位学生如果说对了可以抽第二张卡继续玩。另外一种玩法是让学生在每张卡上写上自己名字的缩写，然后分小组一起玩。第一个学生问"老狼，老狼，几点钟？"同组其他学生轮流说出时间。说对的人可以拿下那张卡。最后谁拿了最多谁就是赢家。

This song borrows the tune of a popular nursery rhyme "London Bridge is falling down". The game that accompanies this rhyme is easy and fun. To play, pick two students to form an arch facing each other, join both hands together and lift their arms up. The rest of the class will form a single line with their hands on the shoulders of the one in front of them, so they can walk under the arch. The class then sings this song. Just as the song ends, the two students will drop their hands down to capture the student who is passing through the arch. That student has to tell the time that the teacher shows him/her. If the student says the time correctly in Chinese, the class gets a point. Otherwise the teacher gets the point.

用《伦敦大桥要塌了》这首歌曲的曲调来练习问时间"现在几点钟？"。先请两个学生到教室前面或中间面对面用手搭起拱门。班上其他同学排队从拱门下穿过去，同时唱着这首歌。音乐停止时，拱门放下，被拦住的学生必须说出教师手上的时间卡。答对了全班学生得一分，答错了老师得一分。

Students can work in pairs or small groups to complete these three assignments to practice telling time in Chinese. To add more fun, make it a timed challenge by seeing how long each team takes to finish all three worksheets correctly.

学生可以配对或分小组来完成这个作业。为了增加趣味性，可以计时看哪一组花的时间最多（少）。

Daily Activities 日常活动

An interesting way to introduce vocabulary related to daily activities is to use TPR to act them out yourself or call on a student to demonstrate the action as you say them in Chinese. Students can then volunteer to guess the meaning in English. You may also wish to include a TPR activity in which you ask the students to recall and act out the actions as they hear them.

After the students are familiar with this new vocabulary, sentences about daily activities can be combined with time for further practice. Making this connection between time and daily activities can help children gain a better sense of time and improve their time-management skills.

教师用TPR法来介绍每日的作息活动。学生一边跟着教师比手划脚，一边跟着念活动名称。稍后教师可以只说口令，学生必须做出动作。等学生都熟悉作息名称和动作以后，可以加上时间来练习。例如：七点钟，我起床。这个练习可以帮助学生加强作息活动的时间观念。

Begin by using TPR to demonstrate the daily activities while introducing the vocabulary words in Chinese. After practicing a few times, show some flash cards with pictures of the daily activities. Ask volunteers to name the activities. Then distribute the worksheets and ask students to cut them and make a mini-book. More advanced students can move on to the extended exercise on page 171. When the book is complete, practice reading the sentences on each page with the whole class. Then encourage individual students to volunteer to read their books in front of the class. Students can also take their books home to read to their family members.

教师用TPR法带领学生做出各种日常活动的动作，同时也一边介绍活动名称。接着教师用图片来测试学生的理解，并加强印象。然后发给同学作业纸，学生必须把图片剪开再装钉成小书。程度较好的学生可以继续完成第171页的延伸练习。教师带领全班朗读小书，并请同学自愿上台朗读，也可鼓励学生把小书带回家念给家人听。

Each sentence in this activity may have a story to tell. Let students take turns to tell why it is the earliest or the latest time that they do each activity.

学生根据个人情况写出不同的作息时间，然后轮流分享他们为什么在这些时候做这些事。

First students will explain each daily activity listed at the bottom in English. Then find the Chinese characters in the word search.

先解释作息活动的英文名称，然后在字谜中找出这些活动的中文名称。

Cultural Link: Emperor Qin Shihuang 秦始皇

The First Emperor, Qin Shihuang, is important in Chinese history. He had many achievements, yet the historians still considered him a "tyrant". This reading activity provides students with an understanding of this important figure in Chinese history.

秦始皇在中国历史上非常重要。他有许多伟大的成就，例如统一中国，统一文字、钱币、度量衡。学生在阅读短文后会对秦始皇的故事有基本的认识。

This is a reading comprehension activity to be completed by students individually or in pairs after they have read the passage about Emperor Qin.

这个阅读测试可由学生在阅读完关于秦始皇的短文后独立或配对完成。

答案： 1.统一；秦　 2.万里长城　 3.蒙古　 4.文字；钱币；度量
　　　 5.兵马俑　 6.西安　 7.虽然；但是；过失

☆ Beginner　🌙 Intermediate　☆🌙 Beginner-Intermediate　🌙○ Intermediate-Advanced　○ Advanced　☺ All

Try It Out! 每月一练

《○ **a. Let's Talk!** 说一说

Notes for Teachers
教学重点

March 三月

March is the month to celebrate Women's History and Foreign Language learning. To support these two topics we have included lessons about famous Chinese women, the community, and countries of the world, with an emphasis on how speaking a second language can be extremely useful in any community in the world.

三月的主题是妇女月和外语教学月。本月活动包括著名的华人女性简介、社区场所、世界各国地理以及各种外语的简短问候词等。

March Calendar 三月月历

☆ **1. Coloring Activity: Hua Mulan** 涂颜色：花木兰 182

We chose Hua Mulan as the cultural theme this month because March is known as Women's History Month in America. Mulan is probably the most famous Chinese woman known to American children because of the popular Disney movies about her. Many children do not realize that Mulan was a real figure in Chinese history. They love hearing the story of this brave young girl who took her father's place in the army to protect him.

以花木兰的故事作为本月月历题材以便彰显妇女月的主题。由于迪士尼电影的宣传，美国儿童对花木兰的故事非常熟悉，但很多小孩不知道花木兰是真实的历史人物。儿童可以借此机会学习花木兰的勇敢和孝顺的精神。

◖○ **2. My March Calendar** 我的三月月历 183

The cultural theme for this month is the story of Mulan. Use the picture on the calendar page to open up a discussion about this fascinating woman. In addition to using the calendar to review numbers, days of the week and special days in March, you may wish to use the calendar to indicate specific activities related to this month's topics. Plan an event around Women's History or Foreign Language Month and put it on the March calendar.

本月的文化主题是花木兰的故事。以月历上的木兰图画开场，与学生讨论著名的中外女性。可以配合妇女月和外语教学月，筹备相关活动，把它们列入三月月历里。月历的其他用途可参照一月月历说明。

◖○ **3. What's Happening in March?** 三月知多少? 184

This fill-in-the-blank worksheet, which is included with each month, allows advanced learners to review numbers, dates, important holidays and events of that month in a familiar and consistent way.

高年级的学生可以在月历的基础上，通过这样的填空题复习数字和星期，熟悉每月重要的日子。

Countries of the World 世界各国

Before beginning this unit, it is helpful to make sure students understand the difference between continents, countries, and states or provinces. Asking students to name countries they have been to is one way to determine if students do in fact know these differences. It is always helpful to have a world map available as a resource, especially for this unit.

开始本课之前，确认学生已经了解洲、国、州、省等概念。可以询问学生去过哪些国家以确定他们知道其中的不同。一份世界地图是必备的教学工具。

☺ **1. Vocabulary Flash Cards: Countries 词卡：国家** 397

An interactive technique to introduce the country names on the vocabulary list is to play a guessing game with students. First, say the name of the country in Chinese, then give a clue about the country. The clue could be the continent on which that country is located or the English translation of the country's Chinese name. The student who guesses correctly can be asked to locate the country on the world map.

可以和学生用互动的方式来学习各国的名称。先念出国家名称，然后给提示（例如：所在洲名或中文翻译名称）。答对者可以在世界地图上指出该国位置。

☾○ **2. Find and Write: Where are these Countries?**
找一找，写一写：这些国家在哪里？ 185

This activity can be completed by students individually or in small groups after a whole group introduction of the Vocabulary Flash Cards on Countries. Students will look at the map, identify each of the countries indicated and write it in the box in pinyin or in Chinese characters.

复习各国家名称以后，学生可以独立或和小组完成此作业。学生可以参考世界地图，找出各国位置，然后用拼音或汉字填写名称。

> 答案： 1. 加拿大　 2. 美国　 3. 墨西哥　 4. 英国　　 5. 德国　 6. 俄罗斯
> 　　　　 7. 韩国　　 8. 日本　 9. 法国　 10. 意大利　11. 中国　 12. 澳大利亚

☾○ **3. Question and Answer: Would You Like to Visit These Countries?**
问一问，答一答：你想不想去这些国家？ 186

After completing the worksheet on page 185, students can work in pairs to take turns asking each other about each country. This can be followed by a survey in which the teacher asks each student which country they most want to visit, recording their responses on the board.

完成前页作业后，学生可以与伙伴互相练习问答彼此的国家。然后，教师可以和全班做问卷调查，看班上同学最想去哪些国家。

☾○ **4. Greeting: Say HELLO in Different Languages 打招呼：你好！** 187

Begin by asking if anyone in class knows how to say "hello" in any language other than English or Chinese. Proceed by practicing how to say "hello" in the languages provided on page 187. Invite students to say "hello" using these languages in front of the class.

首先问学生谁知道如何用英语或中文以外的其他外语来打招呼，然后练习本页的外国语问候词。最后可以请学生上台用这些外语打招呼。

☺ **5. Word Search: Countries around the World 找一找：世界各国** 188

Students can become more familiar with their vocabulary of countries by doing this word search

☆ Beginner　　☾ Intermediate　　☆☾ Beginner-Intermediate　　☾○ Intermediate-Advanced　　○ Advanced　　☺ All

puzzle individually or in small groups.

学生做完这个字谜活动后将会加深对国家名称的印象。

☆ **6. Vocabulary List: Continents** 词表：七大洲 189

Introduce this new vocabulary list of continent names by asking students to name the continents in English. Say each of the continents in Chinese and invite students to guess which continent it is in English. After completing the list, point to each continent on a world map while saying it for the class to repeat in Chinese.

介绍七大洲名称之前，先让学生说出其英语名称。然后教师说出中文洲名，让学生猜是哪一洲。等七大洲介绍完毕后，带领学生在世界地图上找出它们的位置，再用中文念几遍。

☾○ **7. Find and Write: On Which Continent do These Countries Belong?**
找一找，写一写：这些国家在哪些洲？ 190

To complete this activity, students must be familiar with the vocabulary of countries and continents. Students first need to identify each country, and then determine which continent each of the countries is located. Students record the names of the countries under the continent headings in pinyin or in Chinese characters.

学生必须先熟悉各国以及七大洲的中文名称，然后才能完成本页的作业练习。学生必须先辨识国名，才能确定它们在哪些洲，然后再用拼音或汉字填写答案。

> 答案： **北美洲**：加拿大、墨西哥； **南美洲**：巴西； **欧洲**：俄罗斯、德国、法国、英国；
> **亚洲**：日本、中国； **非洲**：南非； **大洋洲**：澳大利亚

Landforms 地形

Landforms are an important topic in the elementary social studies curriculum. In this unit we have developed lessons that allow students to integrate learning Chinese with learning about landforms. Using the map of China is ideal for this purpose because all of the landforms introduced in this unit can be found in China. Some of the activities presented here also include topographical features of other world countries.

地形是小学社会知识课程里的一个重要主题。在此我们提供了一些结合地形与中文学习的活动和作业。由于本课所介绍的地形都能在中国找到，所以建议教师以中国地图作为教具。有些活动也加入了世界其他国家的地形特征。

☆☾ **1. Vocabulary List: Landforms** 词表：地形 191

The 12 landforms introduced in this unit contain some Chinese characters that students may already know. It may be helpful to ask students to identify those characters and discuss the literal translation of each of the words. Ask students if they can think of examples of each of the landforms and if they have visited any of them in the world.

这里所介绍的十二种地形包括了学生已经学过的汉字。可以请学生辨别这些字，并讨论它们各自的意思。问学生他们能否为各种地形提供例子，并谈谈他们是否到过那些地方。

☆☾ **2. Write and Circle: Landforms and Our World**
写一写，圈一圈：地形和我们的世界 192

This activity requires students to share their collective knowledge about places in the world to complete the task. After reading the example given, students must fill in the correct landform that the places belong to, and circle the places that are located in China. To extend this assignment, ask students to locate each of the places on a world map and share their findings with each other.

让学生分享他们对于世界不同地方的知识。看了例子后，学生要填上正确的地形名称，然后圈出位于中国的地方。作为延伸活动，可让学生在世界地图上找出这些地方的位置，并与彼此分享学习收获。

> 答案（括号里为位于中国的地方）：
> 2.（Taklimakan, Gobi）沙漠 3.（Hainan）岛屿 4. 海洋 5. 雨林 6.（Everest）高山
> 7.（Shandong）半岛 8. 深谷 9.（Dongting）湖泊 10.（Tibetan）高原 11. 火山

☆⊆ 3. **Crossword Puzzle: Landforms** 填字谜：地形 193

This crossword puzzle gives students another opportunity to practice using the definitions for each of the landforms to identify and write the correct answers in the puzzle.

这个填字谜让学生练习从各个地形的定义中得出地形的正确名称，并填上答案。

○ 4. **Map Exercise: Locate Places on a World Map Grid** 看地图：环绕地球找一找 194

This activity requires students to identify nine different places on a world map. Students must use map skills to record the locations of these places on the map, and then write the landform that each of these places belong to in Chinese. This lesson is a good example of meeting the Foreign Language standards by connecting Chinese language learning with other subject areas.

这个活动要求学生在世界地图上找出九个地方的位置。学生必须运用读图技巧，找出并写下这些地方在地图上的位置，然后用中文写出它们所属的地形。这个活动结合中文学习与其他学科内容，符合外语学习的标准。

> 答案： 2. H6；沙漠 3. H5；岛屿 4. C3, D3；雨林 5. G5；高山 6. I6, I7；半岛
> 7. H5；河流 8. B6；火山 9. G5；高原 10. B6；湖泊

⊆○ 5. **Art Project: Landform Model** 创意手工：地形模型

Students can create 3-D models of landforms in class using paper mache, clay, or recycled materials. This type of group project is both enjoyable and meaningful to students. Upon completion, students can label the landform project in Chinese and make a presentation to the class about it. (See sample on p. 403)

学生可以在班上用纸型、粘土或循环材料制作立体的地形模型。这个小组活动对学生来说既有趣又有意义。完成后，学生可以为地形模型标上中文名称，介绍给全班同学。（作品展示见第403页）

⊆○ 6. **Research: Choosing a Place to Live** 调查：选择居住的地方

Students can do an online search on the weather for the month of March for each of the following places: the Great Wall, the Himalayan Mountains, Yangtze River, Shanghai and Beijing. Each student should then name the place they would prefer to live and give reasons for their preference.

学生上网查询有关长城、喜马拉雅山、长江、上海和北京在三月份的天气概况，然后从中选出他们想要居住的地方，并提出理由。

⊆○ 7. **Art Project: Postcard Design** 创意手工：明信片制作

Teachers can provide blank index cards for students to do this project. Ask students to design a postcard that illustrates one of the places in China. Imagine they visited that place and they are sending a postcard back to their family and friends telling them how magnificent that place is.

☆ Beginner ⊆ Intermediate ☆⊆ Beginner-Intermediate ⊆○ Intermediate-Advanced ○ Advanced ☺ All

After designing the front side of the postcard, write a message, address and draw a stamp on the reverse side of the postcard.

An alternative would be to let students imagine they own an island or peninsula. They will create their piece of land on a large piece of paper. They will name their island or peninsula, and label all landscapes in Chinese.

教师可以为学生提供空白的卡片，让他们想象自己在中国其中一个地方游玩，现在要寄一张明信片回去，告诉家人朋友那里有多好玩。请学生在卡片上把这个地方画出来，然后在其背面写上文字、地址，并画上一枚邮票。

也可以让学生想象他们拥有一座小岛或半岛，在一张大纸上画出地图，为他们的小岛或半岛命名，并用中文标上所有地形的名称。

My Community 我的社区

Understanding the importance of the community in society is an essential part of the elementary social studies curriculum. This topic provides many opportunities for lessons in the Chinese classroom. Vocabulary surrounding community places and community helpers can be introduced and combined to enhance communication in the target language.

了解社区的重要性是小学社会知识教育的重要课题之一。本主题提供很多课堂活动。学生可以学习社区商店建筑名称、社会人士名称等来进行对话，学以致用。

☆ **1. Vocabulary Flash Cards: My Community 词卡：我的社区** 195

Young learners may need a brief explanation of the definition of community as a place where people live, go to school, work, receive services and have fun. Brainstorm with the class to name different types of places in their own community. Follow this discussion by introducing the Community Vocabulary Flash Cards provided in this unit.

老师可能需要向低年级解释社区的意义：它是住家附近上学、上班、购物和游乐的场所。请学生想出几处社区的重要地点，然后再依次介绍本页其他场所。

☺ **2. Find and Write: Where Can You Find Me?**
找一找，写一写：你在哪里可以找到我？ 196

This activity allows students to incorporate old vocabulary with the new vocabulary provided in this section. First, say each of the words displayed on this activity sheet with students, and then ask where in the community each of the objects can be found. Students can use the Community Vocabulary Flash Cards to find the correct answers and write them in pinyin or in Chinese characters.

The Advanced Search at the bottom of the sheet is an extra challenge for more advanced learners.

本活动可以帮助学生温故知新。先念出本页所列的字，然后问学生在哪儿可以看到或找到这些东西。学生可以参考之前的社区词卡，写出拼音或汉字。程度较好的学生可以继续完成下面的练习。

答案：1. 医院 2. 公安局 3. 学校 4. 图书馆 5. 餐馆 6. 银行 7. 邮局 8. 购物中心

☺ **3. Board Game: Tour Your Community 棋盘游戏：游览社区** 197

Use the worksheet on page 197 to play this game about community places. To play, each player takes a turn rolling the dice. When the dice drops on one of the community places, the player must choose one of the questions to answer (eg. What do you come here for? Who do you see at this place?). Players must answer the question correctly and in a full sentence to earn the points indicated in each section of the board game.

To modify this game for beginners, students can simply call out the community place in Chinese or respond by choosing one of the following words or phrases: often, never, like to go, dislike going, etc. When the teacher decides to stop the game, players will add up their points. The player with the most points wins!

学生可以用第197页的活动来进行社区游览的游戏。首先学生轮流掷骰子，依骰子点数走到社区某处。学生必须答对问题才能取得该处所标示的分数（如你来这里做什么？在这里可以看到哪些人？）。初学者也可以玩此游戏，但只需要用下列程度副词造一完整句子即可得分。累积分数最高的学生便是赢家。

我常常去…… 　　我（从来）没去过…… 　　我最喜欢去…… 　　我不喜欢去……

Use the Community vocabulary flash cards to make connections with the Community Helpers vocabulary flash cards whenever possible.

将社区场所词卡和社会人士词卡作联系，加深学生对社区环境的认识。

Students can work individually or in pairs to complete this activity. Simply rearrange the letters to discover the names of these community helpers. This task is more challenging if students do not use their Community Helpers vocabulary flash cards.

学生可以独立或与伙伴一同完成这个练习。把字母重组找出社会人士的名称。学生如果不参考社会人士词卡，这个练习将更具挑战性。

> **Answer key:** 1. lao shi　2. yi sheng　3. you chai　4. li fa shi　5. jian zhu shi　6. lü shi
> 　　　　　　　7. hu shi　8. nong fu　9. jing cha　10. xiao fang yuan　11. shang ren

Refer to vocabulary words on pages 198-199 to find the answers. For further practice with Community Helpers vocabulary, students can work with each other to read the clues and guess the correct answers.

参考第198-199页的词卡后填写答案。学生可以进一步和伙伴进行问答练习。

> **答案：** 1. 工程师　2. 农夫　3. 警察　4. 护士　5. 老师　6. 邮差
> 　　　　　7. 医生　8. 消防员　9. 记者　10. 牙医　11. 厨师　12. 渔夫

Students can become more familiar with their Community vocabulary by doing this word search puzzle individually or in small groups.

这个字谜将帮助学生加强对社区场所的认识。学生可以独立或与伙伴一起完成。

This word search puzzle gives students an opportunity to identify the Community Helpers vocabulary words in Chinese characters. It can be completed individually or in small groups.

这个字谜帮助学生认读各种社会人士的中文名称。学生可以独立或与伙伴一起完成。

☆ Beginner　🌙 Intermediate　☆🌙 Beginner-Intermediate　🌙○ Intermediate-Advanced　○ Advanced　😊 All

☽◯ 9. Art Project: Chinatown Community 创意手工：唐人街社区模型

Once students understand the concept of a community, they can easily understand the value of a specific community like Chinatown. Discuss the importance of having Chinatown communities in America for the Chinese to engage services and buy goods, and also for non-Chinese to learn about the Chinese culture.

Building a mini Chinatown is a great way for students to learn about this special community. Students can choose a particular place in a community. They will then design a picture or a model of that place and label it in Chinese. Give students limits on the size and materials used according to your specifications. For example, each project is limited to a 6″x4″ cardboard base and all materials used must be recycled items. Students can use boxes, buttons, pictures from magazines and other items. You will be amazed at your students' creativity! It is also possible to create a 3-D Chinatown community to display by using cardstock paper. Please refer to the sample in the Appendices on page 403.

Directions for 3-D Chinatown Community Project:

1. Fold a sheet of cardstock paper in half.

2. Make a 2″ margin on each side of the folded paper.

3. Cut along the margin and stop 2″ away from the end of the paper.

4. Fold this 2″ edge towards the center on each side.

5. Open the paper, pop the center out and push the 2″ margins on each side in.

学生了解社区的概念后，就容易体会像唐人街这样的特定社区的意义。老师可以和学生讨论唐人街对美国华人的重要性，以及它如何促进非华人对中华文化的了解。

制作一个迷你唐人街社区模型可以帮助学生更深入了解唐人街。首先，让学生选择社区里自己喜欢的地点，画图设计模型，然后用中文标示地点名称即成。以第195页介绍的名称为限。所需材料：6″x4″纸卡、纸盒、钮扣、杂志图片等。学生的创意将令你惊奇！学生也可以用薄板制成立体的唐人街模型。

唐人街社区模型制作方法：（参考附录第403页学生作品）

1. 将一张薄板折成一半。

2. 在折线上下端2寸处作记号。

3. 沿记号切开2寸。

4. 把切开部分向内折。

5. 打开薄板，拉出中间部分，上下2寸部分向外折即成。

Famous Chinese Women 著名华人女性

In American schools, March is known as Women's History Month. Students learn about famous women from the past and present. Many schools sponsor contests or other educational activities to recognize the great accomplishments made by women. Women's History Month provides us with an excellent opportunity to introduce some famous Chinese women and their achievements to our students. Learning about these women gives students a deeper understanding of the obstacles women have had to overcome and the tremendous advances they have made in the fields of history, the arts and sciences. This topic is important for all children to learn about, and particularly for Asian girls to know these famous women as role models.

Here are some suggested activities to celebrate Women's History Month:

Stamp of Honor: Design a postage stamp of one of the Chinese women. Be sure to include a picture or photo of the famous woman with some details related to what she is known for.

Picture Dictionary: Make a picture dictionary with at least five famous Chinese women.

Compare and Contrast: Students pick two of the famous Chinese women and write about their similarities or differences. For example: Write the ways Empress Wu Zetian and Hua Mulan are alike. Write the ways Michelle Kwan and Vera Wang are different.

Women's History Trivia Contest: If your school does not already have one, see if it is possible to begin a school-wide Women's History Trivia Contest during the month of March. If this is not possible, conduct a contest within the class using questions related to Chinese women.

Create a Puzzle: Students make their own word search puzzle or crossword puzzle as an assignment for this topic.

Quotes of the Famous: Students can do research to find quotes of famous Chinese women. Collect all the quotes and have a class discussion about them. Mix up all the quotes and challenge the class to match the quote with the person who said it.

在美国学校，三月是妇女月。学生将学习了解古今著名的妇女。很多学校举办庆祝妇女月活动以彰显著名女性的事迹和成就。我们正好借此机会向学生介绍一些著名的华人女性以及她们的成就。由此学生将更能体会过去的女性如何千辛万苦地奋斗才能成为一名杰出的艺术家、科学家，或在其他领域出人头地。这种教育对年幼学生是非常重要的，尤其是提供亚裔女生一些学习的榜样。

以下是一些庆祝妇女月的建议：

荣誉邮票：为其中一位华人女性设计一枚邮票。要加上一张相关图片或照片，并简单介绍她的成就。

图片字典：制作一本拥有至少五位著名华人女性的图片字典。

比较：让学生选出两位著名的华人女性，写出她们之间的异同。例如：写出武则天与花木兰的共同点；写出关颖珊和王薇薇的不同点。

妇女月常识问答赛：若学校没有这种比赛，试试在全校展开这个妇女月常识问答赛。或利用有关华人女性的问题在班上举行比赛。

设计字谜：让学生根据这个主题设计自己的字谜。

名人语录：学生可以搜索资料，查询著名华人女性的语录。收集所有的语录，然后和全班同学一起讨论。将所有语录混淆，让学生们配一配，猜猜语录是谁说的。

⟨○ **1. Picture Cards: Famous Chinese Women 图卡：著名华人女性** 204

Discuss the major achievements of each of the famous Chinese women these picture cards represent. Then challenge students to work in teams to match each woman's name card with the card that is her symbol. The team that matches each of the women with her symbol correctly wins the challenge. One card is left blank for students to include an additional Chinese woman of their choice.

Guess Who?
The name cards can also be used to play this simple game that can be played by two or more players. Each group of players cuts out a set of name cards and puts them in a pile face down on the table. One player picks a card. Other players will guess who that person is by asking "Yes", "No" questions such as: "Is she still alive?" "Is she a politician?" "Was she born in the US?"

If played in pairs, tally the number of questions each player asks. The person who asks the fewest questions at the end of the game will be the winner. If there are more than two players, the player

☆ Beginner ⟨ Intermediate ☆☆ Beginner-Intermediate ⟨○ Intermediate-Advanced ○ Advanced ☺ All

who guesses the person first will get the picture card. The player who holds the most picture cards at the end of the game is the winner.

和学生讨论图卡所代表的华人女性的成就，然后让学生在小组内将各女性的名卡和她所代表的图卡作配对。正确将每位女性的名卡及其相应图卡配对的小组获胜。有一张卡是空白的，让学生填上自己喜欢的华人女性。

猜猜她是谁？

名卡也可以用来玩两个或更多人能玩的简单游戏。每组学生将名卡剪出来，正面朝下叠在桌上。一个学生拿起一张卡，其他学生提问是非题，如"她还在世吗？""她是政治家吗？""她在美国出世吗？"猜猜名卡里的人是谁。

若是两人一起玩，统计彼此所问的问题。问最少问题的学生获胜。若有超过两人一起玩，最先猜对人物的学生便能得到图卡。最后拥有最多图卡的学生获胜。

2. Fact Cards: Famous Chinese Women 资料卡：著名华人女性...................................206

Cut out the name cards on page 205 and the fact cards on pages 206-207. Spread them out on the table either facing up or down, depending on the players' knowledge of the women. The player who can match one name card with two fact cards will win those cards. The player who has the most cards at the end of the game is the winner. Additional cards can easily be added by writing a name card and two fact cards of that person in a pre-cut square similar to the cards provided in these worksheets. Players can always refer to the biographies of these women to find out if they have made a correct match.

将第205页的名卡以及第206-207页的资料卡剪出来，正面朝上或朝下摊开在桌上，视学生对这些女性的熟悉度而定。游戏需两个或更多人一起玩。能够将名卡和两张相应资料卡正确配对的学生将得到这些卡片，最后得到最多卡片的学生获胜。要制作额外的卡片，教师可在预先剪出来的正方形卡片上写下名字和相应的资料。学生在玩游戏时也可以参考这些女性的资料，确定他们的配对是否正确。

3. Online Search: Famous Chinese Women 网上搜索：著名华人女性.......................208

Students can work individually or in pairs to research and do a presentation about one of the famous Chinese women introduced on page 204. Younger learners can display what they have learned on a poster. Older students can present the information they learned through research with a slide presentation or a written report. In addition to relating important and interesting facts about the women they research, all students should indicate why and how these women became so successful.

Before giving this assignment, teachers go over the objectives and requirement for this activity. It is recommended that teachers give a fair rubric guideline (content, accuracy, effort, artistry, etc.)

学生可以独立或配对上网搜索有关第204页所介绍的其中一位著名华人女性的资料，然后把所得资料呈现出来。低年级的学生可以将学习所得列在一张海报上。高年级的可以通过电脑简报或书面报告呈现资料。除了呈现关于该名女性的重要及有趣资料外，所有学生应该说明这些女性如何及为何会如此成功。

在分发这个作业前，教师要先说明它的目的与要求。建议提供公平的评分标准（内容、准确度、所付出的努力、艺术美感等）。

4. Interview: A Famous Chinese Woman 访谈：一位著名华人女性

Divide the class into small groups and give each group the name of a famous Chinese woman to learn about. You may either choose to provide each group with a simple biography about the woman or direct them to do an online search independently. Once they have some information about the famous woman, each group should make up questions and answers that they would ask this woman in an interview. Each group will then choose one member to pretend to be the famous woman and the others in their group will ask her the interview questions in front of the class.

Students can also choose one of the famous Chinese women on the list below to research.

将全班分成小组，给每组一位著名华人女性作为访谈对象。教师可以选择为各组提供关于该女性的简单资料，或引导他们独立进行网上搜索。一旦他们获取关于该名女性的资料，每组就可以设计访谈的题目和答案。之后，每组选出一名组员，扮演该名女性，让其他组员在全班面前和她进行访谈。

以下列出一些额外的著名华人女性供挑选：

古代（有一些是传说人物）： 女娲、嫘祖、西施、孟母、孟姜女、王昭君、杨贵妃、李清照、岳母、林黛玉……

现代： 章子怡（明星）、巩俐（明星）、陈冲（影星）、郎平（女排教练）、邓亚萍（前乒乓运动员）、郭晶晶（奥运金牌跳水运动员）、宋氏姐妹（政治人物）、陈方安生（政治人物）、吴仪（政治人物）、陈冯富珍（世界卫生组织总干事）、林徽因（建筑学家）、王丹凤（老牌女星）、杨丽坤（扮演"阿诗玛"闻名）、严凤英（黄梅戏名伶）、章含之（名媛）、潘虹（影星）、周晓兰（女排运动员）……

Foreign Language Month 外语月

March is also known as Foreign Language Month in the American education system. Many schools sponsor contests or host cultural events that promote and celebrate the learning of foreign languages. We have provided many ideas and suggestion listed in the Appendices. Please refer to pages 378-383.

三月是美国学校的外语教学月。很多学校都举办有关外语的庆祝活动。我们提供了很多适合的教学活动。请参考附录第378-383页。

Spring 春天

Enlarge and color copies of these flash cards to introduce these new Signs of Spring vocabulary words. Students will enjoy coloring their own sets of flash cards for their personal use for review or playing games.

把这些词卡放大，涂色，作为教学工具。学生会喜欢制作自己的一套彩色图卡。可以用词卡进行教学活动或游戏。

Students will be challenged to read and understand some previously learned characters along with the new Signs of Spring vocabulary characters in this activity. Some students may need to use the vocabulary flash cards for support.

本练习可以测试学生对春天词语的掌握能力。必要时老师可以给予协助，或让学生参考学过的词卡来完成作业。

This activity is designed for students to practice writing the Signs of Spring Vocabulary words.

☆ Beginner ℂ Intermediate ☆ℂ Beginner-Intermediate ℂ◯ Intermediate-Advanced ◯ Advanced ☺ All

After completing the sentences, students can color the pictures and practice reading their sentences out loud.

本活动可以帮助学生练习书写有关春天的词语。完成后，学生可以练习大声朗读。

答案：1. 彩虹　2. 太阳　3. 蝴蝶　4. 花儿　5. 风筝　6. 树

☺　**4. Board Game: Spring Fun　棋盘游戏：春天真好玩！** 212

This game is to help the frog find the lotus flower. To play the game, each group of players will need the game board sheet on page 212, a dice, and a plastic chip or other marker for each player. Players take turns to roll the dice, and move their marker along the board. To advance to the number on the dice that they roll, players must say the word for the picture on that number in Chinese. To make this a little more challenging, request that students use the word in a complete sentence. The player who reaches the lotus flower first wins.

学生可以用第212页进行青蛙找莲花的游戏。学生轮流掷骰子，用棋子走棋。学生必须用中文说出骰子点到的图，才能前进至该图。程度较好的学生必须用图名来造句。先到达莲花终点处的便是赢家。

☆☽　**5. Poem: Spring Is Here!　短诗：春天来了！** 213

First, ask students to brainstorm what signs they will see in spring. If possible, the teacher can sketch the signs or show the pictures on the board and introduce the names in Chinese. After students are familiar with the words, teach them the short poem about spring on page 213. Highlight the vocabulary words in pinyin and characters. Students can color the page and add more illustrations of bees and butterflies. Ask volunteers to read the poem in groups in front of the class. Ask students to take this worksheet home and read the poem to their family members.

先问学生春天会看到哪些景象，然后把这些景象很快地用图卡或用粉笔勾画在黑板上并介绍它们的名字。接着带领学生朗读《春天来了》小诗。学生可以涂色并加上蜜蜂蝴蝶等其他象征春天的图画。教师可以邀请自愿学生小组到台上表演朗读。最后鼓励学生将小诗带回家念给家人听。

☽◯　**6. Imagine and Write: Spring Is Beautiful!　想一想，写一写：春天真美丽！** 214

This activity is an extension of the Spring poem activity above. Ask students to close their eyes and use their imaginations to think of a beautiful springtime scene and everything they can see, hear, smell, touch and taste. Afterwards, they can open their eyes and record as many words as possible to describe the scene in the space provided.

本活动是前页小诗的延展。从小诗的意境延伸到用五官来感受春天。先让学生闭上眼睛想象一个美丽的春天景象，可以看到、听到、闻到、摸到、甚至吃到什么？然后睁开眼睛把想象的事物用中文记录下来。

☺　**7. Art Project: Paper Cuts　创意手工：剪纸** 215

Choose one or more of these ideas for students to make a spring paper cut project. If necessary make templates on oak tag for students to trace on colored construction paper. Students can also color and label their work in Chinese. This project can be used to make a nice bulletin board display. (See project sample on p. 403)

这里提供一些设计让学生参考，制作春天剪纸手工。如有必要，可在硬纸板上画出样本，让学生依此描在彩色纸上。学生也可以为自己的作品涂色并用中文命名。完成后可将学生作品展示在布告栏上。（作品展示见第403页）

Cultural Link: Hua Mulan 花木兰

☺ **1. Reading: Hua Mulan 读一读：花木兰** 216

Read the story of Mulan to students. You may also wish to show the movie Mulan to students and compare the two. Here are some questions that can be asked in a discussion about Mulan:

1. What would you do if you were Mulan?
2. Should Mulan have gone to war for her father or stayed at home?
3. Can you think of any other way that Mulan could have kept her family safe?

借妇女月介绍木兰代父从军的故事。老师也可以放映木兰的电影，加深学生的印象。可以和学生讨论书上的木兰和电影里的木兰有何不同？以下几个问题可作参考：

1. 如果你是木兰，你会怎么做？
2. 木兰应该去战场打仗，还是应该留在家里？
3. 你能帮木兰想出别的更好的办法来保护她的家人吗？

☺ **2. Quiz: Hua Mulan 考考你：花木兰** 217

This quiz can be used to assess students' understanding of the reading passage about Mulan. To complete this activity, students will cut out each of the sentence strips, read them and arrange in sequential order.

这个作业能测试学生对之前阅读篇章的理解程度。让学生把印有句子的纸条剪出来，然后按顺序正确排列。

☆((**3. Mini-Book: Hua Mulan 我的小书：花木兰** 218

To make this mini book about Mulan, distribute the worksheets on pages 218-220. Students should then cut out the pages, put them in the correct order and staple together to make a book. Encourage students to illustrate and color the pages and then read it with a partner.

> **Answer key:** Picture 1: Hua Mulan; horse   Picture 2: father; old   Picture 3: man
> Picture 4: brave; parents   Picture 5: woman

读了花木兰的故事，教师可以分发第218-220页的作业，让学生将每一页剪出来，整理好，再请教师把它们钉成小书。鼓励学生在页面上画图以美化小书。

Try It Out! 每月一练

☺ **1. Let's Talk! 说一说** 221

These dialogue drill activities provide an opportunity for students to review and reinforce the learning of vocabulary words such as community places, helpers, and spring signs. They can practice in pairs or in small groups.

会话练习帮助学生复习并加强对学过的生词的掌握。学生可以和伙伴或和小组一起练习。划线的生词可以用其他合适的词语替代。

☆((**2. Let's Write! 写一写** 222
花、国、竹、鱼、朋、友
(For Character Writing Sheets, see pp. 391, 392. 写字练习纸见本书附录 pp. 391, 392。)

Notes for Teachers
教学重点

April 四月

During the month of April, students will have lots of fun learning Chinese with a variety of topics including colors, fruits, animals and inventions from China.

四月有许多有趣的主题，包括颜色、水果、动物以及中国的发明。学生通过学习这些内容，可充分感受到学习中文的乐趣。

April Calendar 四月月历

☺ **1. Coloring Activity: Chinese Inventions** 涂颜色：中国的发明 224

Begin by asking students to identify each of the Chinese inventions on this activity page. Discuss the importance of each of the inventions to the lives of people in ancient and in modern times. How does having these inventions today make life easier? What are some things people would not be able to do if we did not have them?

教师可先引导学生辨认本月月历画上的中国发明，然后讨论每个发明对古代和现代人生活的重要性，如这些发明在今天如何让我们的生活更便利？如果没有这些发明，我们就无法做什么事？

2. My April Calendar 我的四月月历 225

In addition to using the April calendar to review numbers, days of the week, and to mark special days in April, we can use the calendar to create an additional activity using the topic of color words that are introduced this month. Students can be directed to shade in each of the day's boxes with specific colors. One way would be to shade each day of the week with a different color, another way would be to color each week in the month with a different color. A third way would be for students to color even number days with one color and odd number days with another color.

除了用四月月历来复习数字、学星期、以及记下四月的特别节日，我们也可以配合本月的颜色词汇主题，利用月历来设计相关活动。引导学生在每日的格子里涂上指定的颜色。可以为一星期的每一天涂上不同颜色，也可以为一个月的各个星期涂上不同颜色，或为双数日和单数日涂上不同颜色。

3. What's Happening in April? 四月知多少? 226

This fill-in-the-blank worksheet, which is included with each month, allows advanced learners to review numbers, dates, important holidays and events of that month in a familiar and consistent way.

高年级的学生可以在月历的基础上，通过这样的填空题复习数字和星期，熟悉每月重要的日子。

☆ Beginner ☾ Intermediate ☆☾ Beginner-Intermediate ☾○ Intermediate-Advanced ○ Advanced ☺ All

☺ **1. Vocabulary Flash Cards: Colors** 词卡：颜色

Introduce each of the color words by showing large copies of these flash cards and asking students to repeat each of the words after you. Point out the colors of students' clothing for additional practice with each word.

Conduct a survey by asking students to name their favorite color in Chinese and record their answers. Review numbers here too, by counting the number of votes for each color to determine which color is the most popular in the class.

You can also use the color flash cards on page 398 in the Appendices.

放大这些词卡，让学生跟读。也可指出学生衣服的颜色让学生用中文辨认，作为额外练习。

进行问卷调查，请学生用中文说出他们喜欢的颜色并记录下来。统计每种颜色的票数，看哪个颜色在班上是最受欢迎的。教师可借此复习数字。

也可使用附录第398页的颜色词卡。

☆☾ **2. Coloring Activity: The Fish and the Fisherman** 涂颜色：鱼和渔夫

Students refer to the vocabulary words learned in this unit and follow the color code to color this picture. More advanced students can be asked to cross out the given color words and choose their own colors for each number to make their picture unique. Students' work can then be mounted to make a vibrant bulletin board display.

学生应该参考之前所学的颜色词汇，按照颜色指示为这张图画涂色。程度较好的学生无需根据颜色指示涂色，可自行为每个号码设定自己想要的颜色，让图画更特别。之后将学生的作品展示在布告栏上。

☆☾ **3. Coloring Activity: Pagoda** 涂颜色：宝塔

A pagoda is a distinctive multi-story Asian tower with an upward curving roof. Pagodas are commonly seen throughout China. If possible, show students pictures of pagodas from magazines or online. Color the pagoda on this page according to the colors indicated. You may wish to extend the activity by asking students to cut out the pagoda, mount it on a sheet of construction paper and draw a park scene around it, as pagodas are often located in parks in China.

教师可从杂志或网上下载宝塔的图片给学生看。让学生根据练习里所编号的颜色为宝塔涂色。作为延伸活动，可让学生剪出宝塔，贴在彩纸上，然后在其周围画上公园场景。飞檐翘角的宝塔常见于亚洲国家，如中国。

☆☾ **4. Coloring Activity: The Bunny's House** 涂颜色：兔子的家

This is another coloring activity designed for young learners to become more familiar with color words. Students first color the paint buckets according to the colors indicated and then color the house accordingly.

这个活动能帮助低年级学生更加熟悉颜色词汇。学生先为每桶漆写上不同的颜色名称，然后上色，接着依此为图画涂色。

☆☾ **5. Write, Draw, Color: My Color Wheel**
写一写，画一画，涂一涂：我的彩色轮盘

Using this color wheel, students can share information about themselves with their classmates. It

☆ Beginner   ☾ Intermediate   ☆☾ Beginner-Intermediate   ☾○ Intermediate-Advanced   ○ Advanced   ☺ All

also provides the opportunity to address issues related to character education principles such as respect, acceptance, and self-esteem. A bulletin board exhibit of students' work is a terrific way to emphasize diversity in the classroom.

学生可以利用这个彩色轮盘和同学分享有关自己的事物，从中学习如何尊重并接受他人、建立自信。教师可将学生作品展示在布告栏上，借此体现班里的多元性。

Fruits 水果

Enlarge and color copies of the fruit vocabulary flash cards to introduce this set of new vocabulary words. Use familiar sentence patterns to practice with the names of fruits. You may also wish to use real or plastic fruit to make this activity more interesting.

将词卡放大，涂色。让学生用熟悉的句式练习水果词汇。可用真实或塑料水果增添此活动的趣味性。

Students complete this fruit book by drawing pictures of each fruit, cutting and putting the pages together and stapling them. They can then practice reading their books in small groups or in front of the class.

学生可以画出小书里所列的水果，剪出每一页，然后钉起来。接着，他们可以在小组内或给全班朗读他们的小书。

Use a set of fruit vocabulary flash cards or a poster about fruit to review the names and colors of different fruits in Chinese. You may wish to include some less common fruits such as papaya, guava and lychee in this writing activity. Students can then complete the worksheet individually or in small groups.

用一套水果词汇卡或水果图复习不同水果的中文名称和颜色。也可加入一些比较少见的水果，如木瓜、番石榴和荔枝。学生可独立或在小组内完成作业。

This simple survey activity can be completed at home with family members or in class with classmates. Students can then volunteer to share their findings with the class.

这个简单的问卷能够在家里或班上完成。学生在事后可以主动和班上同学分享他们的调查结果。

Many children who are familiar with the book, The Very Hungry Caterpillar, by Eric Carle will enjoy listening to the book's Chinese version. Afterwards, students can fill in the names of fruits in Chinese on the caterpillar activity sheet on page 237 and draw a simple picture about each sentence.

教师先念艾瑞克·卡尔的《好饿的毛毛虫》给学生听。接着，让他们在作业纸上用中文写上水果的名称，并画出相应的水果图。

☆ Beginner ◖ Intermediate ☆◖ Beginner-Intermediate ◖○ Intermediate-Advanced ○ Advanced ☺ All

Animals 动物

☺ **1. Vocabulary Flash Cards: Animals 词卡：动物**

Enlarge and color copies of the Animal flash cards to introduce this new set of vocabulary words. A mixture of sentence patterns can be used to practice with these new words. Students can make their own sets of flash cards for review or to play games with each other.

将词卡放大，涂色。利用不同的句式和学生练习这些新词汇。学生可以制作自己的词卡用来复习或玩游戏。

☆☾ **2. Make a Guess: Who Am I? 猜一猜：我是谁？**

This is a guessing game that students of all ages enjoy. Students draw a picture of an animal they like on a piece of paper and show it to the class. Whoever can name the animal correctly in Chinese first gets a point. Use the following sentence patterns:

Zhè shì bú shì _____?

Zhè shì/bú shì _____.

这个猜谜游戏深受不同年龄层的学生喜爱。让学生在纸上画出他们喜欢的动物，然后给班上同学看。先以中文说出动物正确名称的学生将获得一分。让学生使用以下句式进行问答：

这是不是_____？

这是/不是_____。

☆☾ **3. Make a Guess: Who's Talking? 猜一猜：谁在说话？**

Introduce this activity by explaining that animal sounds are different in other languages. For example, in English we say a dog says, "Woof, woof", and in Chinese we say a dog says, "wang, wang". Proceed by making each of the animal sounds in Chinese for students to guess what animal makes those sounds. Students can then complete this worksheet individually or in small groups.

先解释动物的叫声在其他语言中是不同的。例如，在英文里，狗的叫声是"woof, woof"；在中文里，它的叫声是"汪汪"。接着，发出每一个动物的中文叫声，让学生猜是哪个动物。最后让学生独立或在小组内完成作业。

> **答案：** 1. 猫（cat）；喵喵　2. 羊（sheep）；咩咩　3. 马（horse）；咴咴
> 4. 猪（pig）；咕噜　5. 狗（dog）；汪汪　6. 鸭（duck）；嘎嘎
> 7. 牛（cow）；哞哞　8. 鸡（cock）；喔喔

☺ **4. Song: Old McDonald Had a Farm 儿歌：王老先生有块地**

Review the names of the animals and their sounds. The teacher plays the song and asks students to figure out what animals are mentioned in the song. Then he/she leads the class to read the song lyrics and then sing together. After students are familiar with the song, ask volunteers to perform in groups in front of the class.

先复习动物的名称及其叫声。教师播放歌曲，问学生歌词里的动物有哪些。接着，带领全班朗读歌词，然后一起唱。在学生熟悉歌曲后，请学生以小组方式自愿上来表演给全班看。

☾○ **5. Compare and Write: Which Animal Has...? Which Animal Can...?**
比一比，写一写：谁有……？谁会……？

First, use a set of animal vocabulary flash cards or a poster about animals to review the names of

☆ Beginner　☾ Intermediate　☆☾ Beginner-Intermediate　☾○ Intermediate-Advanced　○ Advanced　☺ All

animals in Chinese. Compare the different animals and ask questions about the different animals' size, colors, and body parts. Then distribute the worksheet and go over the phrases in the word bank. Each student should complete the worksheet and read it together with a partner.

首先，用一套动物词卡或动物图来复习动物的中文名称。接着，比较不同的动物，提出关于不同动物体积、颜色和身体部位的问题。最后，分发作业，讲解词库里的词语。每位学生在完成作业后可以和伙伴一起练习朗读。

Go over the names of each of the animal habitats on the activity sheet with students. Some may be able to guess the meanings based on some of the Chinese characters in the habitat names. Then ask students to write the word for each of the animals under the habitat heading where they belong.

先讲解练习里各个动物栖息地的名称。有些学生或许能辨认名称里的一些汉字，从中猜出它们的意思。接着，让学生根据栖息地写上所属动物的名称。

This activity is designed to help students practice new vocabulary about pets with previously learned color words. Students can use real or imagined pets for this activity.

这个活动让学生配合之前所学的颜色词汇，练习新学的动物词汇。学生可用真实或想象的宠物来完成这个活动。

This activity allows the more advanced students to describe a real or imagined pet in writing, using the vocabulary words that were previously introduced in this unit.

这个活动让程度较好的学生利用本课之前所学过的词汇，描写一只真实或想象的宠物。

Tomb Sweeping Day 清明节

Tomb Sweeping Day is a time to honor one's ancestors and to celebrate the coming of spring. Read the passage and discuss the main ideas with students. Ask students to highlight or underline important vocabulary words. Books, stories and videos about the Tomb Sweeping Day can be used to enhance this lesson.

清明节是扫墓祭祖和欢庆春天到来的日子。让学生阅读短文，然后一起讨论里头的主题，再划出重要的词汇。教师可用关于清明节的书籍、故事和录影来促进本课的教学。

This Cloze exercise can be used as a follow-up activity that students can complete individually or in small groups after reading the passage about the Tomb Sweeping Day.

这个填空作业可以作为跟进活动，让学生在读完短文后独立或在小组内完成。

答案：1. 清明节 2. 中国 3. 四月 4. 祖先 5. 平安 6. 父母 7. 老人 8. 家 9. 踏青 10. 风筝

☆ Beginner   ◖ Intermediate   ☆◖ Beginner-Intermediate   ◖○ Intermediate-Advanced   ○ Advanced   ☺ All

3. Tang Poem: Qingming 唐诗：清明 249

This poem was written by Du Mu, a famous Tang Dynasty poet. Read and discuss the poem with students. Encourage students to do an online search about this poem or other Tang poems.

Advanced students can be challenged to reduce the number of characters in each line of the poem without changing the main idea of the poem.

这首诗是由唐朝著名诗人杜牧所作。和学生一起读这首诗并讨论诗中内容。鼓励学生上网搜索更多关于此诗或其他唐诗的资料。

程度较好的学生可以完成这个富有挑战性的活动——在不改变诗意的情况下，减少每一行的字数。

Cultural Link: Chinese Inventions 中国的发明

**1. Reading: Four Great Inventions from Ancient China
读一读：中国古代四大发明** 251

This reading is about the four great inventions from ancient China: the compass, gunpowder, papermaking and printing. In reading this passage students will learn some interesting facts about these inventions.

这篇短文是关于中国古代四大发明：指南针、火药、造纸术以及印刷术。在阅读短文时，学生将认识和这些发明有关的有趣事实。

**2. Quiz: Four Great Inventions from Ancient China
考考你：中国古代四大发明** 254

Students can work individually or in pairs to answer the questions about the four great inventions of ancient China after reading the passage.

阅读短文后，学生可以独立或配对回答关于中国古代四大发明的问题。

3. Brainstorm and Research: Chinese Inventions 想一想，查一查：中国的发明

Brainstorm with students to make a list of all the inventions they can think of that come from China. Students can work in teams to research their favorite invention and try to make a model of it to present to the class.

和学生一起讨论，列出他们可以想到的来自中国的发明。学生可以和小组一起对他们喜欢的发明进行资料搜索，然后试着做出相关模型，呈现给班上同学。

4. Draw and Write: What Came from China 画一画，写一写：中国的发明 255

Complete this table of inventions by filling in the missing pictures or words.

填上图画或文字以完成这个发明表。

5. Crossword Puzzle: Chinese Inventions 填字谜：中国的发明 256

Help students to review the names of the Chinese inventions listed at the bottom of the page before they work on this crossword puzzle.

教师先让学生复习列在下方的中国发明名称，然后再完成这个填字谜。

Help students to review the names of the Chinese inventions listed at the bottom of the page before they work on this word search.

教师先让学生复习列在下方的中国发明名称，然后再完成这个字谜。

This activity provides students with knowledge about Chinese culture and inventions. Begin by asking students to work in pairs to see how many answers they can guess on page 258. After naming each of the answers correctly in English, teach the name for each in Chinese. Students can then discuss which item they think is most interesting or useful in the world today.

这个活动帮助学生更深入了解中华文化与发明。先让学生配对完成第258页的练习，看看他们能够猜对几题。在用英文写出正确答案后，教师可教导学生相应的中文名称。接着，学生可以讨论哪个发明在现今世界是最有趣或最有用的。

> **Answer key:** 1. abacus   2. paper   3. gunpowder   4. compass   5. rice   6. tea
> 7. ice-cream   8. noodles   9. chopsticks   10. umbrella   11. kite

Try It Out! 每月一练

This dialogue drill activity engages students by talking about the topics that are closely related to them. Students also enjoy role-play activities. Call volunteer students to perform in front of the class.

这个对话练习让学生谈论和他们密切相关的话题。可融入角色扮演，请学生自愿上来表演。

左、右、东、西、南、北

(For Character Writing Sheets, see pp. 391, 392. 写字练习纸见本书附录 pp. 391, 392。)

April 四月

☆ Beginner   ◖ Intermediate   ☆◖ Beginner-Intermediate   ◖◯ Intermediate-Advanced   ◯ Advanced   ☺ All

Notes for Teachers
教学重点

May 五月

Food is an essential and accessible part of the learning of Chinese culture. There are so many topics related to food to include in the month of May, beginning with this month's theme of general food items, names and types of Chinese food, how to order food from a Chinese menu and how to use chopsticks.

It is important to remind students to share their knowledge about Chinese language and culture with family members whenever opportunities become available. Eating a meal at a Chinese restaurant is probably the most convenient way for students to apply their learning in the Chinese classroom to a real life situation right in their own community. We have found that allowing students to share their personal experiences encourages them to be more open to speaking Chinese with native speakers and even trying new foods.

食物是中华文化学习里的一个重要部分。五月份有许多和食物相关的主题，包括一般食品、中国菜的种类及名称、如何点中国菜以及如何使用筷子。

若有机会，应该提醒学生和家人分享他们对中文以及中华文化的认识。在中餐馆用餐能让学生将课堂所学应用在自己社区的真实情境里。通过分享个人经历，学生将更积极地使用中文和华人交谈，并尝试新的食品。

SUN	MON	TUES	WED	THU	FRI	SAT
		1	2	3 意大利面 Spaghetti	4	5
6	7	8	9 炒饭 Fried rice	10	11	12
13	14 比萨 Pizza	15	16	17	18	19
20	21	22	23	24	25 捞面 加馄饨汤 Lo mein & wonton soup	26
27	28	29 鸡蛋 Egg 火鸡肉 Turkey 三文治 Sandwich	30	31		

This month's topic about food can be used with the May calendar by adding your school's lunch menu items to the calendar. In many schools the same foods are served on different days of the week. For example, on Mondays chicken nuggets are served and on Tuesdays hamburgers are served. Adding this vocabulary provides the opportunity to practice using the new food vocabulary with the familiar calendar format. If your school does not provide lunch for students, a made up lunch menu can be created for this purpose (see left).

☆ Beginner   ◖ Intermediate   ☆☆ Beginner-Intermediate   ◖○ Intermediate-Advanced   ○ Advanced   ☺ All

You can ask the following sample questions to further enhance learning:

1. What will be served for lunch on May 9?
2. What will be served on the last Tuesday in May?
3. When will Chinese food be served for lunch?

For other uses of the calendar, please refer to the notes on My January Calendar on page 1.

本月份关于食物的主题可以和五月月历相配合。让学生把学校午餐的菜单填在月历上。例如，星期一吃炸鸡块，星期二吃汉堡包。这样能帮助学生通过月历练习新的食物词汇。若学校没有为学生提供午餐，教师可以为此活动虚拟一份午餐菜单。以下问题可作为参考：

一、五月九日的午餐是什么？
二、五月最后一个星期二的午餐是什么？
三、在哪一天会提供中式午餐？

关于月历的其他用途，请参考第1页"我的一月月历"的说明。

☾○ 3. **What's Happening in May? 五月知多少?**

This fill-in-the-blank worksheet, which is included with each month, allows advanced learners to review numbers, dates, important holidays and events of that month in a familiar and consistent way.

高年级的学生可以在月历的基础上，通过这样的填空题复习数字和星期，熟悉每月重要的日子。

Food 食物

The food vocabulary words introduced in this unit are introduced in different categories and presented in contexts that can facilitate conversation about foods. The categories are: Western breakfast foods, Chinese breakfast foods, vegetables, meats, and Chinese menu foods. Following the groups of foods are activities to pick and choose from. Many of the activities provided are for one specific food category, while other ideas can be used to practice with any of the food categories.

为了帮助学生更快掌握同食物有关的对话，本单元介绍的食物词汇分不同种类呈现，并提供使用情境。这些食物种类包括：西式早餐、中式早餐、蔬菜、肉类以及常见中餐。词汇表之后附有相关课堂活动供教师挑选使用。很多活动专为某类食物设计，也有一些活动适用于任何类型的食物。

☆☾ 1. **Vocabulary List: Western Style Breakfast 词表：西式早餐**

☆☾ 2. **Vocabulary List: Chinese Style Breakfast 词表：中式早餐**

A variety of breakfast foods are presented in a cafeteria setting on these pages. This theme can be used to practice the newly introduced vocabulary words. Display enlarged individual pictures of each of the foods in front of the classroom. Students can take turns holding a paper plate and pretending they are selecting their favorite foods.

Copies of these pages can also be distributed to each student to cut out their favorite foods and paste them onto a paper plate. We have also included Western and Chinese eating utensils on these pages. This food vocabulary is useful for students to learn and can be incorporated into some of the dialogues and activities throughout this unit.

我们为西式和中式早餐词汇设定的情境是自助餐厅，这样可以帮助学生练习刚学到的词汇。活动时，在教室前面放置每种食物的放大图片。学生则手持纸盘，依次挑选自己喜欢的"食物"。

也可将这些图片分发给每位学生，由他们把自己喜欢的食物剪下来，贴在纸盘上。我们在图

May 五月

里还加入了西式和中式餐具。这些食物词汇对学生非常有帮助。他们可以将其融入到本单元的某些对话和活动中去。

These foods are presented in a supermarket setting that is familiar to most children. Activities involving identifying different foods, sorting them by category, expressing likes/dislikes and nutrition can all be used with this vocabulary list.

这些食物都呈现在多数学生所熟悉的超级市场里。本单元设有许多活动，如辨别不同的食物、食物分类、表达对食物的喜好/厌恶，以及认识食物的营养价值等。教师可按需挑选，增添学习的趣味性。

To complete this activity worksheet found on page 269, ask students to pretend that they are the manager of a supermarket. As such, they must fill in the correct labels for each of the vegetables displayed in the store.

让学生想象自己是某超级市场的经理，为超市里所陈列的各种蔬菜标上正确的名称。

In this activity which combines math skills and language skills, students can work individually or in pairs to figure out the cost of buying the items on the shopping list found on page 269. Be sure to point out the amounts specified for each of the items on the list.

Answer key: 1. $1.00 2. $1.50 3. $1.50 4. $4.00 5. $3.00 6. $1.50 7. $12.50

这个活动考验学生的数学及语文能力。学生可以独立或和伙伴一起计算出购买购物清单里的食物需要多少钱。记得要列出每样食物的价格。

On this page some common Chinese food dishes are presented on a placemat background. Students can make flash cards and use them to learn the names of the foods. Students can also use this new vocabulary to make sentences about which foods they like and do not like to eat.

这些常见的中国菜以中式餐垫为背景。让学生将词卡剪出来，用它们学习中菜名称。学生也可利用这些新词汇造句，说说他们喜欢和不喜欢的食物。

Create the following scenario for students:

Imagine that your mother is making a special dinner of your favorite food for a dinner party for you. Your grandparents and your best friends will be invited. To prepare for this, you will need to go food shopping. First decide four to five dishes for the menu, and then make a list of groceries you will need to have to make them. Use the pattern provided on page 272 to indicate which food you will need to purchase for the dinner.

为学生设置以下情境：

想象你的母亲将为你和你的好友准备一顿特别的晚餐，所有的菜都是你喜欢吃的。你的祖父母及好友将受邀前来。要准备这些，你必须去买菜。先决定四至五道菜，然后依此准备购物清单。利用第272页列出你需要购买的食材。

☆ Beginner   ☾ Intermediate   ☆☾ Beginner-Intermediate   ☾○ Intermediate-Advanced   ○ Advanced   ☺ All

☆◖ **9.** **Draw and Label: My Favorite Food** 画一画，写一写：我爱吃的食物

Students draw and label the foods they like most from the given vocabulary list(s). Use the sentence patterns: Wǒ ài chī; Wǒ zuì ài chī; Wǒ xǐ huan chī; Wǒ zuì xǐ huan chī...

让学生画出他们最喜欢的食物，然后利用所学过的食物词汇为图画写上名称。练习时可使用以下句式：

我爱吃……。我最爱吃……。　我喜欢吃……。我最喜欢吃……。

☺ **10.** **Art Project: My Chinese Placemat** 创意手工：我的中餐具垫

Students can use any combination of vocabulary words in this unit to design a placemat that they can use at home. Provide each student with a large sheet of construction paper. They can cut out and paste pictures from the vocabulary sheets or draw their own pictures. Label each item in Chinese pinyin and/or characters and make up a border pattern. If possible, laminate students' work.

学生可以利用本单元里任何组合的词汇，设计一张能在家里使用的餐具垫。为每个学生提供一大张彩色纸，让他们把从词汇表剪出来的图片贴在上面，或在彩纸上自行画图。为每个食物标上汉语拼音和/或汉字，并设计花边。

◖◯ **11.** **Integrated Activity: Ordering Food from a Chinese Menu**
综合活动：点中国菜 273

The worksheets on pages 273-275 will help students learn the names of some popular food found on a Chinese menu and some of the basic sentence patterns needed to ask for these food in a Chinese restaurant.

On page 273 we have provided a sample menu with examples of different beverages, appetizers, soups, main dishes, and desserts. Practice saying each example with students and discuss whether or not they like each of the items listed.

On page 274 students must fill in their own choices from the selections to indicate their preferences for the beverage, appetizer, soup, main course and dessert on the menu. Students can then practice reading their answers to become more familiar with saying their favorite food in Chinese.

On page 275 we have provided a dialogue for students to use in a role play between a waiter and a customer. To make this more like a real restaurant situation, prepare a table or desk in the classroom with a placemat or tablecloth and place settings of paper plates, cups, and plastic ware. Students can volunteer to pretend to be the waiter or customer to act out this role play scene. Remind students to practice using what they have learned the next time they visit a Chinese restaurant and to share their experience with the class afterwards.

第273-275的练习能让学生认读一些在中式菜单上非常受欢迎的菜名，以及在中餐馆点菜时常用的一些基本句式。

第273页是一份菜单，里头列有饮料、开胃菜、汤、主食以及甜品。和学生练习念出每道菜的名称，谈谈他们喜不喜欢这些菜。

在第274页，学生必须根据菜单上的菜，填上他们想要的饮料、开胃菜、汤、主食以及甜品。接着，学生可以练习念出他们的答案，熟悉用中文说出他们喜欢的食物。

第275页关于侍者和顾客之间的对话，能让学生用来进行角色扮演。要做得更逼真些，可以在班前摆放桌子和椅子，桌上铺上餐具垫和桌布，并摆放纸盘、纸杯和塑料餐具。让学生自愿扮演侍者或顾客。提醒他们下次光顾中餐馆时，要练习课堂上所学到的词汇和对话，然后和班上同学分享。

◖◯ **12.** **Decode the Word Search: Chinese Food** 数字解码：中国菜的秘密 276

Decode the numbers to figure out the correct words from the Chinese Food vocabulary list.

将数字解码并找出正确的字。

13. Reading: Food Pyramid 读一读：食物金字塔 277

The food pyramid is used as a tool for children to understand the important food groups necessary for a healthy diet. Use the food pyramid diagram to introduce the different food groups. Review foods introduced and ask students to name three foods that are included in each of the food groups.

食物金字塔能帮助孩子了解健康饮食中的重要食物类别。用食物金字塔来介绍不同的食物类别。复习之前所介绍的食物，让学生说出每个食物类别中的三样食物。

14. Role Play: My Chinese Restaurant 角色扮演：我的中餐馆

In this activity students will pretend that they own a Chinese restaurant. They must first make up a name for the restaurant, then make a menu with prices for each item. We suggest using dollar amounts from $1 to $10. Students can then use the menu to role play asking questions using the patterns "Nǐ yǒu méi yǒu (food name)?" and "(food name) duō shǎo qián?"

设置情境，让学生想象自己开设中餐馆。他们必须先为餐馆取名，再设计菜单，列出每道菜的价格。价格范围建议在一至十元之间。之后，学生可以使用菜单进行角色扮演，利用"你有没有（食物名称）？"和"（食物名称）多少钱？"这两个句式提问。

15. Role Play: My Farm Stand 角色扮演：我的菜摊

This activity is basically the same as the one above; except that students will pretend that they own a farm that has a farm stand. They will need to make up a name for their farm stand and list the items for sale and the prices for each. Students can then take turns role playing buying and selling produce. If possible, use plastic fruits and vegetables for this activity.

这个活动基本上和之前的相同，不过学生会假设他们拥有一家农场，要为他们的菜摊取名并为所售卖的蔬果标价。学生可以轮流扮演买卖蔬果的不同角色。建议在活动中使用塑料水果和蔬菜。

16. Survey: Favorite Food 问卷：爱吃的中国菜 278

In this teacher-directed activity students are asked whether or not they like to eat the various food listed on the chart. Students can then determine the most and least popular food among their classmates. If this activity is done by more than one class, the results of each class survey can then be compared with each other.

此活动由教师主导。问学生是否爱吃列在表里的中国菜。学生可凭此断定同学们最爱吃或最不爱吃的菜。若有超过一班进行此活动，可相互比较各班的问卷结果。

17. Write and Say: Favorite Food and Healthy Food
写一写，说一说：爱吃和健康的食物 279

This activity allows students to express whether or not they like different foods and how often they eat certain foods. Students can also practice talking about whether foods they eat are healthy or unhealthy using the information provided in the food pyramid. After completing the worksheet by writing names of foods in the headings provided, students can practice reading their answers with each other.

此活动让学生利用"喜欢"、"不喜欢"、"常常吃"、"不常吃"、"从没吃过"等词汇来表达对食物的喜好以及食用次数。他们也将利用所学到的食物金字塔知识，讨论健康和不健康的食物。填上食物名称后，他们可以和伙伴一起练习对话。

☺ 18. Word Search: Chinese Food 找一找：中国菜 280

After the review of the names of Chinese food items on page 271 and page 273, students will enjoy this word search activity.

复习了第271和273页的中国菜名称后，学生将会觉得这个活动非常有趣，并乐在其中。

☺ 19. Bingo Game: Food 宾果游戏：食物

Students can fill in any vocabulary that they learned in the lesson to play this game. (Use the Bingo template on page 394 for this activity.)

学生可以填上他们在本课所学过的词汇。（用附录第394页的宾果游戏卡来进行本活动。）

☺ 20. Song: Rainbow Sister 儿歌：虹彩妹妹 281

Teach students the words and melody to sing this folk song. It is possible to find recordings of this popular folk song to use in your classroom.

《虹彩妹妹》是一首源自中国内蒙古绥远的民谣。先教导学生歌词里的词汇以及旋律。可能的话，在班上播放这首通俗民谣，促进学习。

☺ 21. Folk Dance: Chopsticks Dance 民族舞蹈：筷子舞

Chopsticks are commonly used in Chinese folk dances. Some basic movements include tapping the chopsticks while raising them up and down, from right to left, and while turning around. After practicing these movements with students, make up a simple chopstick dance for students to perform to the song Rainbow Sister.

筷子常被用于中国民族舞蹈中。一些基本的动作包括在上下、左右移动筷子以及转身的同时拍击筷子。和学生练习动作后，设计一个简单的筷子舞，让学生配合《虹彩妹妹》这首歌来跳。

☺ 22. Game: Musical Chopsticks Challenge 游戏：音乐筷子挑战

Introduce the lesson about using chopsticks by reading a story about chopsticks or telling a personal experience. Explain that people in China, Korea, and Japan typically use chopsticks on a daily basis. We suggest letting students know that learning how to use chopsticks is not easy for everyone, even adults, and that it is okay if they are not able to do it well.

To set up for the chopstick challenge, request that each student ask for chopsticks in Chinese and practice holding them. Then hand out a plastic bowl filled with Styrofoam peanuts for students to practice with. When the music begins students should remove their Styrofoam peanuts from the bowl one at a time. When the music stops, students should count up the number of pieces that they have removed. Next, students should quickly put the pieces back in the bowl to begin again. This time allow the music to play a little longer and when it stops, students are to count the number of pieces again. The challenge is to have a higher score on the second round and most students will be successful in doing this.

Another way for students to practice using chopsticks is for students to pass a Styrofoam peanut back and forth to each other without dropping it. Tell students to keep track of the number and try to surpass it each time. This activity can be done with two students or in small groups.

通过阅读有关筷子的故事或讲述自己的亲身经历，引出本课主题。向学生说明中国人、韩国人和日本人每天都会使用筷子。最好让学生知道学习使用筷子对任何人都不容易，即便是成人也是如此，所以就算他们用得不好也没关系。

May 五月

首先要求每名学生用中文索取筷子并练习使用，为筷子挑战赛热身。然后分发塑料碗，碗里装满塑料泡沫"花生"。音乐开始，学生用筷子从碗里夹出"花生"，每次只限一粒。音乐结束时，计算夹到的"花生"总数。然后尽快把夹出的"花生"放回碗里，开始下一轮。这次音乐时间可以稍长，音乐结束，再次计算夹到的"花生"数目。筷子挑战赛的目的是看谁能在第二轮得到比第一轮更高的分数，大多数学生都能成功。

另一种练习方式是学生之间用筷子传递这种塑料泡沫"花生"，让他们记住传递的数目，尽量下一次能超过上一次的数目。此活动可由两名学生合作完成，也可以小组为单位进行。

For this activity, students can pretend that they are helping out at home by putting the family's groceries in the refrigerator. Follow the directions on the worksheet to put each food in its proper place inside the refrigerator. Further discussion about this activity can be generated by discussing which of the items students actually have in their refrigerators at home.

Teachers may engage the students into the activity using this sentence:
冰箱里，冰箱里，冰箱里有什么？
Bīng xiāng li, bīng xiāng li, bīng xiāng li yǒu shén me?

让学生想象自己在帮家人把食物放进冰箱里。按照练习上的指示，将各食物分类放在冰箱的正确位置。可将活动加以延伸，让学生谈谈自己家里的冰箱是否也有这些食品。

教师可用上述句子引导学生进行活动。

Mother's Day 母亲节

Following the instructions of the paper-cutting project, students will fold the paper and cut out the heart-shaped pattern with teacher's assistance if necessary. Then, they will paste the project in a card and write Mother's Day messages. (See project sample on p. 403)

让学生把纸折起来，剪出心形图案。接着，把它贴在卡片上，然后写上母亲节祝语。（作品展示见第403页）

Copy this certificate on pink or yellow paper if possible. Students can decorate, write their mother's name and sign the certificate. Make sure students are able to read the message on the certificate so that they can proudly present it to their mother on Mother's Day!

将此证书印在粉红或黄色的彩纸上。学生可以在上面点缀一番，然后签名。确保学生能念出证书上的祝语，好让他们在母亲节当天可以自豪地献给自己的妈妈。

Students are encouraged to replace the underlined words with other words learned in this unit.

鼓励学生以本单元里所学过的其他词汇来取代划上横线的词汇。

Cultural Link: Tea-Drinking 中国茶

Drinking tea is an important part of Chinese culture. Most Chinese drink tea on a regular basis.

☆ Beginner ◖ Intermediate ☆☆ Beginner-Intermediate ◖○ Intermediate-Advanced ○ Advanced ☺ All

May 五月

Students are usually surprised that tea comes from plants that grow in China. Show different types of tea leaves and allow students to smell them.

This short passage helps less advanced students to learn about the legendary story of discovering tea, how tea are produced and the variety of green tea, black tea and scented tea.

喝茶是中华文化里的一个重要部分。多数华人都经常喝茶。学生总是对茶叶来自中国的事实感到惊奇。给学生看不同种类的茶叶，并让他们闻一闻。

这篇短文帮助低年级学生认识茶是如何被发现的、茶的制作过程，以及不同种类的绿茶、红茶和花茶。

2. **Quiz: Tea-Drinking** 考考你：中国茶

This activity is a follow-up exercise of the reading passage that will help students improve and reinforce their reading comprehension skills.

这个活动是之前阅读短文的延伸，能提升并强化学生的阅读理解能力。

答案：1. 神农　　　　　2. 柴、米、油、盐、酱、醋、茶
　　　3. (2)、(3)、(1)　4. 绿茶：龙井；红茶：铁观音；花茶：茉莉花茶

3. **Mini Book: My Tea Book** 我的小书：中国茶

Make a pot of tea and allow it to cool while students work on their mini tea books. At the end of the lesson give those students who wish to try it a little taste of tea.

Answer key: rice; oil; tea; tea; Chinese; Shen Nong; leaves; hot; teapot; water; lid; health.

在学生制作小书的当儿，可泡一壶茶并让它冷却。在结束这堂课前，让有兴趣品尝的学生尝尝茶的味道。

Try It Out! 每月一练

a. **Let's Talk!** 说一说

1. **What Do You Want For Dinner?** 你晚餐想吃什么？

2. **What Do You Want For Breakfast?** 你早餐想吃什么？

3. **What's A Food Pyramid?** 食物金字塔是什么？

First review the vocabulary learned in the food section, next students will role play and practice these short dialogues with the teacher. Then students practice in pairs with the teacher's assistance. When students are comfortable with the conversation, ask volunteers to pair up and perform in front of the class.

先复习食物主题里的词汇，再让学生和教师练习这些对话，进行角色扮演。然后在教师的协导下让学生配对练习。在学生熟悉对话后，请他们以配对方式自愿上来表演给同学看。

b. **Let's Write!** 写一写
春、夏、秋、冬、风、雨
(For Character Writing Sheets, see pp. 391, 392. 写字练习纸见本书附录 pp. 391, 392。)

May 五月

Notes for Teachers
教学重点

June 六月

June Calendar 六月月历

☺ **1. Coloring Activity: Dragon Boat Festival** 涂颜色：端午节 294

This coloring page is about the Dragon Boat Festival, one of the major festivals in Chinese culture. Introduce the festival by telling the tragic story of the famous Chinese poet, Qu Yuan, who is featured on this page. The "zong zi" and dragon boats which are important in the celebration of the Dragon Boat Festival are also represented on this page. Images of real dragon boat races, which have become popular in many cities across the world, can easily be found online and downloaded to share with your students.

本月主题是端午节，它是中华文化里最重要的节日之一。先述说本页主角——诗人屈原的悲剧故事作为导入，然后再谈谈本页里的粽子和龙舟。这些都是庆祝端午节时不可缺少的。龙舟赛在世界各地已越来越普遍，其照片也容易在网上找到，教师可将之下载与学生分享。

☽○ **2. My June Calendar** 我的六月月历 295

The topics of this month include Dragon Boat Festival, Father's Day, Sports and Insects. The topic about Sports can be used with the June calendar by adding your school's sports team practices to the calendar (see below). You can further enhance learning by asking the following sample questions:

June Sport Team Practices

SUN	MON	TUES	WED	THU	FRI	SAT
					1	2
3	4 棒球 Baseball	5	6	7	8 网球 Tennis	9
10	11	12	13 篮球 Basketball	14	15	16
17	18 棒球 Baseball	19	20	21	22 网球 Tennis	23
24	25	26	27 篮球 Basketball	28	29	30

1. What sport practices are held on alternate Mondays?
2. What sport practices are held on alternate Wednesdays?
3. When does the tennis team meet?

For other uses of the calendar, please refer to the notes on My January Calendar on page 1.

本月学习主题包括端午节、父亲节、休闲活动、球类运动和昆虫。关于运动的主题可以和六月月历相配合，让学生把学校球队练习时间填在月历上（见左图）。接着，可以提问以下参考问题以促进学习：

☆ Beginner ☾ Intermediate ☆☆ Beginner-Intermediate ☾○ Intermediate-Advanced ○ Advanced ☺ All

June 六月

1. 哪个球队的练习是每两个星期一进行一次的？

2. 哪个球队的练习是每两个星期三进行一次的？

3. 网球队的练习是在什么时候？

关于月历的其他用途，请参考第1页"我的一月月历"的说明。

This fill-in-the-blank worksheet, which is included with each month, allows advanced learners to review numbers, dates, important holidays and events of that month in a familiar and consistent way.

高年级的学生可以在月历的基础上，通过这样的填空题复习数字和星期，熟悉每月重要的日子。

We highly recommend presenting each student with a Chinese Language Achievement Certificate at the end of the school year. On page 384 we have provided a certificate that should be signed by the teacher and principal and, if possible, copied on red paper. If this certificate is not appropriate for your situation, it is easy to adapt a certificate template to reflect your program's specifications.

在学年结束前，建议给每个学生颁发中文奖状。我们在第384页提供了一个奖状样板，让教师和校长在上面签字后印在红纸上。若此奖状不适用，可以根据个别课程的特点自行修改奖状样板。

Leisure Activities 休闲活动

This set of flash cards can be used to introduce some activities that children enjoy in their free time. Try using TPR by modeling and directing students to act out each activity as it is being said. Individual students can then volunteer to act out one of the activities while the other students try to name the activity in Chinese. For additional practice students can volunteer to name one activity that they enjoy doing and one that they do not enjoy.

这套词卡可用来介绍孩子在闲暇时所喜欢进行的活动。试着用TPR教学法来引导学生做出每项活动的动作。之后，个别学生可以自愿做出某项活动的动作，让其他学生用中文猜是哪个活动。作为额外练习，学生可自愿举出他们喜欢做的一项活动以及不喜欢做的活动。

Completing and reading this mini-book about their leisure activities provide students with an opportunity to use the new vocabulary in a meaningful context. Using the time phrases such as "frequently", "rarely", "never", and expressing their likes, students will enjoy talking about their favorite activities and learn about their classmates.

此活动能让学生在相关的语境中使用休闲活动词语和时间副词，如"常常"、"很少"、"从来不"等，并用它们来表达自己的喜好。学生将乐于和同学分享彼此喜欢的活动。

This song is a good one to introduce in spring as more people spend time outdoors. Adding body movements encourages children to participate as well as remember the song's lyrics.

这首歌非常适用于春天，因为此时大家会到户外活动。加入肢体动作能鼓励学生积极参与，同时也加深他们对歌词的印象。

☆ ☾ **1. Vocabulary Flash Cards: Ball Games 词卡：球类运动**

This set of flash cards introduces some of the most popular sports that are played with balls. After introducing each sport, ask students to stand up if they enjoy playing that sport. Write the name of each sport on the board or chart paper and the number of students in the class that enjoy playing each sport. You may also wish to bring in some of the balls used to play these sports and ask students to name them in Chinese.

这套词卡介绍一些受欢迎的球类运动。在介绍每项运动后，若学生喜欢那项运动，可请他们站起来。把每项运动的名称写在白板上或纸表上，同时记录喜欢各项运动的学生总数。也可把和这些运动有关的不同球类带到班上，让学生用中文说出它们的名称。

☆ ☾ **2. Vocabulary Flash Cards: More Sports 词卡：其他运动**

This set of flash cards introduces more sports that are popular among school-age children. Use the same activity above to find out how many students in the class participate in these sports.

这套词卡介绍另外一些颇受学生欢迎的运动。用上述方法找出班上有多少同学参与这些运动。

☆ ☾ **3. Write and Draw: My Favorite Sport 写一写，画一画：我最喜欢的运动**

In this activity students are to choose the sport that is their current favorite and one that they would like to learn to play in the future. As students share their responses with the class, tally the answers to find out which activities are most popular with that class.

学生可把他们目前最喜欢的运动，以及他们将来想学的运动写下来、画出来。当学生与班上同学分享答案时，教师可将答案记录下来，看看这一班最受欢迎的运动有哪些。

☆ ☾ **4. Chant: Sports 顺口溜：运动**

Students work in teams to create a chant using their sports vocabulary list to fill in their favorite sports. Encourage teams to practice repeatedly for a class chant competition. After each group performs, students can enter a secret ballot and vote for the chant they like best.

学生以小组形式创作顺口溜。他们可以利用所学过的运动词汇填写他们喜欢的运动。鼓励各组勤加练习以进行朗读比赛。在各组表演后，让学生投选出表现最好的小组。

☆ ☾ **5. Art Project: My Weekly Schedule on Sports 创意手工：运动时间表**

Students will cut out the two wheels and put them together with a paper fastener. They can then practice asking each other about their weekly schedule in Chinese by saying: Xīng qī___, nǐ zuò shén me?

让学生剪出轮盘，用铜扣钉将它们钉牢。之后，学生就可以用中文练习问彼此每星期的活动有哪些："星期____，你做什么？"

☾ ○ **6. Reading: Yao Ming 读一读：姚明加油！**

Although many students have heard of Yao Ming, the famous basketball player from China, they probably do not realize how tall he is. Before reading the passage about him, measure his height on a wall in the classroom and mark it with a piece of colored tape. This visual aid makes learning about this great athlete even more interesting for students. **Note:** Yao Ming is 7'6" tall (2.29m).

To expand this lesson students can replace Yao Ming's name and basketball with other names and sports using the reading model.

☆ Beginner ☾ Intermediate ☆☾ Beginner-Intermediate ☾○ Intermediate-Advanced ○ Advanced ☺ All

June 六月

虽然很多学生都认识从中国来的著名篮球员姚明，但他们或许不知道他到底有多高。在阅读有关他的短文前，教师可在课室的墙上量出他的身高，然后用彩色胶带纸标出来。这种直观教具能增添学习的趣味性。**注：姚明身高为 7'6"（2.29米）。**

作为延伸活动，学生可以用其他名字和运动来替代姚明和篮球。

Father's Day 父亲节

In America and many other countries, Father's Day is celebrated on the 3rd Sunday in June. Children enjoy making gifts for their father for this special day. The projects below can be modified for children in the class who do not have a father.

在美国和许多国家，父亲节是在六月的第三个星期天。孩子们喜欢为父亲制作礼物，在这个特别的日子送给他们。如果班上有学生没有父亲，也可将以下的活动建议稍作调整以适用于其他送礼对象。

☺ **1. Art Project: No.1 Dad Badge/Gold Medal 创意手工："爸爸第一名"徽章** 309

This Father's Day project is a perfect way to show and tell one's father how much he means to him/her. Students will need to color, cut, sign their name and practice reading the words.

这个父亲节手工能很好地表达孩子对父亲的爱。让学生涂色，剪出丝带，签名，然后练习念出上面的文字。

☺ **2. Art Project: Super Dad Certificate 创意手工：超级爸爸奖** 310

Students will trace the Chinese characters, color, and fill in their name and the date. Students can practice reading their certificates to each other so that they will be able to read it to their father on Father's Day.

让学生描出汉字，涂色，然后填上他们的名字和日期。学生可以彼此练习，互念出自己奖状上的文字，以便能够在父亲节念给父亲听。

☺ **3. Art Project: Father's Day Shirt Card 创意手工：父亲节卡片** 311

This Father's Day shirt and tie card is easy for children of all ages to make. (See sample on p. 404)

Instructions:

1. Fold the paper in half. The hearts will be hidden inside the card.
2. Cut along the dotted lines and fold the two sides down to look like a collar.
3. Use construction paper to cut a tie shape (bow tie or regular tie) and paste it on the center of the shirt.
4. Write the words "爸爸，我爱你" in the empty hearts inside the shirt card.
5. Add decorations to complete this special Father's Day card.

对各年龄层的孩子来说，这个父亲节卡片是非常容易制作的。（作品展示见第404页）

指示：

1. 将纸张对折。印有文字和空心的那一面折在内侧。
2. 沿着虚线剪纸，然后将两边往下折，做成衣领。
3. 用彩色纸剪出一条领带或领结，然后贴在上衣的中间。
4. 在卡内空心处写上"爸爸，我爱你"。
5. 点缀这张卡片以增添美感。

This poem uses simple similes such as sun, rainbow, lighthouse and hero to express love for a father figure. Practice reading this poem with the whole class, then allow students to practice reading it together in small groups. Encourage students to take the poem home and read it to their father.

诗中利用简单的比喻，如太阳、彩虹、灯塔和英雄，来表达对父亲的爱。和全班一起练习朗读这首诗，然后让学生在小组内练习。鼓励他们带回家念给父亲听。

Insects 昆虫

This set of flash cards can be used to introduce the names of nine insects that are familiar to students in Chinese. Learning about insects in Chinese will help to reinforce the learning about insects that is part of the elementary curriculum.

这套词卡介绍九种昆虫的中文名称。这些昆虫都是学生所熟悉的。作为小学课程的一部分，学习昆虫的中文名称有助于巩固学生对昆虫的认识。

Introduce or review the words "dà" and "xiǎo" using objects of different sizes in the classroom. Students can then apply the two new words to describe the insects on the activity sheet. Color words can also be added to create more opportunities for speaking about insects.

利用不同大小的物件，在班上介绍或复习"大"、"小"二字。之后学生可以利用这两个新词形容活动纸上的昆虫。也可以加入彩色词汇以制造更多讨论昆虫的机会。

This worksheet consists of two parts.

1. **Insect Survey:** Give students a set amount of time to go around the classroom and interview each other using the sentence patterns provided. This survey encourages students to practice using the new vocabulary and to review numbers.

2. **Let's Catch:** Provide one set of insect cards for each group using the insect vocabulary sheet cut into cards. Students place cards face down in the center. As each card is turned up, the student who slaps it first and names it correctly in Chinese will write his/her initials in the box next to that insect.

这个活动分成两部分。

1. **昆虫问卷：** 让学生在规定的时间内用第315页的问题互访，这能让他们练习新学的词汇，并复习数字。

2. **捉虫乐：** 为每一组提供一套昆虫词卡。学生把卡面朝下摆在中间。当每张卡被翻过来时，最先拍到词卡并且说出卡中昆虫正确名称的学生，将能把他/她的名字写在那只昆虫旁边的格子里。

It is important for young students to observe the body parts of insects and learn to distinguish them. This activity is designed to relate to the school curriculum and reinforce their learning about the body parts of insects.

辨认昆虫的身体部位能提高小学生的观察力。此活动配合学校课程，强化学生对昆虫的身体部位的学习。

☆◖ 5. Fill in the Blanks: Are You Afraid Of These Insects?

Some children are afraid of insects and some children love them. This activity provides an interactive exercise to engage students in a conversation drill and express their fear about certain insects.

有些孩子怕昆虫，有些却喜欢昆虫。此练习具有互动性，让学生参与对话，表达他们对某些昆虫的恐惧。

◖○ 6. Reading: Story of the Silkworm 读一读：蚕丝的故事

Silk making is one of the important inventions of China. This reading is about the discovery of silk and how it was produced to make clothing and other items.

丝绸是中国的重要发明之一。此活动简单浅白地介绍丝绸是如何被发现并制成衣服和其他用品的。

◖○ 7. Quiz: Story of the Silkworm 考考你：蚕丝的故事

Students can work individually or in pairs to complete this activity after reading the passage.

读了短文后，学生可以独立或和伙伴一起完成这个作业。

> 答案： 1. 黄帝 2. 西陵氏 3. 嫘祖 4. 桑树 5. 丝绸 6. 丝路
> 7. 衣服；扇子 8. 五千多年 9. 蚕茧

◖○ 8. Sequencing: How To Make Silk 排列顺序：丝的制作

This activity requires students to number the steps in the silk making process in the correct order.

这个活动要求学生列出丝绸制作步骤的正确顺序。

> 答案： (1) 采桑叶；(2) 养蚕；(3) 晒干蚕茧；(4) 抽丝；(5) 蚕丝染色；(6) 纺纱织布

◖○ 9. Compare: Life Cycles of the Butterfly and the Silkworm Moth

It is important for young students to observe the life cycle of the insects. Learning about the life cycle is part of the school curriculum. Students will find it interesting to compare it with the life cycle of the silkworm moth.

Note: Butterfly and silkworm moth go through a similar life cycle, except that the butterfly turns from the egg to a butterfly and silkworm moth turns from the egg to a moth at the final stage.

让学生观察昆虫的生命周期通常是学校课程的一部分。学生会很有兴趣去比较昆虫和蚕蛾的生命周期。

注：蝴蝶和蚕蛾的生命周期是相似的，只是蝴蝶从卵最后变成蝶，而蚕蛾从卵最后变成蛾。

> **Answer key:**
>
> | Similarities | Differences |
> |---|---|
> | 1st stage : Egg is the same. | 4th stage : The egg of the butterfly turns to a butterfly; |
> | 2nd stage: Larva is the same. | the egg of the silkworm turns to a moth. |
> | 3rd stage : Pupa is the same. | |

June 六月

Cultural Link: Dragon Boat Festival 端午节

The Dragon Boat Festival is an important festival in Chinese culture. It is held on the 5th day of the 5th month on the lunar calendar. On this day people celebrate by participating in or watching dragon boat races and eating steamed rice packages called "zong zi". Although dragon boat races originated in China, dragon boat races are held in many cities around the world each year.

端午节在农历的五月初五，是中华文化里的一个重要节日。在这天，人们通过参与或观赏龙舟赛以及吃粽子来庆祝端午节。虽然龙舟赛源自中国，但每年也都在世界上很多有华人的地方举行。

Students will learn about the story of the Dragon Boat Festival from this simple and plain passage. The important vocabulary words are in bold so that teachers may reinforce and explain.

Although historical records indicate that Qu Yuan jumped into the river and committed suicide, teachers should be cautious when telling the story of Qu Yuan to young children and should avoid bringing up the topic of suicide.

学生将通过这篇浅显的短文认识端午节。重要的词汇都加黑了，便于教师讲解。虽然历史记载屈原是投江自尽的，但教师在讲述屈原的故事时应该小心，避免带入自杀的课题。

This activity will help students to better understand the definitions of the selected vocabulary words and improve their reading skill.

这个活动能帮助学生更好地了解指定词汇的意思，提升阅读能力。

> 答案：龙舟比赛 —— dragon boat races；
> 爱国诗人 —— Qu Yuan；
> 治理国家 —— govern the country；
> 不同意 —— is not agreeable；
> 战乱 —— chaos and wars；　读书人——scholar；
> 罢免 —— remove from office；
> 粽子 —— rice dumplings wrapped with bamboo or reed leaves；
> 从此 —— from this date on；　建议——suggest

After learning the story of the Dragon Boat Festival, students will enjoy this hands-on art project of making a paper dragon boat. Follow the directions to form the body of the boat. Cut out the boat head and the tail, then glue or staple them to both ends of the body to form a dragon boat. (See sample on p. 404)

认识了有关端午节的由来，学生将会喜欢这个制作纸龙舟的活动。根据指示做成船身。剪出船头和船尾，将它们贴在或钉在船身两端，做成龙舟。（作品展示见第404页）

☆ Beginner　❆ Intermediate　☆❆ Beginner-Intermediate　❆❍ Intermediate-Advanced　❍ Advanced　☺ All

Try It Out! 每月一练

☆☾ **a. Let's Talk!** 说一说

1. **Hobbies and Sports** 爱好和运动

   Students will practice these short dialogues by using the learned vocabulary words of the topics of sports and leisure activities. The third dialogue even provides an opportunity for students to review and expand their conversation about the sports which are associated with the seasons.

   学生将利用所学过的运动和休闲活动词汇来练习这些对话。第三个对话可让学生进行和季节性运动相关的谈话。

☾◯ **b. Let's Write!** 写一写

江、河、玉、石、衣、刀

(For Character Writing Sheets, see pp. 391, 392. 写字练习纸见本书附录 pp. 391, 392。)

Notes for Teachers
教学重点

July 七月

July Calendar 七月月历

☺ **1. Coloring Activity: Independence Day** 涂颜色： 美国独立日

America's Independence Day is on the 4th of July. This is a national holiday in America and many Americans observe the day by participating in or watching parades, having picnics and watching fireworks at night. Students who are from America can share their personal experiences with this holiday. Students who are not from America can be asked to share how they celebrate their country's national day.

美国独立日是在七月四日。这是美国的公定假日，许多美国人都会通过参加或观赏游行、野餐和在夜晚欣赏烟火来欢庆这一天。从美国来的学生可以和同学们分享他们的个人经历。其他同学可以分享他们如何庆祝自己国家的国庆节。

☽◯ **2. My July Calendar** 我的七月月历

By this point in the school year most students will be able to fill in the numbers of the July calendar independently. Students can then color the calendar red, white, and blue to represent America's Independence Day or the colors of their nation's flag.

到学年的这个阶段，多数学生应该能够独立填写七月月历上的数字。接着，让他们将月历涂上红、白和蓝色，标志美国独立日，或涂上他们自己国家国旗的颜色。

☽◯ **3. What's Happening in July?** 七月知多少?

This fill-in-the-blank worksheet, which is included with each month, allows advanced learners to review numbers, dates, important holidays and events of that month in a familiar and consistent way.

高年级的学生可以在月历的基础上，通过这样的填空题复习数字和星期，熟悉每月重要的日子。

National Day 国庆节

☺ **1. Vocabulary Flash Cards: Independence Day** 词卡： 美国独立日

Identify and discuss each of these vocabulary words related to America's Independence Day. Introducing this set of words presents the opportunity to make connections with other cultures by comparing different foods eaten for a national holiday celebration or popular symbols for different countries.

讨论每一个和美国独立日有关的词语。介绍这些词语时，也可以比较不同国家的国庆节所吃的食物，或不同国家的著名象征物，作为文化联系。

☆ Beginner ☾ Intermediate ☆☾ Beginner-Intermediate ☾◯ Intermediate-Advanced ◯ Advanced ☺ All

☆ ☾ **2. Match and Write: Independence Day** 连一连，写一写：美国独立日 334

This vocabulary exercise requires students to match individual characters to make words related to Independence Day. Students must then provide the pinyin and English translation for each of the words.

这个词汇练习要求学生连接单词，组成和美国独立日相关的词语。接着，学生必须为每个词语提供拼音和英文翻译。

> 答案： 1. 美国、měi guó、America；   2 自由女神、zì yóu nǚ shén、Statue of Liberty；
> 3. 烟火、yān huǒ、fireworks；   4. 热狗、rè gǒu、hotdog；
> 5. 老鹰、lǎo yīng、eagle；   6. 国旗、guó qí、flag；
> 7. 七月四日、qī yuè sì rì、   8. 野餐、yě cān、picnic；
>   4th of July；   9. 游行、yóu xíng、parade.

☆ ☾ **3. Word Search: Independence Day** 找一找：美国独立日 335

This word search puzzle gives students the opportunity to practice reading and become more familiar with the new Independence Day vocabulary words.

这个字谜让学生能够练习阅读刚学过的美国独立日词语，加深印象。

☺ **4. Coloring: National Day around the World** 涂颜色：世界各国的国庆节 336

Many children love to learn about the designs of different flags from around the world. On this worksheet students are required to color the flags correctly and write each of the country's date of independence. This exercise is a good review of color words, months, and numbers.

许多学生喜欢认识世界各国国旗的图案。在这个作业里，学生必须为各国国旗涂上正确的颜色，并写上其国庆节的日期。这个活动有助于复习颜色词汇、月份和数字。

> **Answer key:** Mexico – May 5; China – October 1; Korea – August 15;
> South Africa – April 27; Israel – May 14.

☾○ **5. Write, Draw, Color: My Country's National Day**
写一写，画一画，涂一涂：我的国庆节 337

Students will feel proud to complete this worksheet that features a picture of their country's flag. Depending on the class make up, it may be necessary to provide an online resource or World Almanac for some students to refer to in order to complete this activity. In addition to drawing and coloring their nation's flag correctly, students are required to fill in the colors of their flag in Chinese.

这个活动让学生展示自己国家的国旗。视学生的背景，或许有必要提供网上资源或世界年鉴，让一些学生作为参考，来完成这个活动。除了正确画出国旗并涂上颜色，学生还必须以中文为自己国家的国旗标上颜色名称。

┌─────────────────┐
│ **Craft Fun 手工乐** │
└─────────────────┘

☺ **1. Peking Opera: Introduction and Face-Painting** 京剧：简介和脸谱涂色 338

Color a sample of each of the worksheets included to introduce the four main character roles in Peking Opera and the colors that are used to represent them. This provides an opportunity to review

☆ Beginner ☾ Intermediate ☆☾ Beginner-Intermediate ☾○ Intermediate-Advanced ○ Advanced ☺ All   **61**

the color words and to discuss the attributes associated with each of the characters. Students can then use the worksheets to color their copies of the Peking Opera masks. To supplement this activity images or video clips of Peking Opera can be shown to the class. (See sample on pp. 404-405)

为每页的脸谱涂色，然后用来介绍京剧里的四种主要角色以及不同颜色的代表。这能让学生复习颜色词汇，并讨论每个角色所代表的性格特征。之后，学生可以在自己的活动纸上为这些京剧脸谱涂色。要增添活动的趣味性，可在班上播放京剧的图片或录影。（作品展示见第404–405页）

☺ **2. Origami Fun: Pinwheel 趣味折纸：风车** 342

Paper folding is an ancient art form that is popular in both China and Japan. To do origami, it is best to use special origami paper, but, colored copy paper cut into squares can be used as a substitute. We suggest making a sample of the project to become familiar with the process before demonstrating the steps to the class. Encourage children who complete each step quickly to assist other students who may have more difficulty following the steps. (See sample on p. 405)

折纸是一种古代的艺术形式，在中国和日本非常受欢迎。要进行折纸，最好是用特制的纸张；剪成四方形的彩色纸也可以用来折纸。我们建议先做出一个样本以熟悉整个过程，再示范给学生看。可鼓励做得快的学生去帮助较慢的学生。（作品展示见第405页）

☺ **3. Art Project: Tangram Fun 创意手工：七巧板** 343

Tangram is an ancient Chinese puzzle game. It is a square that is divided into seven pieces: two big triangles, one medium triangle, two small triangles, one square and one parallelogram. To do this activity, students each need to cut out the seven tangram pieces found on page 343. You may wish to challenge students to reassemble the cut out pieces to make a square before moving on to the game.

To play this game, all seven pieces must lay on a flat surface, with one piece touching the other without overlapping to form a shape of animal, house, bird or other figures. This game not only helps young students build up geometrical skills, but also helps develop their imagination and creativity. (See sample on p. 405)

The book, Grandfather Tang's Story, can be read in conjunction with this tangram activity.

七巧板是一种中国的古老游戏。它是由一块四方形板切成七小块，其中包括两个大三角形、一个中三角形、两个小三角形、一个正方形和一个平行四边形。要进行这个活动，每个学生必须剪出第343页的七小块。你可以让学生将剪出来的七小块再重组成四方形，然后开始玩七巧板的游戏。

游戏的规则是把七小块平放，可以随意变换位置，但每块必须互相衔接，且不可重叠，用这七小块组成动物、房子、鸟或其他图像。这个游戏不但可以帮助幼童建立几何图形概念，还可以让他们发挥想像力和创造力。（作品展示见第405页）

Cultural Link: Four Treasures of the Study 文房四宝

○ **1. Reading: Chinese Calligraphy and Painting 读一读：中国书法和中国画** 345

Calligraphy and painting are often considered the two most important skills and disciplines of the Chinese scholars in ancient time. To perform good artwork, scholars used good tools known as "Wenfang Si Bao" which means "Four Treasures of the Study". They are brush, inkstick, paper and inkstone.

☆ Beginner ☾ Intermediate ☆☾ Beginner-Intermediate ☾○ Intermediate-Advanced ○ Advanced ☺ All

The reading passage discusses the importance of a scholar to be highly skilled in the arts of calligraphy and painting.

书法和绘画常被认为是中国古代文人必备的两项最重要的技艺，而文人中不可少的工具就是"文房四宝"——笔、墨、纸、砚。

阅读短文谈论文人能书能画的重要性。

This follow-up activity can help students improve reading comprehension skills in Chinese.

这个跟进活动帮助学生提升中文阅读理解能力。

答案： 1. 必备的；   2. 笔、纸；   3. 不仅、而已、独特的；
       4. 性格、思想；   5. 画中有诗；
       6. 人物画；   7. 除了、之外

This activity reinforces grammar usage and helps students improve their writing skills in Chinese.

这个活动强化语法的使用，帮助学生提升他们的中文写作能力。

简答题答案： 1. 琴、棋、书、画
           2. 笔、墨、纸、砚
           3. 山水画、花鸟画、人物画
           4. 因为它们可以当作书画作品的装饰，增加美感，
             还能帮助我们辨识作者，了解作者的思想和感情。

Try It Out! 每月一练

a. **Let's Talk!** 说一说

Students can work with partners to practice these dialogues about nationalities and countries. They can change the nationality or country name to describe themselves if necessary.

学生可以配对练习这些关于国籍和国家的对话。如有需要，他们也可以更换国籍或国名来形容自己。

足、身、豆、草、虫、鸟

(For Character Writing Sheets, see pp. 391, 392. 写字练习纸见本书附录 pp. 391, 392。)

July 七月

☆ Beginner   ☾ Intermediate   ☆☾ Beginner-Intermediate   ☾○ Intermediate-Advanced   ○ Advanced   ☺ All

Notes for Teachers
教学重点

August 八月

August Calendar 八月月历

☺ **1. Coloring Activity: Summer Vacation** 涂颜色：暑假 352

Summer is a popular time of year for families to enjoy their vacation time together. This topic provides a good opportunity for students to share about their favorite family outings or trips. Use the picture on this page to begin a discussion about summer vacation with students. Afterwards students may color this page as they wish.

夏天是全家一起度假的好时光。这个主题让学生分享他们喜欢的家庭郊游活动或旅行。利用这一页的图画作为起点，和学生讨论暑假。之后再让学生为图画涂色。

2. My August Calendar 我的八月月历 353

Students can use this month's calendar to discuss when their families will go on vacation or participate in different summer activities. Use an enlarged copy of the calendar, and, as students volunteer information about themselves, put it on the calendar. Summer vacation and leisure activities are enjoyable topics that most students will be motivated to share about.

For other uses of the calendar, please refer to the notes on My January Calendar.

学生可以用本月月历讨论全家的暑假度假计划或者其他活动安排。将月历放大，把学生所分享的内容填在里面。暑假和休闲活动都是大家喜欢谈论的课题。

关于月历的其他用途，请参考第1页"我的一月月历"的说明。

3. What's Happening in August? 八月知多少？ 354

This fill-in-the-blank worksheet, which is included with each month, allows advanced learners to review numbers, dates, important holidays and events of that month in a familiar and consistent way.

高年级的学生可以在月历的基础上，通过这样的填空题复习数字和星期，熟悉每月重要的日子。

Summer Fun 夏天乐

☆ **1. Vocabulary Flash Cards: Summer Activities** 词卡：夏天活动 355

This set of flash cards introduces some popular activities that many people enjoy during the summer months. To help students become more familiar with these new words after introducing them, ask students if they have ever tried each of the activities. Students can also practice interviewing each other about which activities they enjoy most.

☆ Beginner   ☾ Intermediate   ☆☾ Beginner-Intermediate   ☾◯ Intermediate-Advanced   ◯ Advanced   ☺ All

这套词卡介绍许多人在暑假时所喜欢进行的活动。为了帮助学生在认识新词汇后对它们更熟悉，可问学生他们是否有尝试过这些活动。学生可以练习访问彼此关于他们最喜欢的活动。

Students pick three activities that they love the most to write about and draw to complete this mini-book. They will share their drawings and favorite activities when they present their mini-book to the class.

学生写下并画出他们最喜欢的三个活动，然后和班上同学分享。

This set of flash cards introduces words for things people commonly see at a beach. If possible, use pictures of beach scenes from advertisements or from the Internet to ask students which objects from the vocabulary list that they see. Students can share their responses by answering in a complete sentence using the new words

这套词卡介绍海滩上常见的东西。可能的话，拿广告或互联网上的海滩照片给学生看，问他们在照片里看到哪样东西是他们新学到的词汇。学生可利用新词汇以完整句子回答。

For additional practice with these new words about things to see and do on the beach, students can circle the correct word that corresponds with each of the pictures on this page.

让学生圈出和图片相应的正确词汇，作为额外练习。

This set of flash cards introduces words for things that people bring to the beach. To make learning this set of words more lively, use a real beach bag filled with some of the items on the list to demonstrate what you usually take on a trip to the beach. Students can also be asked to draw a picture of a large beach bag and draw and label five things they usually take with them to the beach. Afterwards they can share and compare their items with the class.

这套词卡介绍人们带到海滩的东西。要增添学习趣味，可使用一个真的海滩包，在里头放一些词卡上所列的东西，展示给学生看。也可让学生画一张大的海滩包，里头再画他们常带到海滩的五样东西，并标上名称。之后，他们可以和同学分享并比较各自的物品。

This activity is a good follow up activity to be done after students learn the new words related to the beach.
这个活动能巩固学生之前所学的海滩词汇。

This activity gives students further practice with using the new Beach Words vocabulary.
这个活动让学生进一步练习使用海滩词汇。

答案： 1. 海滩　　2. 烤肉　　3. 铲子　　4. 晒太阳　　5. 太阳眼镜
　　　　　6. 冲浪板　　7. 海鸥　　8. 救生员　　9. 游泳衣

☆ Beginner　⟨ Intermediate　☆⟨ Beginner-Intermediate　⟨○ Intermediate-Advanced　○ Advanced　☺ All

答案：1. 对　　2. 不对　　3. 对　　4. 不对　　5. 对　　6. 对
7. 不对　　8. 对　　9. 不对　　10. 对　　11. 对　　12. 不对

☺ **12. Jeopardy Game: 60 Questions Review** 按铃抢答：60个复习题

Here at the end of the month we introduce an exciting game that challenges students to recall a great deal of the information covered in Chinese Treasure Chest. It is based on the popular American TV game show called Jeopardy in which contestants compete to answer questions from different categories. The categories we have made include: Chinese to English; English to Chinese; Social Studies; Culture; and Chinese Characters. The teacher can choose the appropriate sample questions provided to fit into these five categories. The easiest questions are $100 questions and the most difficult are $500. The use of a buzzer system such as Eggspert makes playing this game ever more fun for students.

How to Play:
A member of the team picks a category and value (e.g., Animals, $100)

Variations:
Divide the class into teams. Give each team a few minutes to agree upon their team name. When the class is ready to begin, one player from each team will come forward to a predetermined place in the classroom.

If possible, have a buzzer system such as Eggspert available

☆ Beginner　☾ Intermediate　☆☾ Beginner-Intermediate　☾◯ Intermediate-Advanced　◯ Advanced　☺ All

for students to play with. Otherwise, provide each team with a different noise maker to make a sound when a player is ready to respond to a question. Including these props makes playing this game much more exciting and fun for children.

The teacher then begins by choosing a category for the first question and the amount that will be awarded for answering correctly. The player who responds with the correct answer wins that amount for the team and is allowed to choose the category from which the next question will be asked. The game continues this way for as long as the teacher decides to play. This can be determined by a dollar amount or by time.

The following sample questions from topics 1-8 can be used for the Chinese to English, English to Chinese and Chinese Characters categories. Of course, teachers can substitute the words to include specific vocabulary to review with students. For the Chinese Characters category we recommend making large flash cards with characters for students to identify by reading and/or translating.

Sample Chart

学校 School	数学 Numbers	颜色 Colors	家庭 Family	文化 Culture
$100	$100	$100	$100	$100
$200	$200	$200	$200	$200
$300	$300	$300	$300	$300
$400	$400	$400	$400	$400
$500	$500	$500	$500	$500

(Students may pick their top 5 choices of the categories.)

1. **School:**
1) What does "shū bāo" mean?
2) What does "xué xiào" mean?
3) How do you say "teacher" in Chinese?
4) How do you say "pencil" in Chinese?
5) Name one direction that teachers give to students in Chinese. (Stand up, sit down, raise your hand, please, no talking, pay attention etc.)

2. **Numbers:**
1) What number is "jiǔ shí wǔ"?
2) How do you say "12" in Chinese?
3) What is the number before/after "sān shí sān"?
4) Say today's date in Chinese.
5) Read the following characters: 十、九、八、七、六、五、四、三、二、一.

3. **Colors:**
1) Name the color of "píng guǒ" in Chinese.
2) Name one thing that is "huáng sè". (Teacher decide if the answer should be in Chinese or English)
3) Say the name of the Chinese lucky color in Chinese.
4) Say 2 colors on what you are wearing in Chinese.
5) Answer the question in Chinese: 熊猫是什么颜色的? xióng māo shì shén me yán sè de?

4. **Family:**
1) How do you say "mother" in Chinese?
2) How do you say this person in Chinese? (Teacher show flash card of a family member in characters or pinyin)
3) Say all your family members in Chinese.
4) Answer the question: 你的妹妹叫什么名字? Nǐ de mèi mei jiào shén me míng zì?
5) What does "Wǒ ài wǒ de jiā" mean?

5. Animals:

1) Name one zodiac animal in Chinese and English.
2) What is "tiger" in Chinese?
3) Name one animal that can fly in Chinese and English.
4) Name the zodiac sign of this year in Chinese and English.
5) Translate: 我喜欢狮子和老虎.
   Wǒ xǐ huan shī zi hé lǎo hǔ.

6. Body Parts:

1) How do you say "nose" in Chinese?
2) What does "dù zi" mean?
3) Name one body part that a fish doesn't have in Chinese.
4) Answer the question in Chinese: 你有几个眼睛? Nǐ yǒu jǐ gè yǎn jing?
5) Sing the first part of the song "Head, Shoulders, Knees and Toes" in Chinese and point to them. (Answer: 头、肩膀、膝盖、脚趾头; Tóu, jiān bǎng, xī gài, jiǎo zhǐ tou.)

7. Sports:

1) What does "lán qiú" mean?
2) How do you say "baseball" in Chinese?
3) Name one of your favorite sports in Chinese and English.
4) Name one of the popular sports in China/America/Brazil, etc.
5) Translate: 哥哥常常去打网球。
   Gē ge cháng cháng qù dǎ wǎng qiú.

8. Food and Fruits:

1) What is the most popular beverage in China?
2) Name one food item in the Chinese menu.
3) How do you say "rice" in Chinese?
4) Name the food that rabbits love to eat the most.
5) Answer the question: 你喜欢吃什么水果/蔬菜? Nǐ xǐ huan chī shén me shuǐ guǒ/shū cài?

9. Social Studies:

1) What is the 3rd biggest country in the world?
2) Why was the Great Wall of China built?
3) What is China's capital?
4) What is the largest city in China?
5) What is the official language spoken in China?
6) What is the longest river in China?
7) In what city were the Terra-cotta soldiers and horses found?
8) Name 2 countries that border China.
9) Name one of China's deserts.
10) Name 2 main attractions that people visit in China.

10. Culture:

1) What are the two lucky colors in Chinese culture?
2) Name one way that people celebrate the Chinese New Year.
3) How many animals are in the Chinese zodiac?
4) What do people eat to celebrate the Mid-Autumn Festival?
5) What is the traditional food eaten for birthday celebrations in China as a symbol of long life?
6) Why does Chinese New Year fall on a different day each year?
7) Why do people sweep their floors before the New Year period? Or name two ways that Chinese families prepare for the New Year.
8) Name one way that Chinese people celebrate the Dragon Boat Festival.
9) Name one thing that was invented in China.
10) Name the four treasures that Chinese people use for calligraphy and painting.

☆ Beginner   ℂ Intermediate   ☆ℂ Beginner-Intermediate   ℂ○ Intermediate-Advanced   ○ Advanced   ☺ All

在八月结束时，可介绍一个刺激好玩的游戏来考一考学生在本套书中所学到的知识。这是一个改编自美国高收视电视节目"Jeopardy"的游戏，参赛者必须从不同组别中选题作答。我们在此所设的组别有：中译英、英译中、社会知识、文化以及汉字。 教师可从下列参考题目中选出适当的纳入这五大组别。最简单的题目值100元，而最难的题目值500元。计时铃声的使用会让这个游戏更有趣。

玩法：每组派一名组员选择组别和题值（如：动物；$100）

不同玩法：

将全班分成几组，让他们为自己的组取名。当大家都准备好后，让每组派一名组员到教室里的指定位置。

可能的话，设置一个计时铃声系统让学生玩。不然，为每组提供一个不同的声响器，在参赛者准备回答问题时可以发出声音。添加这些道具能够让游戏更刺激好玩。

首先，教师选择第一道问题的组别以及正确答题后所能得到的数额。正确答题的参赛者将为他/她的组赢得数额，并可以选择下一道问题的组别。游戏的长短由教师决定。这可以通过所得数额或时间决定。

以下参考题目中的前八大主题，可以用在中译英、英译中以及汉字的组别里。教师可更换题目中的词语，以便和学生一起复习某些特定词语。对于汉字组别的题目，我们建议制作大词卡，上面印有汉字，让学生通过阅读和/或翻译进行辨认。

---

1. 学校：

1) 什么是"shū bāo"？
2) 什么是"xué xiào"？
3) 如何用中文说"teacher"？
4) 如何用中文说"pencil"？
5) 用中文说出教师给学生的一项指示。（站起来、坐下、请举手、不要说话、注意看等）

2. 数字：

1) "Jiǔ shí wǔ"的数字是什么？
2) 如何用中文说"12"？
3) "Sān shí sān"之前/之后的数字是什么？
4) 用中文说出今天的日期。
5) 念出这些汉字：十、九、八、七、六、五、四、三、二、一。

3. 颜色：

1) 用中文说出"píng guǒ"的颜色。
2) 举出一件黄色的东西。（教师可决定答案应该是中文的还是英文的。）
3) 用中文说出一个中国吉祥颜色的名称。
4) 用中文说出你衣服上的两种颜色名称。
5) 用中文回答这个问题：熊猫是什么颜色的？

4. 家庭：

1) "Mother"在中文怎么说？
2) 你如何用中文称呼这个人？（教师出示一张词卡，上面印有一个家庭成员的称谓。可以是拼音或汉字。）
3) 用中文称呼你的家人。
4) 回答这个问题：你的妹妹叫什么名字？
5) "我爱我的家"的意思是什么？

5. 动物：

1) 用中文和英文说出一个生肖动物的名字。
2) "Tiger"在中文怎么说？
3) 用中文和英文说出一个会飞的动物。
4) 用中文和英文说出今年的生肖年份。
5) 将"我喜欢狮子和老虎。"这句话翻译成英文。

6. 身体部位：

1) 如何用中文说"nose"？
2) "Dù zi"是指哪一个身体部位？
3) 用中文说出鱼所没有的身体部位。
4) 用中文回答问题：你有几个眼睛？
5) 用中文唱英文儿歌《Head, Shoulders, Knees and Toes》，并指出这些身体部位。

---

7. 体育：

1) "篮球"的意思是什么？

2) "Baseball"中文怎么说？

3) 用中文和英文说出你喜欢的一项运动。

4) 举出在中国/美国/巴西所流行的一项运动。

5) 将"哥哥常常去打网球"翻译成英文。

8. 食物和水果：

1) 什么饮料在中国最受欢迎？

2) 举出中式菜单里的一道菜。

3) "米饭"中文怎么说？

4) 举出兔子最爱吃的食物。

5) 回答这个问题：你喜欢吃什么水果/蔬菜？

9. 社会知识：

1) 世界上面积第三大国家是哪一国？

2) 为什么要建造中国万里长城？

3) 中国的首都是什么？

4) 中国最大的城市是什么？

5) 中国的官方语言是什么？

6) 中国最长的河流是什么？

7) 兵马俑是在哪一个城市被发现的？

8) 举出两个和中国毗邻的国家。

9) 举出中国的一个沙漠。

10) 举出人们到中国时会观光的两个主要景点。

10. 文化：

1) 中华文化里的两个吉祥颜色是什么？

2) 举出人们庆祝农历新年的其中一种方式。

3) 中国的生肖有几个动物？

4) 人们庆祝中秋节时会吃什么？

5) 在中国庆寿时所吃的代表长寿的传统食物是什么？

6) 为什么每年的农历新年都在不同的日子？

7) 为什么人们在农历新年前要扫地？或举出华人家庭准备农历新年的两种方式。

8) 举出华人庆祝端午节的一种方式。

9) 举出在中国发明的一样东西。

10) 举出华人在书画时所用的文房四宝。

Cultural Link: Zheng He 郑和

○ 1. **Reading: Zheng He and His Seven Voyages**
读一读：郑和下西洋 367

Zheng He, the greatest explorer in Chinese history, is known for his seven voyages to the western oceans. This reading provides a brief introduction about his background, his adventurous voyages, and his contributions to the world.

Most western school children learn about the famous European explorers and their discoveries; Christopher Columbus in 1492, Vasco Da Gama in 1498, and Ferdinand Magellan from 1519-1521. However, Zheng He completed his voyages decades before theirs and his fleets were significantly larger.

In 2005, China celebrated the 600th anniversary of this great explorer whose voyages and contributions to the world should be recognized and remembered.

August /八月

☆ Beginner 《 Intermediate ☆《 Beginner-Intermediate 《○ Intermediate-Advanced ○ Advanced ☺ All

Reference:
Zheng He's Seven Voyages to the Western Ocean:

Voyage	Years	Places Visited
1st	1405 – 1407	Siam, Sumatra, Malacca, Sri Lanka, etc.
2nd	1407 – 1409	Siam, Java, Malacca, Sri Lanka, etc.
3rd	1409 – 1411	Siam, Java, Sumatra, Malacca, Sri Lanka, etc.
4th	1413 – 1415	Arabian Peninsula, Hormuz, East Africa, etc.
5th	1417 – 1419	Java, Malacca, Hormuz, East Africa, etc.
6th	1421 – 1422	Siam, Sri Lanka, Hormuz, East Africa, etc.
7th	1431 – 1433	Red Sea and Mecca, etc.

Compare with the other explorers:

Explorer	Year of Voyages	Number of Ships	Size of the Ship	Number of People
Zheng He	1405 – 1433	48 – 317	400 ft.	28,000
Columbus	1492	3	90 ft	90
Magellan	1519 – 1521	5	100 ft.	265

郑和是中国历史上最伟大的航海家，他以七次下西洋闻名。这篇短文简单介绍了郑和的背景、航程以及贡献。

多数西方的孩子都了解一些著名的欧洲探险家的事迹，如：哥伦布于1492年发现美洲新大陆、达迦马于1498年航海到印度、麦哲伦于1519–1521年率领船队首次环航地球等等。不过，郑和在这些欧洲探险家开始航行探索的几十年以前就完成了他的航程，而且随行的舰队更壮大。

在2005年，中国庆祝了这位伟大航海家下西洋600周年，肯定他所做的贡献。

参考资料：

航程	年份	所到之地
第一次	1405 – 1407	暹罗、苏门答腊、马六甲、斯里兰卡等
第二次	1407 – 1409	暹罗、爪哇、马六甲、斯里兰卡等
第三次	1409 – 1411	暹罗、爪哇、苏门答腊、马六甲、斯里兰卡等
第四次	1413 – 1415	阿拉伯半岛、霍尔木兹、东非等
第五次	1417 – 1419	爪哇、马六甲、霍尔木兹、东非等
第六次	1421 – 1422	暹罗、斯里兰卡、霍尔木兹、东非等
第七次	1431 – 1433	红海、麦加等

☆ Beginner ☾ Intermediate ☆☾ Beginner-Intermediate ☾○ Intermediate-Advanced ○ Advanced ☺ All

与其他航海家比较：

航海家	航行年份	舰队数量	船舰体积	人数
郑和	1405 – 1433	48 – 317	400 ft.	28,000
哥伦布	1492	3	90 ft	90
麦哲伦	1519 – 1521	5	100 ft.	265

○ **2. Quiz: Zheng He 考考你：郑和** 369

This follow-up activity helps students review the content of the reading passage. It will improve students' reading comprehension skill.

这个跟进活动能帮助学生复习阅读短文的内容，从而提升他们的阅读理解能力。

> 答案： 1. 郑和下西洋一共七次。
> 2. 因为明成祖派他到国外推广外交，宣传中国文化。
> 3. 郑和最远到达非洲东岸。他是在第四次航行时到达的。
> 4. 郑和从中国带了丝绸、茶叶、金银和瓷器等物品作为礼物。
> 5. 郑和从外国带回香料、象牙、药品、珍珠和珍奇的动物。
> 6. 郑和下西洋大大地推动了全世界的航海事业。

Try It Out! 每月一练

☆ ☾ **a. Let's Talk! 说一说**

1. Do You Like to Go to the Beach? 你喜欢去海滩吗？ 370

2. Where Are You Going This Summer? 这个暑假你要去哪里？ 370

Students will first review vocabulary words of summer activities and sea animals before practicing these dialogue drills. The teacher can role play with the entire class using the dialogues. Then, ask students to practice in pairs while the teacher walks around and provides assistance. If time permits, ask students to volunteer role playing in front of the class in pairs.

先让学生复习夏天活动以及海洋生物的词汇，再练习这些对话。教师可带领全班进行角色扮演。接着，让学生配对练习，教师从旁给予协助。若时间允许，可请学生以配对形式自愿上来表演给全班同学看。

☆ ☾ **b. Let's Write! 写一写** 371

金、门、贝、言、食、舟

(For Character Writing Sheets, see pp. 391, 392. 写字练习纸见本书附录 pp. 391, 392。)

☆ Beginner   ☾ Intermediate   ☆☾ Beginner-Intermediate   ☾○ Intermediate-Advanced   ○ Advanced   ☺ All

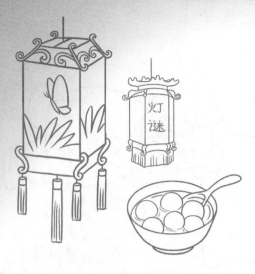

一月
January

Calendar	一月月历
Zodiac Animals	十二生肖
Chinese New Year (Spring Festival)	农历新年（春节）
Lantern Festival	元宵节
Try It Out!	每月一练
Let's Talk!	说一说
Let's Write!	写一写

shí 十 èr 二 shēng 生 xiào 肖

January 一月

年 _____

xīng qī rì 星 期 日	xīng qī yī 星 期 一	xīng qī èr 星 期 二	xīng qī sān 星 期 三	xīng qī sì 星 期 四	xīng qī wǔ 星 期 五	xīng qī liù 星 期 六

What's Happening in January?
一月知多少？

jīn tiān shì　　　　　yuè　　　　rì
1. 今天是＿＿＿＿月＿＿＿＿日。

míng tiān shì　　　　yuè　　　　rì
2. 明天是＿＿＿＿月＿＿＿＿日。

zuó tiān shì　　　　　yuè　　　　rì
3. 昨天是＿＿＿＿月＿＿＿＿日。

jīn tiān shì xīng qī
4. 今天是星期＿＿＿＿＿＿＿。

yī yuè yǒu　　　　　　　　　　tiān
5. 一月有＿＿＿＿＿＿＿＿天。

yī yuè zhōng tè bié de rì zi shì
6. 一月中特别的日子是＿＿＿＿＿＿＿＿。

xīn nián shì　　　　　　　yuè　　　　rì
7. 新年是＿＿＿＿＿月＿＿＿＿日。

yī yuè de dì yí gè xīng qī wǔ shì　　　yuè　　　rì
8. 一月的第一个星期五是＿＿月＿＿日。

yī yuè de zuì hòu yí gè xīng qī yī shì　　yuè　　rì
9. 一月的最后一个星期一是＿＿月＿＿日。

de shēng rì shì　　　yuè　　　rì
10. ＿＿＿＿＿＿＿的生日是＿＿月＿＿日。
(a person's name)

shǔ lǎo shǔ 鼠/老鼠	niú 牛	hǔ lǎo hǔ 虎/老虎	tù tù zi 兔/兔子
lóng 龙	shé 蛇	mǎ 马	yáng 羊
hóu hóu zi 猴/猴子	jī 鸡	gǒu 狗	zhū 猪

Find and Color: Who Are the Winners?
找一找，涂一涂：谁赢了？

The emperor announced, "The first 12 animals to reach the finish line will have a year named after them!" Color the 12 animals that are the winners in the race.

Cut and Paste: What Is the Next Zodiac Animal?
剪一剪，贴一贴：下一个生肖是什么？

Year 1999	Year 2000	Year 2001
tù zi 兔子	lóng 龙	
Year 2003	**Year 2004**	**Year 2005**
yáng 羊	hóu zi 猴子	
Year 2008	**Year 2009**	**Year 2010**
lǎo shǔ 老鼠	niú 牛	

jī 鸡	lǎo hǔ 老虎	shé 蛇

Matching Activity: Zodiac Animal Matching
配对游戏：生肖配一配

Cut out the pinyin words and Chinese characters below. Paste each next to its animal picture.

	Pinyin	**Chinese Character**

lǎo shǔ	lóng	mǎ	gǒu	yáng	niú
龙	狗	羊	牛	老鼠	马

Compare: Are They the Same or Different?
说一说，比一比：它们哪里相同？哪里不同？

Say the names of the following animals. Then compare each pair of animals listed below and point out their similarities and differences. The first one has been done for you. For the last question, fill in any two animals and compare them.

1. 牛和羊：牛和羊都有四只脚、都吃草、颜色不同。

2. 龙和蛇：_____

3. 鸡和兔：_____

4. 老虎和猴子：_____

5. 老鼠和牛：_____

6. _____：_____

Bonus: Can you use two zodiac animals to make up a Chinese idiom?
Hint: Try an online search of "Chinese idioms".

jī fēi gǒu tiào
(For example: 鸡飞狗跳)

1. _____ 2. _____

名字：＿＿＿＿＿＿＿＿＿＿＿＿＿＿ ＿＿＿＿月＿＿＿＿日

Vocabulary Review: Who Am I?
词汇练习：我是谁？

Fill in the blanks.

1. wǒ shuō　wō wō wō 我说：“喔喔喔……” (I say, "Cockle doodle doo.")	wǒ shì 我是＿＿＿＿＿＿＿＿＿。
2. māo ài zhuī wǒ 猫爱追我。 (Cats love to chase me.)	我是＿＿＿＿＿＿＿＿＿。
3. wǒ huì fēi 我会飞。 (I can fly in the sky.)	我是＿＿＿＿＿＿＿＿＿。
4. wǒ huì pá shān 我会爬山。 (I can climb mountains.)	我是＿＿＿＿＿＿＿＿＿。
5. wǒ de bèi ràng rén qí 我的背让人骑。 (People love to ride on my back.)	我是＿＿＿＿＿＿＿＿＿。
6. wǒ ài shuì jiào 我爱睡觉。 (I love to sleep.)	我是＿＿＿＿＿＿＿＿＿。
7. wǒ jiào　sī sī sī 我叫：“嘶嘶嘶……” (I say, "sssssssss.")	我是＿＿＿＿＿＿＿＿＿。
8. wǒ ài chī hú luó bo 我爱吃胡萝卜。 (I love to eat carrots.)	我是＿＿＿＿＿＿＿＿＿。
9. wǒ shuō　miē miē miē 我说：“咩咩咩……” (I say, "Baa baa.")	我是＿＿＿＿＿＿＿＿＿。
10. wǒ jiào　wāng wāng wāng 我叫：“汪汪汪……” (I say, "Woof, woof.")	我是＿＿＿＿＿＿＿＿＿。
11. wǒ shuō　mōu mōu mōu 我说：“哞哞哞……” (I say, "Moo, moo.")	我是＿＿＿＿＿＿＿＿＿。
12. wǒ ài chī xiāng jiāo 我爱吃香蕉。 (I love to eat bananas.)	我是＿＿＿＿＿＿＿＿＿。

82

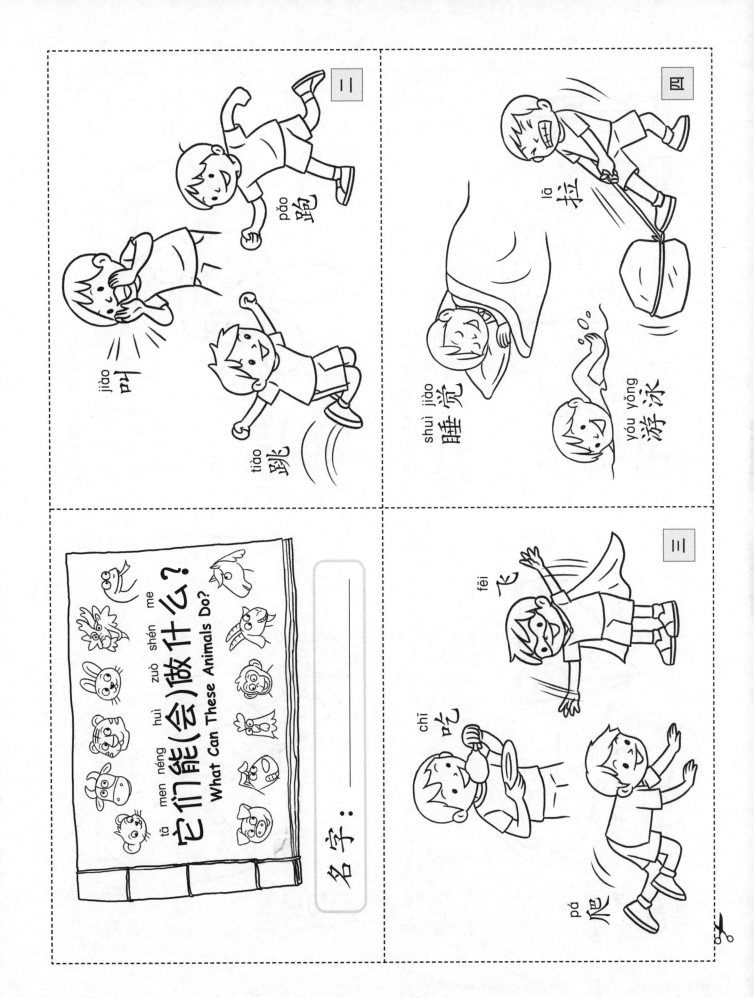

pǎo
跑

jiào
叫

tiào
跳

二

lā
拉

shuì jiào
睡觉

yóu yǒng
游泳

四

fēi
飞

chī
吃

pá
爬

三

tā men néng huì zuò shén me
它们能（会）做什么？
What Can These Animals Do?

名字：

六

niú 牛 (Ox)

niú huì
牛会 ___ 车。
chē
The ox can pull a cart.

八

tù 兔 (Rabbit)

tù zi huì
兔子会 ___ 。
The rabbit can jump.

五

shǔ 鼠 (Rat)

lǎo shǔ ài
老鼠爱 ___ 乳酪。
rǔ lào
The rat loves to eat cheese.

七

hǔ 虎 (Tiger)

lǎo hǔ huì
老虎会 ___ 山。
shān
The tiger can climb mountains.

Note: Besides "乳酪", "cheese" is also known as "起士".
qǐ shì

+

shé
蛇
(Snake)

shé huì
蛇会 ──○
The snake can swim.

+二

yáng
羊
(Goat)

yáng ài   cǎo
羊爱 ── 草○
The goat loves to eat grass.

九

lóng
龙
(Dragon)

lóng huì
龙会 ──○
The dragon can fly.

+一

mǎ
马
(Horse)

mǎ huì
马会 ──○
The horse can run.

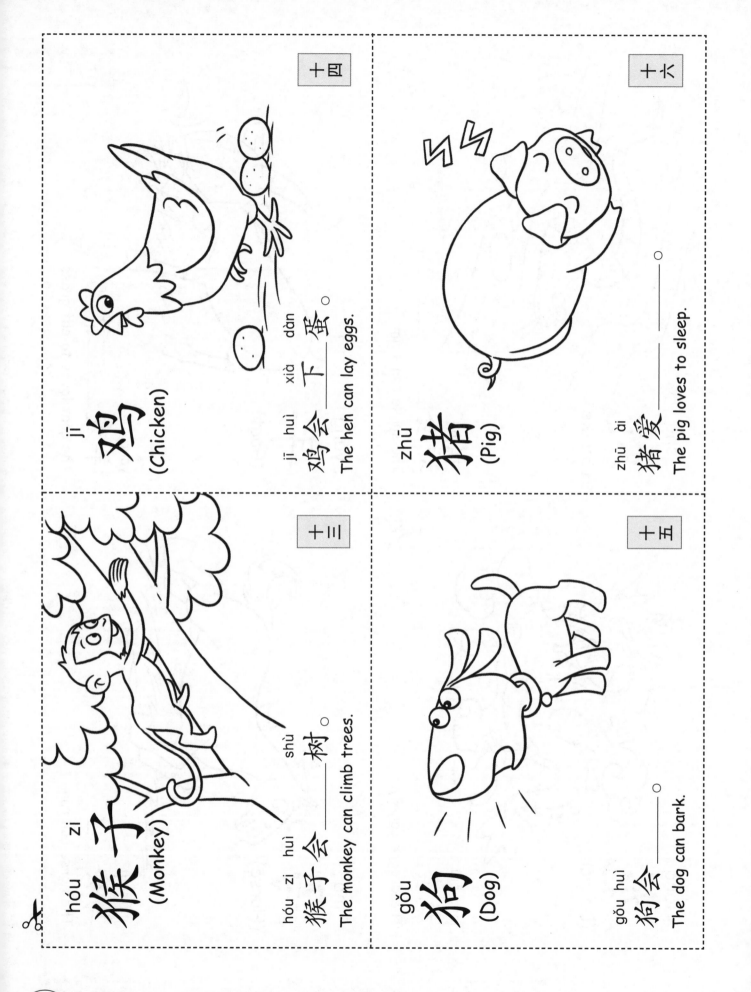

十四

jī
鸡
(Chicken)

jī huì xià dàn
鸡会 下 蛋。
The hen can lay eggs.

十六

zhū
猪
(Pig)

zhū ài
猪爱 ——。
The pig loves to sleep.

十三

hóu zi
猴子
(Monkey)

hóu zi huì shù
猴子会 树。
The monkey can climb trees.

十五

gǒu
狗
(Dog)

gǒu huì
狗会 ——。
The dog can bark.

名字：＿＿＿＿＿＿＿＿＿＿＿＿＿＿＿ ＿＿＿月＿＿＿日

Reading: Chinese Zodiac Personality Traits
读一读：你的生肖个性

shǔ
鼠
1972, 1984, 1996, 2008
You are very popular. You are good at art and like to invent things.

niú
牛
1973, 1985, 1997, 2009
You are hardworking and patient. You are a good listener and have very strong ideas.

hǔ
虎
1974, 1986, 1998, 2010
You are brave and sensitive. People respect you for your deep thoughts and brave actions.

tù
兔
1975, 1987, 1999, 2011
You are talented and loving. You like to talk, and many people trust you.

lóng
龙
1976, 1988, 2000, 2012
You are proud and energetic. You have good health and lots of energy.

shé
蛇
1965, 1977, 1989, 2001
You are wise and good looking. You love good books, food, music, and art. You will have good luck with money.

mǎ
马
1966, 1978, 1990, 2002
You are cheerful and efficient. You like to compliment others.

yáng
羊
1967, 1979, 1991, 2003
You are kind and artistic. You are very friendly.

hóu
猴
1968, 1980, 1992, 2004
You are very wise and funny. You can always make people laugh. You are also very good at solving problems.

jī
鸡
1969, 1981, 1993, 2005
You are very honest and hardworking. You have many talents.

gǒu
狗
1970, 1982, 1994, 2006
You are loyal and honest. You can always keep secrets. Sometimes you worry too much.

zhū
猪
1971, 1983, 1995, 2007
You are fortunate and sincere. You are a good student. You always finish projects or assignments on time.

Writing Activity: What Zodiac Animal Sign Do They Have?
写一写：他们属什么生肖？

Complete the wheel by filling in one or two personality traits represented by each zodiac animal sign. You may refer to the chart on page 87.

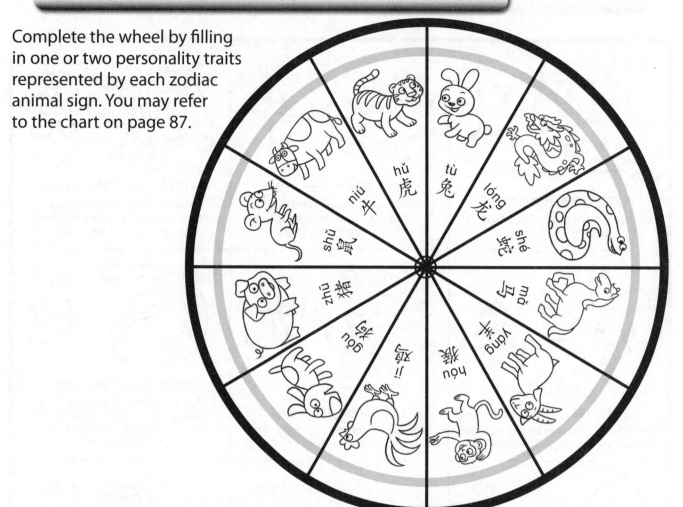

What zodiac animal sign do your family and friends have? Fill in the blanks.

1. I was born in the Year of the _____.

    I am very_____.

2. My_____ was born in the Year of the _____.

    He/She is very_____ and _____.

3. My_____ was born in the Year of the_____.

    He/She is very_____ and _____.

4. My_____ was born in the Year of the _____.

    He/She is very_____ and _____.

Word Search: Zodiac Animals ❶
找一找：生肖 ●

Write the animal names in English:

1. 猪 zhū: _____
2. 老虎 lǎo hǔ: _____
3. 鸡 jī: _____
4. 老鼠 lǎo shǔ: _____
5. 马 mǎ: _____
6. 兔子 tù zi: _____

7. 牛 niú: _____
8. 蛇 shé: _____
9. 龙 lóng: _____
10. 猴子 hóu zi: _____
11. 羊 yáng: _____
12. 狗 gǒu: _____

Find the above pinyin words in the word search puzzle below.

```
c j l m z k l i g t c i a
g n i e o a a a x b k w z
c l u t d i d m o l y h c
n i l e i a m e d h u o e
n t e k a g e m l n u u g
h a x h c y c d y a n z b
g p k e p g t y l g d i h
x y a n g y u g o u j t m
p w d s y h j m n s a c a
k b x i s i b e g u b u e
c s d o a y e k m l y d h
l v a e x h y c m t i h b
i l y d h c o g o z h a g
h s g m u s t x u j o l c
k d y h u m k t o h d j e
```

Word Search: Zodiac Animals ❷
找一找：生肖 ⚊

How many times can you find these animal names in the word search?
Fill in the blanks.

1. 牛： ＿＿＿＿个。　4. 龙： ＿＿＿＿个。

2. 山羊： ＿＿＿＿个。　5. 老虎： ＿＿＿＿个。

3. 马： ＿＿＿＿个。　6. 兔子： ＿＿＿＿个。

山	羊	马	大	龙	田	老	水
小	生	龙	小	马	牛	虎	龙
牛	龙	小	田	生	龙	生	牛
水	生	水	龙	兔	子	田	马
龙	牛	龙	山	马	生	生	山
田	兔	老	大	龙	羊	龙	水
马	子	牛	虎	山	田	大	小
大	老	虎	龙	羊	龙	水	牛

Art Project: Chinese Zodiac Lantern
创意手工：生肖灯笼

Instructions:

1. Draw the animals that are missing.
2. Color each animal and cut out the lantern shape.

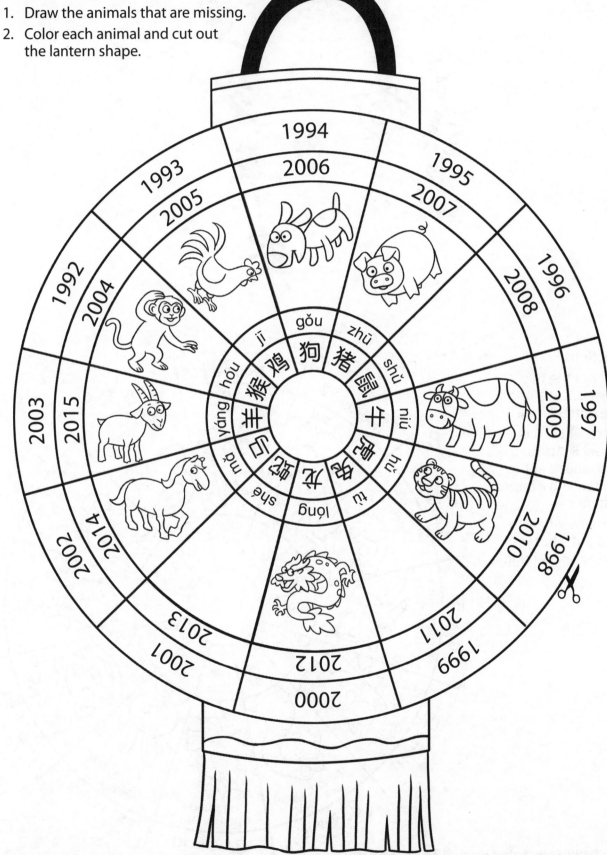

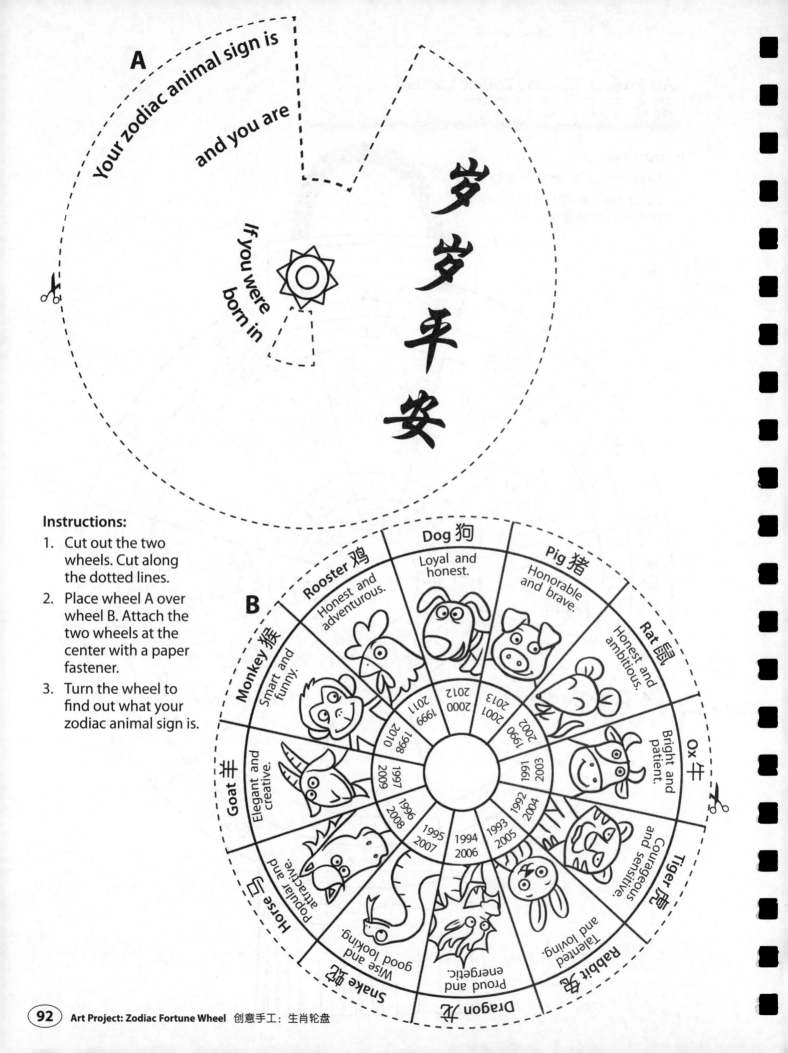

A

Your zodiac animal sign is

and you are

If you were born in

岁岁平安

Instructions:

1. Cut out the two wheels. Cut along the dotted lines.
2. Place wheel A over wheel B. Attach the two wheels at the center with a paper fastener.
3. Turn the wheel to find out what your zodiac animal sign is.

B

Dog 狗
Loyal and honest.

Rooster 鸡
Honest and adventurous.

Pig 猪
Honorable and brave.

Rat 鼠
Honest and ambitious.

Monkey 猴
Smart and funny.

Ox 牛
Bright and patient.

Goat 羊
Elegant and creative.

Tiger 虎
Courageous and sensitive.

Horse 马
Popular and attractive.

Rabbit 兔
Talented and loving.

Snake 蛇
Wise and good looking.

Dragon 龙
Proud and energetic.

1998 2010
1999 2011
2000 2012
2001 2013
1990 2002
1991 2003
1992 2004
1993 2005
1994 2006
1995 2007
1996 2008
1997 2009

hěn jiǔ yǐ qián zhōng guó yǒu yí gè hěn cōng míng de huáng dì   tā guǎn lǐ quán tiān xià
很久以前，中国有一个很**聪明的**皇帝。他管理全天下

suǒ yǒu de shì qing   kě shì huáng dì jiàn jiàn lǎo le   cháng cháng wàng jì shì qing   yě
所有的事情。可是，皇帝渐渐老了，常常**忘记**事情，也

wàng jì shí jiān   tā xiǎng le hěn jiǔ   zhōng yú xiǎng chū le yí gè hǎo bàn fǎ   huáng dì
忘记时间。他想了很久，终于想出了一个好办法。皇帝

hěn xǐ huan dòng wù   tā xiǎng yòng shí èr zhǒng dòng wù lái jì suàn shí jiān   dàn shì yào rú hé
很喜欢**动物**，他想用十二种动物来计算时间。但是要如何

tiāo xuǎn zhè shí èr zhǒng dòng wù ne   wèi le gōng píng qǐ jiàn   tā jué dìng jǔ bàn yì chǎng
挑选这十二种动物呢？为了公平起见，他决定举办一场

sài pǎo
赛跑。

dì èr tiān huáng dì zhào jí suǒ yǒu de dòng wù   tā shuō   dà jiā hǎo   jīn tiān
第二天，皇帝**召集**所有的动物。他说："大家好！今天

wǒ men yào jǔ bàn yì chǎng dòng wù sài pǎo   zuì xiān yóu guò tiān hé   pǎo dào zhōng diǎn de
我们要举办一场动物赛跑，**最先**游过天河、跑到终点的

shí èr zhī dòng wù   kě yǐ dài biǎo wǒ men zhōng guó lái jì suàn shí jiān   yī dào dá de
十二只动物，可以代表我们中国来计算时间。依到达的

shùn xù   měi yì zhī dòng wù dài biǎo yì nián   měi shí èr nián chóng fù yí biàn
顺序，每一只动物代表一年。每十二年重复一遍。"

sài pǎo kāi shǐ le   suǒ yǒu de dòng wù dōu pīn mìng de pǎo   dào le tiān hé
赛跑**开始**了。所有的动物都拼命地跑。到了天河

biān   lǎo shǔ qǐng qiú niú zài tā guò hé   niú dā ying le   dāng niú gāng cóng shuǐ zhōng shàng
边，老鼠**请求**牛载它过河，牛答应了。当牛刚从水中上

àn shí   lǎo shǔ yòng lì yí tiào   fēi kuài de pǎo dào le zhōng diǎn   yīn cǐ lǎo shǔ dé le
岸时，老鼠用力一跳，飞快地跑到了终点，因此老鼠得了

dì yī míng   suí hòu shì niú   hǔ   tù   lóng   shé   mǎ   yáng   hóu
第一名。随后是牛、虎、兔、龙、蛇、马、羊、猴、

jī   gǒu   zhū   zuì hòu sài pǎo jié shù le
鸡、狗、猪。**最后赛跑结束了。**

zhè jiù shì shí èr shēng xiào de gù shi
这就是十二生肖的故事。

Long, long ago in the ancient Middle Kingdom which we know as China today, there lived a very wise emperor. The emperor was a very important man who had a lot of things on his mind because he had to take care of all the affairs of the people and creatures that lived in the Middle Kingdom. The emperor was getting older and so was becoming more and more forgetful. He was especially worried about how he was getting the years all mixed up in his mind. He couldn't remember the things that happened in each year.

One day while he was thinking about this problem, the emperor decided to name the years after animals because he loved animals. He felt that 12 would be a good number to pick, and, similar to a clock going round in rotation, the animals would also make a cycle. But he did not know which 12 animals to choose. The emperor was known to be a very fair ruler and did not believe he should choose his favorite animals. After some careful thought, he came up with a brilliant idea.

The next morning he called all the animals in the kingdom together and said, "Today we are going to have a great race. The first 12 animals to swim across the River of Heaven and cross the finish line will have the special honor of having a year named after them!"

Well, of course, all the animals were very excited because they all wanted to have a year named after them. The race began and the animals went as fast as they could. When it was time to cross the river, the clever rat, knowing that the ox was a strong swimmer, climbed on his back to get a free ride across the river. Just as the ox was climbing out of the river, the rat jumped off, hurried across the finish line and took first place.

After the rat, came the ox, tiger, rabbit, dragon, snake, horse, goat, monkey, rooster, dog, and finally the pig. The race ended. From this day on these 12 animals have had the special honor of having a year named after them.

Vocabulary Review: Story of the 12 Zodiac Animals
词汇练习：十二生肖的故事

Match the words in Column A with the words in Column B.

(Column A)

十二生肖
shí èr shēng xiào

请求
qǐng qiú

召集
zhào jí

聪明的
cōng míng de

最先
zuì xiān

结束
jié shù

开始
kāi shǐ

最后
zuì hòu

忘记
wàng jì

动物
dòng wù

赛跑
sài pǎo

重复
chóng fù

(Column B)

wise

ended

asked

animals

first

at last

race

repeated

summoned (called)

12 zodiac animals

began

forgot

Quiz: Story of the 12 Zodiac Animals
考考你：十二生肖的故事

动物	最先	最后	开始
结束	十二生肖	重复	请求
赛跑	忘记	聪明的	召集

1. 很久以前，中国有一个很_____皇帝。

2. 可是，皇帝渐渐老了，常常_____事情，也忘记时间。

3. 皇帝很喜欢_____，他想用十二种动物来计算时间。

4. 为了公平起见，他决定举办一场_____。_____到达终点的动物可以代表中国计算时间。

5. 第二天，皇帝_____所有的动物。

6. 每一只动物代表一年。每十二年_____一遍。

7. 赛跑_____了。所有的动物都拼命地跑。

8. 到了天河边，老鼠_____牛载它过河。

9. _____赛跑_____了，这就是_____的故事。

10. 依顺序写出十二生肖的名称：

_____、_____、_____、_____

_____、_____、_____、_____

_____、_____、_____、_____

Math Fun: Chinese Zodiac Animals
算一算，数一数：十二生肖

中国新年用十二种动物来代表，称为十二生肖。每一生肖代表一年，以鼠年开始，以猪年结束。然后再重复一次，顺序不变。

On the Chinese calendar, every year is represented by an animal. There are 12 zodiac animals that make a rotation. The cycle begins with the Rat and ends with the Pig. Each animal sign is repeated every 12 years and always follows the same order.

请回答下面问题：

jīn nián shì　　　　　nián　zhǎo chū nà ge shēng xiào　bìng tú shang hóng sè
1. 今年是＿＿＿＿＿年。找出那个生肖，并涂上红色。

qù nián shì　　　　　nián　zhǎo chū nà ge shēng xiào　bìng tú shang huáng sè
2. 去年是＿＿＿＿＿年。找出那个生肖，并涂上黄色。

míng nián shì　　　　　nián　zhǎo chū nà ge shēng xiào　bìng tú shang lán sè
3. 明年是＿＿＿＿＿年。找出那个生肖，并涂上蓝色。

sān nián qián shì　　　　　nián　zhǎo chū nà ge shēng xiào　bìng tú shang lǜ sè
4. 三年前是＿＿＿＿＿年。找出那个生肖，并涂上绿色。

shí èr nián hòu shì　　　　　nián
5. 十二年后是＿＿＿＿＿年。

挑战题（Challenge）：

1. 莉莉今年十岁，属马。他的哥哥属牛。
   莉莉的哥哥比她大＿＿＿＿＿岁。

97

shēng xiào
生肖

gōng xǐ fā cái
恭喜发财

biān pào
鞭炮

jiǎo zi
饺子

wǔ lóng wǔ shī
舞龙/舞狮

jú zi
桔子

shǒu suì
守岁
stay up late on New Year's Eve

yú
鱼

hóng bāo
红包

Word Search: Chinese New Year
找一找：农历新年

Find the 11 pinyin words from the box below in the Word Search.

i	a	u	u	a	z	u	h	n	o	s
o	e	x	w	i	h	n	c	a	y	a
h	s	o	b	u	a	g	i	p	e	a
i	a	c	a	f	i	x	g	n	o	g
u	g	f	e	b	g	y	j	a	z	a
s	j	y	j	n	g	w	p	w	j	o
u	a	u	e	i	j	n	u	h	c	a
o	e	h	z	s	a	l	o	s	p	a
h	s	h	i	i	o	o	n	h	h	a
s	o	n	b	n	x	s	z	s	y	i
b	i	j	g	w	i	i	i	i	e	g

What do these words mean in English?

1. 春节 chūn jié: ＿＿＿＿＿＿＿＿＿＿

2. 红包 hóng bāo: ＿＿＿＿＿＿＿＿

3. 桔子 jú zi: ＿＿＿＿＿＿＿＿＿＿

4. 生肖 shēng xiào: ＿＿＿＿＿＿

5. 鞭炮 biān pào: ＿＿＿＿＿＿＿＿

6. 鱼 yú: ＿＿＿＿＿＿＿＿＿＿＿＿＿

7. 饺子 jiǎo zi: ＿＿＿＿＿＿＿＿＿

8. 舞狮 wǔ shī: ＿＿＿＿＿＿＿＿＿

9. 守岁 shǒu suì: ＿＿＿＿＿＿＿＿

10. 舞龙 wǔ lóng: ＿＿＿＿＿＿＿＿

11. 恭喜发财 gōng xǐ fā cái: ＿＿＿＿＿＿＿＿＿＿＿＿＿＿＿＿＿

Note: "春节" and "农历新年" both mean "Chinese New Year".

名字： _____   _____ 月 _____ 日

Vocabulary Review: Chinese New Year
词汇练习：农历新年

Fill in the blanks in pinyin or characters using the words below:

gōng xǐ fā cái 恭喜发财	shǒu suì 守岁	hóng bāo 红包	chūn jié 春节	jiǎo zi 饺子
wǔ lóng / wǔ shī 舞龙／舞狮	yú 鱼	shēng xiào 生肖	biān pào 鞭炮	jú zi 桔子

1. The animal signs related to people's age and personality.

2. A food served as the last dish on Chinese New Year's Eve and represents "surplus".

3. A food served on Chinese New Year's Eve and represents "gold treasure".

4. A special lucky envelope that children receive from adults on Chinese New Year.

5. A special performance that brings good luck and is associated with drums and firecrackers.

6. A fruit that sounds like "good luck".

7. A kind of small explosive that creates noise and smoke that will scare the evil spirits away.

8. The custom of staying up late on Chinese New Year's Eve.

9. A common greeting that people say throughout the period of Chinese New Year.

10. Another name for Chinese New Year.

dōng guā táng
冬瓜糖
winter melon candy

guā zi
瓜子
melon seeds

jīn jú
金桔
kumquats

guì yuán
桂圆
longan

huā shēng
花生
peanut

nián gāo
年糕
rice cake

fā gāo
发糕
steamed sponge cake

lián zi
莲子
lotus seeds

fèng lí sū
凤梨酥
pineapple tarts

Note: Festive snacks for Chinese New Year may vary in different parts of China.

Survey: What Food Do You Like to Eat during Chinese New Year?
问卷：你喜欢吃什么新年食品？

Instructions:

1. Using the dialogue below, conduct a survey in your class to find out which foods your classmates like to eat and which foods they do not like.

2. Check ✔ under the "喜欢" (Like) column if your classmates like to eat each of the foods; check ✘ under "不喜欢" (Dislike) column if they do not.

nǐ xǐ huan chī guā zi ma
Ⓐ 你喜欢吃<u>瓜子</u>吗？

wǒ xǐ huan   bù xǐ huan chī guā zi
Ⓑ 我喜欢 / 不喜欢吃<u>瓜子</u>。

nǐ xǐ huan chī   ma
Ⓐ 你喜欢吃＿＿＿＿＿＿吗？

wǒ xǐ huan   bù xǐ huan chī
Ⓑ 我喜欢 / 不喜欢吃＿＿＿＿＿＿。

Number of students asked in the survey		喜欢	不喜欢	喜欢	不喜欢	喜欢	不喜欢	喜欢	不喜欢	喜欢	不喜欢	喜欢	不喜欢	喜欢	不喜欢	喜欢	不喜欢	喜欢	不喜欢
	十人																		
	九人																		
	八人																		
	七人																		
	六人																		
	五人																		
	四人																		
	三人																		
	二人																		
	一人																		

Popular food for Chinese New Year

Rhyme: Chinese New Year Is Coming!
数来宝：新年到！

咚咚锵，咚咚锵，
咚咚咚锵咚咚咚锵。

Dōng dōng qiāng, dōng dōng qiāng,
dōng dōng dōng qiāng dōng dōng dōng qiāng.

(Sound imitation of the gongs and drums)

新年好，新年好。
穿新衣，戴新帽。
恭喜新年，春来到！

Xīn nián hǎo, xīn nián hǎo.
Chuān xīn yī, dài xīn mào.
Gōng xǐ xīn nián, chūn lái dào!

Happy New Year! Happy New Year!
Wear new clothes. Wear new hats.
Welcome the New Year. Welcome Spring!

* *

咚咚锵，咚咚锵，
咚咚咚锵咚咚咚锵。

Dōng dōng qiāng, dōng dōng qiāng,
dōng dōng dōng qiāng dōng dōng dōng qiāng.

(Sound imitation of the gongs and drums)

新年好，新年好。
拿红包，放鞭炮。
舞龙舞狮，真热闹！
真－热－闹！

Xīn nián hǎo, xīn nián hǎo.
Ná hóng bāo, fàng biān pào.
Wǔ lóng wǔ shī, zhēn rè nào!
Zhēn － rè － nào!

Happy New Year! Happy New Year!
Get the red envelopes. Set off the firecrackers.
Dragon dances, lion dances, so amazing!
A－M－A－Z－I－N－G!

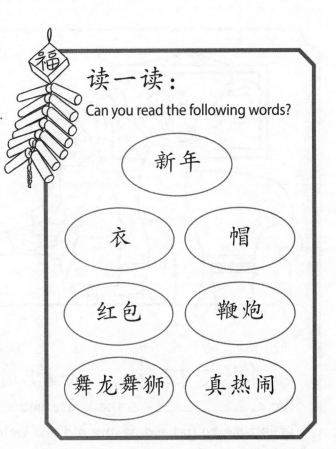

读一读：

Can you read the following words?

新年

衣　　帽

红包　　鞭炮

舞龙舞狮　　真热闹

103

guò xīn nián
过新年
Chinese New Year Celebration

名字：_____

wǒ men dà sǎo chú　　qù jiù yíng xīn
我们大扫除，去旧迎新。

We c_____ the house and s_____ the floor.

It is time to get rid of the old and welcome the _____ year.

wǒ men tiē chūn lián　jiǎn chūn huā　dà jí dà lì
我们贴春联，剪春花，大吉大利。

We put up red c_____ and p_____ c_____ on doors and windows for good luck.

wǒ men mǎi xīn yī fu　jiǎn tóu fa　xīn nián kuài lè
我们买新衣服，剪头发，新年快乐。

We buy new c_____ and get h_____ to start the new year.

On Chinese New Year's Eve

四

wǒ men huí jiā chī nián yè fàn　　tuán tuán yuán yuán

我们回家吃年夜饭，团团圆圆。

We go home for a big family r_____ dinner on New Year's Eve.

✂ -

五

wǒ men chī jī　　yā　　yú　　jiǎo zi　　nián gāo hé huǒ guō

我们吃鸡、鸭、鱼、饺子、年糕和火锅，

jí xiáng rú yì

吉祥如意。

We eat c_____, d_____, f_____, d_____,

rice cakes and hotpots. All are symbolic of good luck and good wealth.

On Chinese New Year

wǒ men xiàng dà ren bài nián   suì suì píng ān

我们向大人拜年，岁岁平安。

We say "G_____" to grown-ups and receive red
_____ for good luck.

wǒ men fàng biān pào   kàn wǔ lóng wǔ shī   qìng zhù xīn nián

我们放鞭炮，看舞龙舞狮，庆祝新年。

We set off the _____ and watch the lion dance and dragon
parade to celebrate the New Year.

名字：＿＿＿＿＿＿＿＿＿＿＿＿＿＿＿ ＿＿＿＿月＿＿＿日

Character Code Challenge: Chinese New Year Message ❶
解码游戏：新年密语 ➊

Use the character codes below to solve the secret message about Chinese New Year.

A：一	B：二	C：三	D：四	E：五	F：六
G：七	H：八	I：九	J：十	K：口	L：手
M：人	N：天	O：木	P：心	Q：日	R：月
S：山	T：水	U：火	V：上	W：下	X：大
Y：小	Z：中				

下五　下五一月　月五四　六木月

七木木四　手火三口　一天四　水木

山三一月五　一下一小　五上九手

山心九月九水山

yī 一 one	èr 二 two	sān 三 three	sì 四 four	wǔ 五 five	liù 六 six	qī 七 seven
bā 八 eight	jiǔ 九 nine	shí 十 ten	kǒu 口 mouth	shǒu 手 hand	rén 人 person	tiān 天 sky
mù 木 wood	xīn 心 heart	rì 日 sun	yuè 月 moon	shān 山 mountain	shuǐ 水 water	huǒ 火 fire
shàng 上 up	xià 下 down	dà 大 big	xiǎo 小 small	zhōng 中 middle		

Character Code Challenge: Chinese New Year Message ❷
解码游戏：新年密语 ⬤

Use the character codes below to solve the secret message about Chinese New Year.

A：木	B：月	C：下	D：田	E：手	F：一
G：火	H：人	I：小	J：男	K：口	L：二
M：水	N：大	O：牛	P：耳	Q：子	R：三
S：山	T：上	U：女	V：目	W：心	X：四
Y：日	Z：中				

心人牛二手　一小山人　木三手　山手三目手田

心小上人　上人手　人手木田山　木大田　上木小二山

牛大　上牛　山日水月牛二小中手　人木耳耳日

月手火小大大小大火山　木大田

手大田小大火山

mù 木 wood	yuè 月 moon	xià 下 down	tián 田 field	shǒu 手 hand	yī 一 one	huǒ 火 fire
rén 人 person	xiǎo 小 small	nán 男 man	kǒu 口 mouth	èr 二 two	shuǐ 水 water	dà 大 big
niú 牛 cow	ěr 耳 ear	zǐ 子 child	sān 三 three	shān 山 mountain	shàng 上 up	nǚ 女 female
mù 目 eye	xīn 心 heart	sì 四 four	rì 日 sun	zhōng 中 middle		

名字：_____   _____月_____日

dà jí dà lì
大吉大利
May you have lots of good luck and fortune.

jí xiáng rú yì
吉祥如意
May you have good fortune in all your affairs.

chū rù píng ān
出入平安
May you have peace wherever you go.

sì jì píng ān
四季平安
May you have peace throughout the four seasons.

wǔ fú lín mén
五福临门
May the five good fortunes come through your door.

lǎo shào píng ān
老少平安
May everyone in your family be safe and sound.

110

Art Project: Chinese New Year Couplets
创意手工：对联

Fold here

名字：_____ _____月_____日

Note: *Refer to instructions on p. 9.*

名字：_____ _____月_____日

年年有余
Abundance

Instructions:

1. Trace a template of 9" circle on red construction paper to make the body of the fish.
2. Cut out a triangle from the circle to form a mouth.
3. Staple the small triangle piece to the opposite side to form a tail.
4. Color the picture of the fish above. Cut it out and paste it in the center of the red fish.
5. Add a fish eye above the mouth.
6. Decorate the fish with a pattern or a lucky message.

Note: See sample on p. 400.

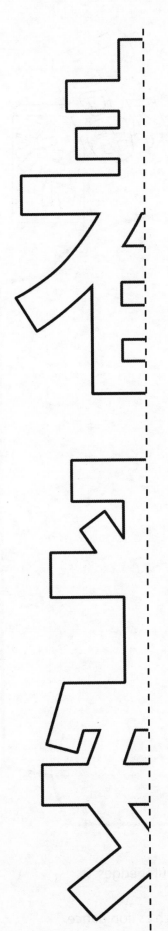

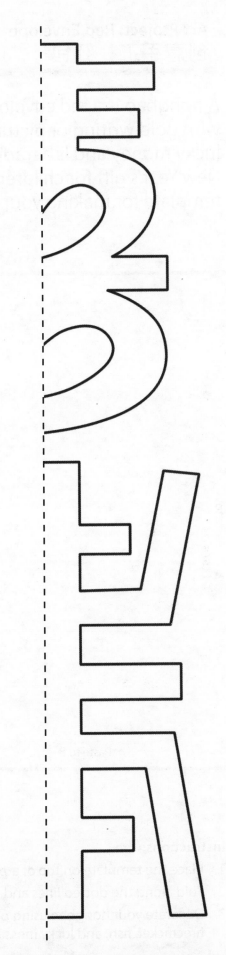

Art Project: Red Envelope
创意手工：红包

A hongbao is a red envelope decorated with gold writing or pictures. It contains lucky money and is a traditional Chinese New Year's gift for children. Below is a template for making your own hongbao.

Flap

Paste to A

A

Paste to B

B

Instructions:

1. Place the template on top of a piece of red paper and cut along the outer edges.

2. Fold along the dotted lines and paste the paper as indicated.

3. Decorate your hongbao using popular Chinese New Year symbols such as lion dance, firecracker, fish, and lucky messages. Or, you can decorate it with your own design.

Art Project: Firecrackers
创意手工：鞭炮

1

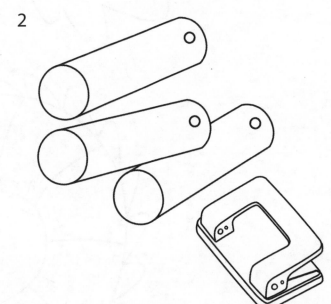

2

Materials needed:
- Red paper 3″ x 4″ – 6 pieces
- Red paper 2″ x 6″ – 1 piece
- Red yarn 1 ½ ft. – 1 piece

Instructions:

1. Roll the small red paper into a tube and staple it.
2. Punch a hole on the top of each tube.
3. Thread the yarn into each hole and make a knot.
4. Write a lucky message on the big red paper and tie it to the tail.

3

4

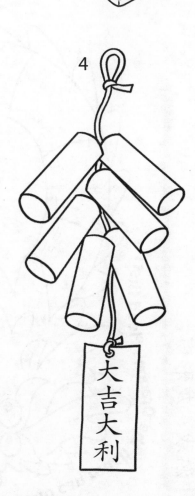

Game: Chinese New Year Dragon Board Game
游戏：龙形棋

Who can reach the Dragon's Head first?

Game: Chinese New Year Qs and As
问答游戏：农历新年知多少

今年是什么 生肖年？ What is the animal sign for this year? **2 Points**	一共有几 个生肖？ How many Zodiac animals are there? **2 Points**	动物赛跑， 谁跑第一名？ Who is the winner in the Zodiac Race? **1 Point**
十二生肖最后 一名是谁？ Who is the 12th winner in the Zodiac Race? **2 Points**	十二生肖里 有没有猫？ Is the cat one of the Zodiac animals? **2 Points**	今年农历新年 是几月几日？ When is Chinese New Year this year? **3 Points**
新年的吉祥 颜色是什么？ What is the good luck color for Chinese New Year? **1 Point**	小孩子过年会收 到什么礼物？ What do children receive from adults on Chinese New year? **2 Points**	农历新年 又叫什么？ What is the other name for Chinese New Year? **3 Points**
鱼在过年 时代表什么？ What does fish symbolize in Chinese New Year? **2 Points**	为什么过年要穿红 衣服和新衣服？ Why do Chinese people wear red and new clothes on Chinese New Year? **1 Point**	红包里面 装了什么？ What is inside the red envelopes? **1 Point**
为什么过年 要放鞭炮？ Why do Chinese people light firecrackers during Chinese New Year? **2 Points**	元宵节是 什么时候？ When is the Lantern Festival? **2 Points**	请说一句 新年吉祥话。 Say one good luck greeting in Chinese. **3 Points**

名字：_____ _____月_____日

Song: Happy New Year!
新年歌：恭喜！恭喜！

měi tiáo dà jiē xiǎo xiàng
每条大街 小 巷，
From big streets to little lanes,

měi gè rén de zuǐ li
每个人的 嘴 里，
People clamor shine or rain.

jiàn miàn dì yí jù huà
见面第一 句 话，
Voices ring with merry calls,

jiù shì gōng xǐ gōng xǐ ā
就是恭喜 恭 喜。啊！
Happy new year to all! … Hah!

gōng xǐ gōng xǐ
恭喜恭喜
Happy, happy greetings to all!

gōng xǐ nǐ ya
恭喜你呀！
gōng xǐ gōng xǐ
恭喜恭喜

gōng xǐ nǐ
恭喜你！
Happy New Year to you all!

120

Recipe: Dumplings
下厨乐：包饺子

Ingredients

1 lb. Chinese cabbage

2 scallions

2 cloves of garlic, finely chopped

2 tsp. fresh ginger, finely chopped

1 tbsp. soy sauce

1 tbsp sesame oil

1 tsp. salt

1 tbsp. cornstarch

1 lb. lean ground pork

1 10-oz. package prepared dumpling wrappers (available at Asian food stores)

Steps

Part 1:

1. Finely chop the Chinese cabbage and scallions and put them in a mixing bowl.

2. Add the soy sauce, salt, cornstarch, and pork. Mix well with a spoon.

3. Place 1 teaspoon of filling on each wrapper.

4. Fold the wrappers into half circles. Moisten the edges with water, and press them together to seal.

Part 2:

1. In a large pot, bring 2 quarts of water to a boil.

2. Put in the dumplings and cover the pot. When the water starts boiling, add 1 cup of cold water.

3. Repeat this step twice. When the water boils for the third time, the dumplings are done.

4. Serve with 1/4 cup of soy sauce mixed with 2 tablespoons of vinegar. Makes 4 dozen dumplings.

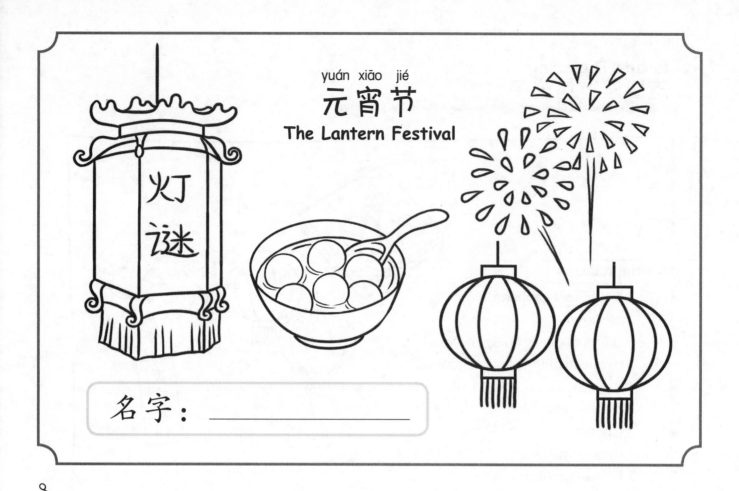

yuán xiāo jié
元宵节
The Lantern Festival

名字：＿＿＿＿＿＿＿＿＿

一

zhēng yuè shí wǔ shì yuán xiāo jié   tā shì chūn jié de zuì hòu yì tiān
正月十五是元宵节。它是春节的最后一天。

The ＿＿＿＿＿＿＿ day of Chinese New Year is the ＿＿＿＿＿＿＿ Festival.
It marks an end to the 15 days of Chinese New Year celebration.

zhè yì tiān shì xīn nián yǐ hòu kàn dào de dì yí gè mǎn yuè

这一天是新年以后看到的第一个满月。

On this day, we see the first f_____ m_____ of the New Year.

wǒ men chī   yuán xiāo   dài biǎo quán jiā tuán yuán

我们吃 "元宵" 代表全家团圆。

We eat sweet, round dumplings called "_____ _____" to symbolize family togetherness.

四

wǒ men shàng jiē qù kàn huā dēng   wǔ lóng hé yān huǒ
我们上街去看花灯、舞龙和烟火。

People dress up and head to the street to see l_____,
dragon _____, and f_____.

✁ -

五

外黄内白，
猴子最爱。
（猜一水果）
Yellow outside,
white inside.
Monkey's favorite
treat. (a fruit)

wǒ men cāi dēng mí   zhēn yǒu qù
我们猜灯谜，真有趣。

We guess _____ attached to lanterns. It is a lot of fun for everyone.

Art Project: Chinese Lantern Paper Cut
创意手工：灯笼剪纸

Follow the instructions below to make this paper cut.

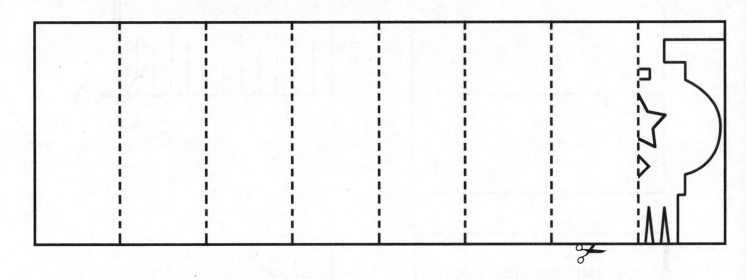

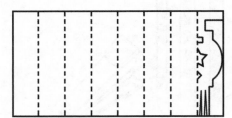

1. Cut out the whole piece of paper.

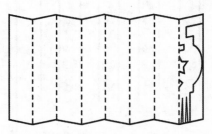

2. Fold along the dotted lines.

3. Maintaining the folds, cut out the shape of the lantern.

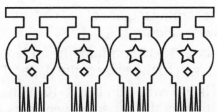

4. Unfold the paper to get the Chinese lantern paper cut.

Art Project: Chinese New Year Lantern
创意手工：新年灯笼

a.

b.

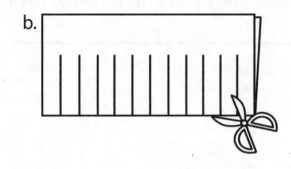

c.

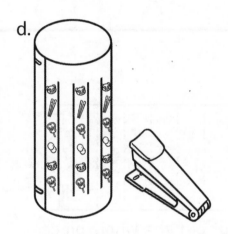

d.

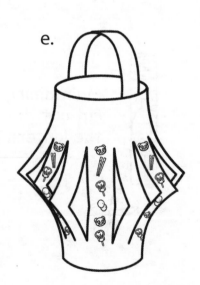

e.

Steps:

1. Fold a rectangular piece of red construction paper lengthwise. (Figure a)

2. Make about 10-12 cuts from the folded side and leave about 1 inch to the edge of the paper. (Figure b)

3. Unfold it and write numbers 1-10 in Chinese on the top and bottom of the paper between cuts. (Figure c)

4. Decorate alternate cuts with Chinese symbols, such as kites, pandas, dragons, chopsticks, fans, and so on. (Figure c)

5. Roll the paper into a tube with words and decoration facing outward. Staple the edges. (Figure d)

6. Decorate a 6" x 2" strip of construction paper and staple it across one end of the lantern to make a handle. (Figure e)

7. Press the top to make the cut strips protrude outward. (Figure e)

Riddle Game: Riddles for Lantern Festival
猜一猜：趣味灯谜

1. 没根不用种，打开像朵花，
四季都会开。（猜一物）

It can grow but has no roots,
Opens like a flower,
Seen all year round.
(an object)

2. 有风不用它，没风可生风，不动
不凉，越动越凉。（猜一物）

It is useless when it is windy,
It makes wind when there is none,
When you don't move it, it is not cool,
When you move it, it becomes cool.
(an object)

3. 两只脚一样长，
甜酸苦辣一起尝。（猜一物）

It has two feet of the same length.
It takes up everything sweet, sour,
bitter or spicy.
(an object)

4. 头上几根羽毛，人人拿来玩，
最爱空中跳舞。（猜一物）

It has a few feathers on its head,
Everyone likes to play with it,
It loves to dance in the air.
(an object)

5. 嘴长肚子大，不吃饭和菜，
爱喝白开水，也爱吐黄水。
（猜一日常用品）

Long mouth and big belly; does not eat rice
or vegetables; loves to drink clear water;
yellow water pours from it. (an object)

6. 门边贴上红彩衣，一左一右
写满字，喜庆日子便出来。
（猜一物）

Two red strips stuck on two sides of the
door; left and right, each filled with words;
they show up on happy occasions. (an object)

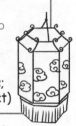

7. 外表绿色，内里空心，
熊猫最爱它。(猜一植物)

Green on the outside,
Hollow on the inside,
Giant Panda's favorite.
(a plant)

8. 圆形两兄弟，长得一样高，
互追追不到，合作向前走。
（猜一物）

Like two round-shaped brothers; exactly the
same height; always chasing each other; and
working together to move forward. (an object)

9. 身体用纸造，纸里包住火，
拿着夜行乐趣多。（猜一物）

Its body is made of paper,
Fire fills its inside,
Lots of fun to hold at night.
(an object)

10. 白里透红，生日祝寿。
（猜一食品）

White inside and red outside,
Eaten on birthdays for long life.
(a food)

11.
脖子能伸缩，手脚可收藏，
水陆能生存，一生寿命长。
（猜一动物）
Its neck can stretch.
Its feet can hide.
It can survive in water and on land.
It has a long life. (an animal)

12.
白宝宝，爱吃叶，自筑房子，
人们作衣裳。（猜一昆虫）
It has a white body.
It loves to eat leaves.
It builds its own home.
People use it to make clothes.
(an insect)

13.
身结红果，引它发火，
声大如雷，好运便来。
（猜一物）
Its body is covered in red; when lit, it
lights up the sky; sounds like loud thunder;
makes good luck come your way. (an object)

14.
日吃数十斤，初生粉红皮，
渐成黑白衣，圆圆胖胖好
脾气。（猜一动物）
Eats a lot every day; pink when it is
born; gradually turns black and white;
chubby and cheerful. (an animal)

15.
皮制面皮，肚子空心，
不打不发声，越打越欢喜。
（猜一物）
Leather skin. Hollow belly. If you don't
beat it, it has no sound. If you beat it
hard enough, it feels happy. (an object)

16.
有时像桔子，有时像香蕉，
看得见，摸不到。
（猜一自然景象）
Sometimes it looks like an orange. Sometimes
it looks like a banana. You can see it, but you
cannot touch it. (a natural thing)

17.
兄弟两个，一东一西，
可以听到，不能见到。
（猜一脸上器官）
Two brothers, one right, one left.
They hear each other, but they cannot
see each other. (a sense organ)

18.
外黄内白，猴子最爱。
（猜一水果）
Yellow outside, white inside.
Monkey's favorite treat.
(a fruit)

19.
可大可小，可长可短。
只能前进，不能退后。
(猜一抽象物)
They can be big or small, long or short.
They can only go forward. They cannot go
backward. (an abstract concept)

20.
有面没有口，有脚没有手。
虽有四只脚，自己不会走。
（猜一物）
It has a face but no mouth. It has legs
but no hands. Even though it has four
legs, it cannot walk. (an object)

名字：＿＿＿＿＿＿＿＿＿＿＿＿＿＿ ＿＿＿月＿＿＿日

Let's Talk!
说一说

Dialogue 1

nǐ shì nǎ yì nián chū shēng de
(A) 你是哪一年出生的？

wǒ shì　　　　　　　chū shēng de
(B) 我是＿＿＿＿＿＿出生的。

nà nǐ shǔ shén me
(A) 那你属什么？

wǒ shǔ
(B) 我属＿＿＿＿＿＿。

Dialogue 2

nǐ zuì xǐ huan nǎ yí gè shēng xiào
(A) 你最喜欢哪一个生肖？

wǒ zuì xǐ huan
(B) 我最喜欢＿＿＿＿＿＿。

wèi shén me
(A) 为什么？

yīn wèi
(B) 因为＿＿＿＿＿＿

yòu　　　　　　yòu
又＿＿＿＿＿＿又＿＿＿＿＿＿。

Dialogue 3

guò xīn nián yào shuō shén me jí xiáng huà
(A) 过新年要说什么吉祥话？

xīn nián kuài lè　　gōng xǐ fā cái
(B) 新年快乐！恭喜发财！

nǐ huì zěn me qìng zhù xīn nián
(A) 你会怎么庆祝新年？

(B) ＿＿＿＿＿＿＿＿＿＿＿＿＿＿＿

(Mention at least two activities.)

名字：＿＿＿＿＿＿＿＿＿＿＿＿ ＿＿＿月＿＿＿日

Let's Write!
写一写

tiān sky	天	天		
mǐ rice	米	米		
zǎo morning	早	早		
tǔ soil	土	土		
duō more	多	多		
shǎo some	少	少		

二月
February

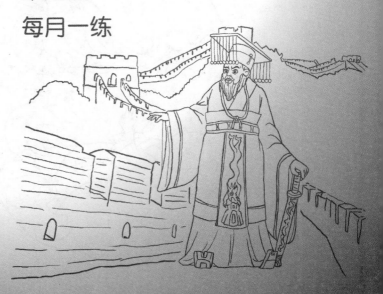

qíng
rén
jié

____ 年

xīng qī rì 星期日	xīng qī yī 星期一	xīng qī èr 星期二	xīng qī sān 星期三	xīng qī sì 星期四	xīng qī wǔ 星期五	xīng qī liù 星期六

What's Happening in February?
二月知多少？

jīn tiān shì　　　　　yuè　　　　rì
1. 今天是＿＿＿月＿＿＿日。

míng tiān shì　　　　　yuè　　　　rì
2. 明天是＿＿＿月＿＿＿日。

zuó tiān shì　　　　　yuè　　　　rì
3. 昨天是＿＿＿月＿＿＿日。

jīn tiān shì xīng qī
4. 今天是星期＿＿＿＿＿。

èr yuè yǒu　　　　　　　　　tiān
5. 二月有＿＿＿＿＿＿＿天。

èr yuè zhōng tè bié de rì zi shì
6. 二月中特别的日子是＿＿＿＿＿。

qíng rén jié shì　　　　　　yuè　　　　　rì
7. 情人节是＿＿＿月＿＿＿日。

èr yuè de dì yí gè xīng qī èr shì　　　yuè　　　rì
8. 二月的第一个星期二是＿＿月＿＿日。

èr yuè de zuì hòu yí gè xīng qī wǔ shì　　yuè　　rì
9. 二月的最后一个星期五是＿＿月＿＿日。

de shēng rì shì　　　yuè　　　rì
10. ＿＿＿＿＿的生日是＿＿月＿＿日。
　　(a person's name)

134

Number Chart: 1-100
认一认：一到一百

0	líng	零	10	shí	十	20	èr shí	二十
1	yī	一	11	shí yī	十一	30	sān shí	三十
2	èr	二	12	shí èr	十二	40	sì shí	四十
3	sān	三	13	shí sān	十三	50	wǔ shí	五十
4	sì	四	14	shí sì	十四	60	liù shí	六十
5	wǔ	五	15	shí wǔ	十五	70	qī shí	七十
6	liù	六	16	shí liù	十六	80	bā shí	八十
7	qī	七	17	shí qī	十七	90	jiǔ shí	九十
8	bā	八	18	shí bā	十八	100	yī bǎi	一百
9	jiǔ	九	19	shí jiǔ	十九	1,000	yī qiān	一千

一	二	三	四	五	六	七	八	九	十
十一	十二	十三	十四	十五	十六	十七	十八	十九	二十
二十一	二十二	二十三	二十四	二十五	二十六	二十七	二十八	二十九	三十
三十一	三十二	三十三	三十四	三十五	三十六	三十七	三十八	三十九	四十
四十一	四十二	四十三	四十四	四十五	四十六	四十七	四十八	四十九	五十
五十一	五十二	五十三	五十四	五十五	五十六	五十七	五十八	五十九	六十
六十一	六十二	六十三	六十四	六十五	六十六	六十七	六十八	六十九	七十
七十一	七十二	七十三	七十四	七十五	七十六	七十七	七十八	七十九	八十
八十一	八十二	八十三	八十四	八十五	八十六	八十七	八十八	八十九	九十
九十一	九十二	九十三	九十四	九十五	九十六	九十七	九十八	九十九	一百

名字： _____ _____月_____日

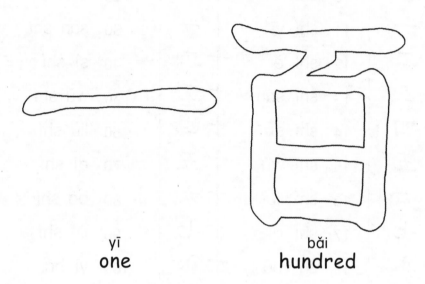

yī
one

bǎi
hundred

Directions:

1. Color "一百".
2. Cut on the dotted line.
3. Ideas for decoration:
    (a) write big and small "一百" in the blank space;
    (b) draw 100 objects;
    (c) create your own images.
4. Tie a string to the two edges on top and hang it up.

Fill in the missing numbers and color the hearts lightly.

名字：_____

月 _____ 日 _____

Math Fun: Ways to Make 100
趣味数学：加起来100

Fill in the blanks with the correct numbers to make 100. The first one has been done for you.

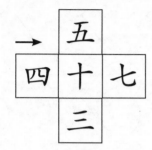   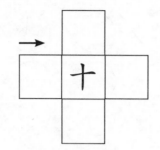   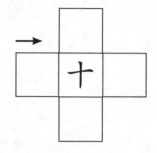

__47__ + __53__ = 100   __21__ + _____ = 100   __73__ + _____ = 100

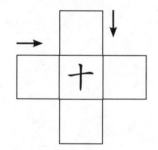   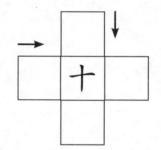

_____ + __44__ = 100   _____ + __35__ = 100

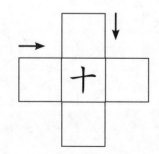   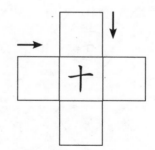   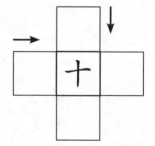

_____ + _____ = 100   _____ + _____ = 100   _____ + _____ = 100

名字： _____

____ 月 ____ 日

| Initials | b, p, m, f, d, t, n, l, g, k, h, j, q, x, zh, ch, sh, r, z, c, s, w, y |
| Finals | a, o, e, ei, ai, ie, ao, ou, an, en, ang, ong, er, i, u, ü |

Instruction:
Use the above initials and finals to think of 100 words that you know. Write the character, pinyin and its English meaning in each space provided. The first one has been done for you. You may refer to a book or dictionary. (Use one box for one character.)

我 wǒ	I						

Story-telling: A Little Love Story
讲故事：小小爱情故事

One day a boy and girl were walking in a park hand in hand on a warm summer day.

Suddenly they heard a loud clap of thunder and saw a bolt of lightning strike across the sky...

Then it started to rain...

Quickly they searched for a shelter...

They were very nervous...

Dry and safe from the storm, the two stood holding each other until the storm passed...

After the storm they continued their walk in the park...

ài
爱

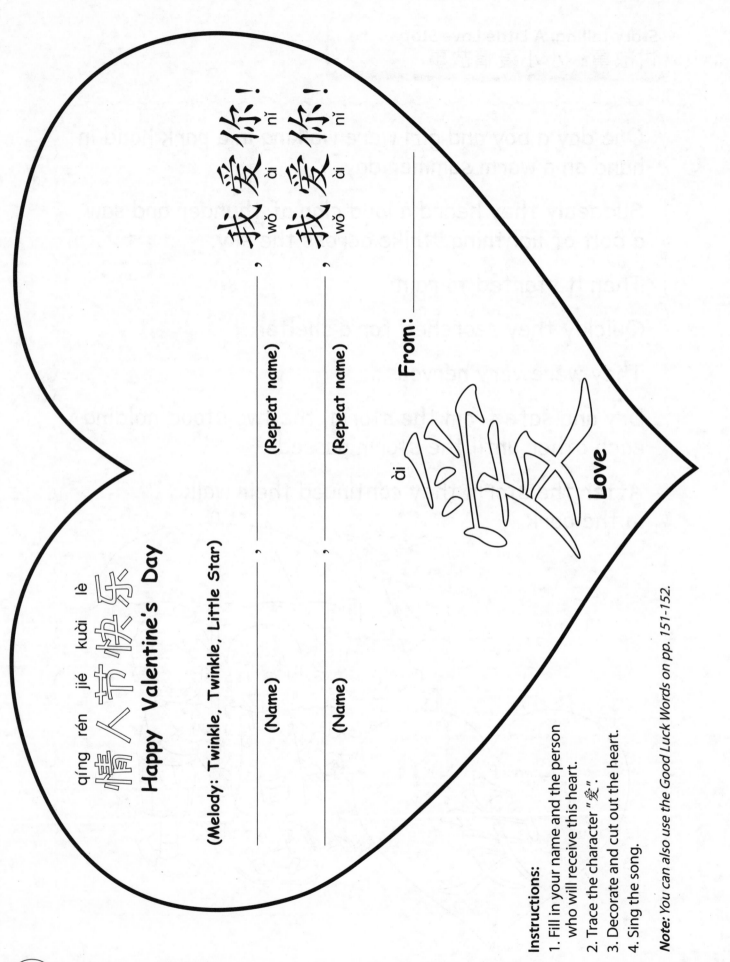

qíng rén jié kuài lè
情人节快乐
Happy Valentine's Day

(Melody: Twinkle, Twinkle, Little Star)

_____ , _____ ,
(Name)   (Repeat name)

wǒ 我 爱 ài 你 nǐ !

_____ , _____ ,
(Name)   (Repeat name)

wǒ 我 爱 ài 你 nǐ !

ài

Love

From: _____

Instructions:
1. Fill in your name and the person who will receive this heart.
2. Trace the character "爱".
3. Decorate and cut out the heart.
4. Sing the song.

Note: You can also use the Good Luck Words on pp. 151-152.

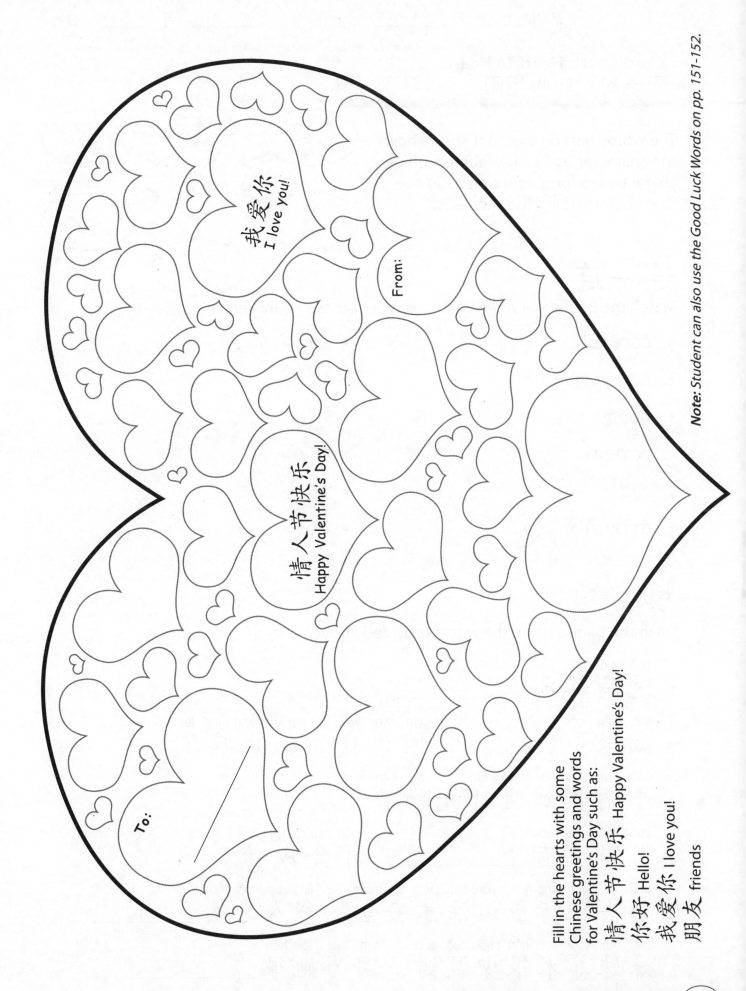

我爱你
I love you!

From:

情人节快乐
Happy Valentine's Day!

To:

Note: Student can also use the Good Luck Words on pp. 151-152.

Fill in the hearts with some
Chinese greetings and words
for Valentine's Day such as:
情人节快乐 Happy Valentine's Day!
你好 Hello!
我爱你 I love you!
朋友 friends

Word Chart: Heart to Heart
配一配：心心相印

The word chart on the right shows how the character "心" can combine with other characters to form new words. Go over them before doing the exercises.

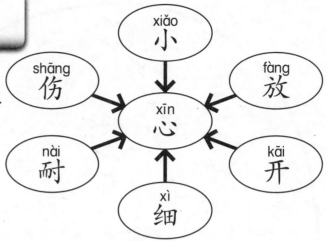

连一连

Match the English words with the correct Chinese equivalents.

1. careful   •   • 伤心

2. not worried •   • 小心

3. happy   •   • 细心

4. patient   •   • 耐心

5. sad   •   • 开心

6. attentive   •   • 放心

填空题

Fill in the blanks using the words provided above.

　　guò mǎ lù yào
1. 过马路要_____。

　　wǒ hěn   yīn wèi wǒ de māo shēng bìng le
2. 我很_____，因为我的猫生病了。

　　xiǎo míng shōu dào shēng rì lǐ wù hěn
3. 小明收到生日礼物很_____。

　　zuò shì yào yǒu   cái huì chéng gōng
4. 做事要有_____，才会成功。

　　chū qù lǚ xíng yīng gāi zhù yì ān quán   jiā rén cái huì
5. 出去旅行应该注意安全，家人才会_____。

　　mèi mei suàn shù hěn shǎo zuò cuò   yīn wèi tā hěn
6. 妹妹算术很少做错，因为她很_____。

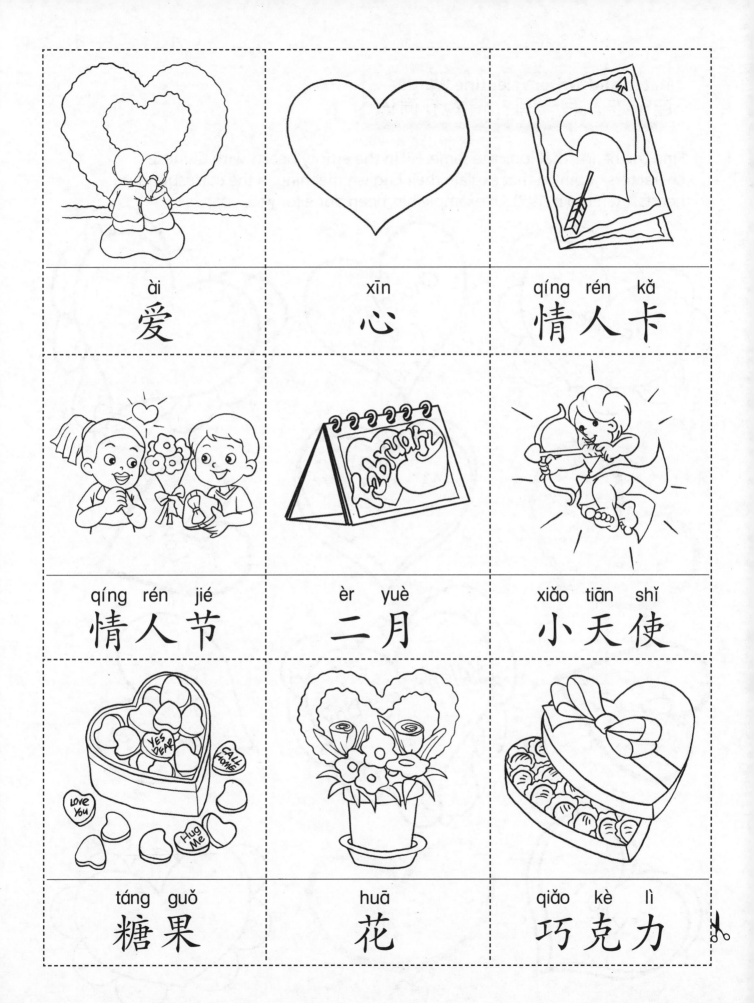

ài
爱

xīn
心

qíng rén kǎ
情人卡

qíng rén jié
情人节

èr yuè
二月

xiǎo tiān shǐ
小天使

táng guǒ
糖果

huā
花

qiǎo kè lì
巧克力

Match and Write: Valentine Words
连一连，写一写：情人节词语

Find the hearts that look the same. Fill in the empty hearts with Chinese characters or pinyin that explain their English meaning in the corresponding hearts. (Refer to p. 147) An example has been done for you.

Flowers

Chocolate

February

Love

Valentine's Day

Heart

二月

Word Puzzle: Valentine's Day
填字谜：情人节

Fill in the missing letters to complete the pinyin spelling for each of the Valentine words. Write the Chinese characters or English words on the space provided. The first one has been done for you.

1. qiǎo kè lì ＿＿＿＿＿＿＿＿＿ 巧克力 , ＿＿＿＿＿＿＿＿ Chocolate

2. x__n ＿＿＿＿＿＿＿＿＿, ＿＿＿＿＿＿＿＿

3. xiǎo tiā__ shǐ ＿＿＿＿＿＿＿＿＿, ＿＿＿＿＿＿＿＿

4. tán__ guǒ ＿＿＿＿＿＿＿＿＿, ＿＿＿＿＿＿＿＿

5. è__ yuè ＿＿＿＿＿＿＿＿＿, ＿＿＿＿＿＿＿＿

6. qiǎo k__ lì ＿＿＿＿＿＿＿＿＿, ＿＿＿＿＿＿＿＿

7. xī__ ＿＿＿＿＿＿＿＿＿, ＿＿＿＿＿＿＿＿

8. qíng rén __ié ＿＿＿＿＿＿＿＿＿, ＿＿＿＿＿＿＿＿

9. à__ ＿＿＿＿＿＿＿＿＿, ＿＿＿＿＿＿＿＿

10. èr yu__ ＿＿＿＿＿＿＿＿＿, ＿＿＿＿＿＿＿＿

Arrange the underlined letters from above to write the surprise three-word phrase in the blanks below.

＿＿ ＿＿ ＿＿ ＿＿ ＿＿ ＿＿ ＿＿ ＿＿ ＿＿ ＿＿ ＿＿ ＿＿ (in pinyin)

＿＿＿＿＿＿＿＿＿＿＿＿＿＿＿＿＿＿＿＿＿ (in characters or English)

Word Puzzle: Valentine's Day
填字谜：情人节

名字：_____ _____月_____日

Pattern Challenge: Valentine Words
找规律：情人节词语

Read the words aloud and find the pattern in each line. Fill in the blanks with the word that should come next in the pattern. Write your answer in characters or pinyin and illustrate in the space provided.

Write in characters or pinyin below	Draw a picture below
1 xiǎo tiān shǐ xīn 小天使 心 小天使 心 小天使	
2 táng guǒ huā 糖果 糖果 花 花 糖果 糖果 _____	
3 ài xīn 爱 心 爱 心 爱 _____	
4 èr yuè 二月 花 爱 二月 _____ 爱 二月	
5 qiǎo kè lì qíng rén kǎ 巧克力 情人卡 糖果 巧克力 _____ 糖果	
6 爱 _____ 情人卡 情人卡 爱 爱 情人卡 情人卡	
7 巧克力 爱 小天使 _____ 爱 小天使	
8 _____ qíng rén jié 情人节 情人节 二月 情人节 情人节	

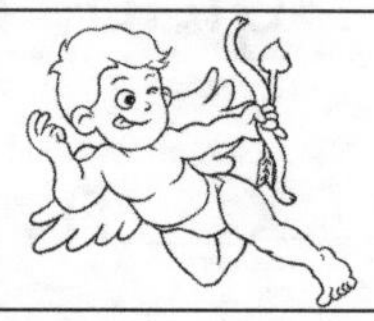

(148)

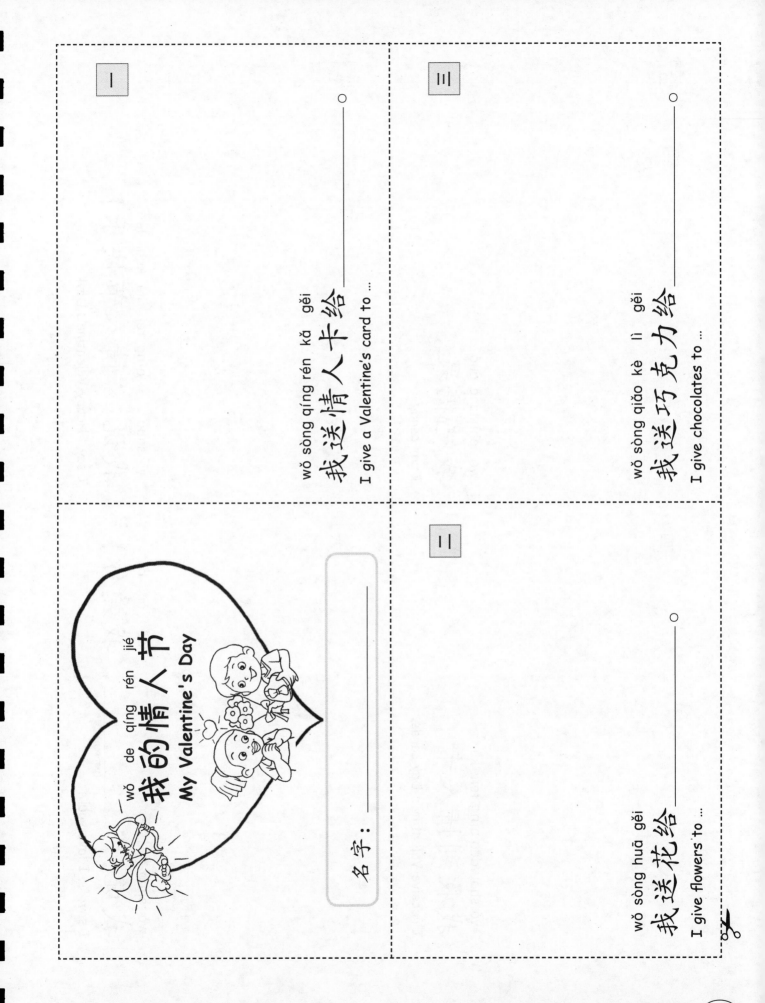

一

wǒ sòng qíng rén kǎ gěi
我送情人卡给 ————————
I give a Valentine's card to ...

三

wǒ sòng qiǎo kè lì gěi
我送巧克力给 ————————
I give chocolates to ...

wǒ de qíng rén jié
我的情人节
My Valentine's Day

名字：————————

二

wǒ sòng huā gěi
我送花给 ————————
I give flowers to ...

wǒ chī táng guǒ
我吃糖果。
I eat candy.

wǒ shuō　　qíng rén jié kuài lè
我说："情人节快乐！"
I say, "Happy Valentine's Day!"

wǒ shōu dào qíng rén kǎ
我收到情人卡。
I receive Valentine's Day cards.

　　　　　　　　wǒ ài nǐ
wǒ shuō
我说："＿＿＿＿，我爱你！"
　　　　　(person)
I say, "... I love you!"

ài 爱 love	爱 爱 爱 爱 爱 爱 爱 爱 爱 爱
lì 力 power	力 力
jí 吉 good luck	吉 吉 吉 吉 吉 吉
zhì 智 wisdom	智 智 智 智 智 智 智 智 智 智 智 智
kāng 康 health	康 康 康 康 康 康 康 康 康 康 康

xǐ 喜 happiness	喜 喜 喜 喜 喜 喜 喜 喜 喜 喜 喜 喜
měi 美 beauty	美 美 美 美 美 美 美 美 美
lù 禄 good fortune	禄 禄 禄 禄 禄 禄 禄 禄 禄 禄 禄 禄
ān 安 peace	安 安 安 安 安 安
shòu 寿 longevity	寿 寿 寿 寿 寿 寿 寿

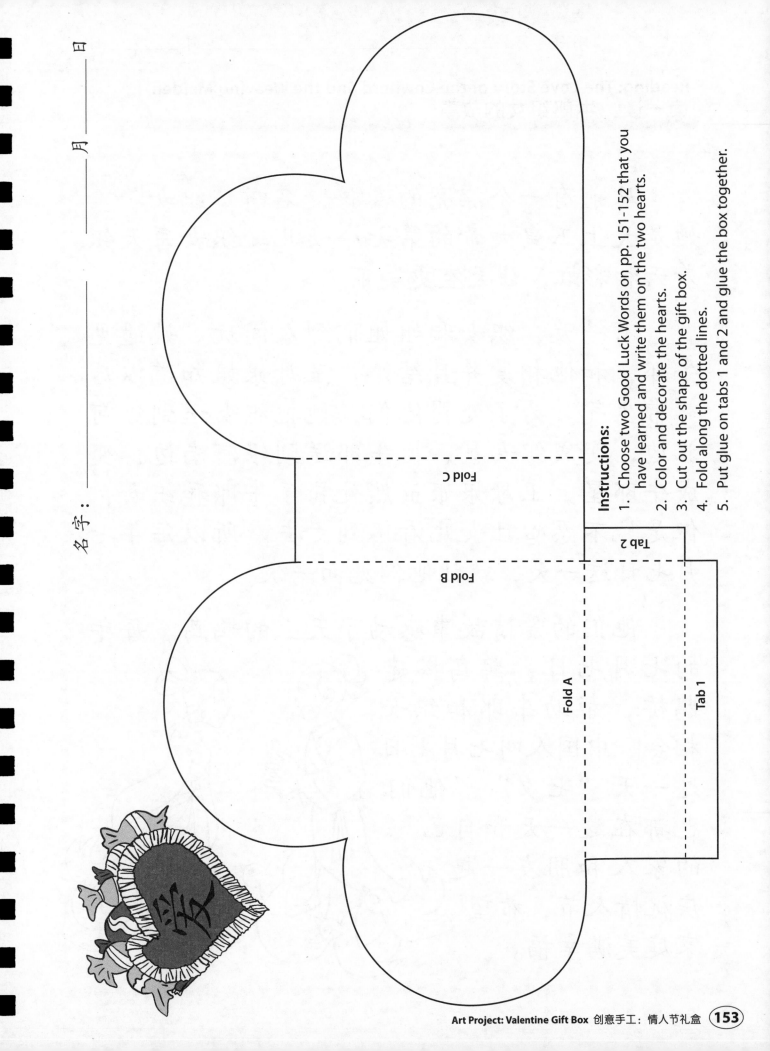

名字：———— 月———— 日————

Fold C

Fold B

Tab 2

Fold A

Tab 1

Instructions:

1. Choose two Good Luck Words on pp. 151-152 that you have learned and write them on the two hearts.
2. Color and decorate the hearts.
3. Cut out the shape of the gift box.
4. Fold along the dotted lines.
5. Put glue on tabs 1 and 2 and glue the box together.

Reading: The Love Story of the Cowherd and the Weaving Maiden
读一读：牛郎织女的故事

从前有一个漂亮的女孩，名叫"织女"。她是天上玉皇大帝的第七个女儿。织女每天织着云和彩虹，让天空更美丽。

有一天，织女和姐姐们到人间玩。她遇见牛郎，和他相爱并且结婚。王母娘娘知道以后非常生气。为了处罚他们，她把织女送到银河北边，变成织女星，把牛郎送到银河南边，变成牛郎星。王母娘娘虽然处罚了牛郎和织女，但是她不忍心让女儿看不到丈夫。所以每年七月七日这一天，就让他们见面一次。

他们的爱情故事感动了天上的鹊鸟。每年的七月七日，鹊鸟搭建鹊桥，帮助牛郎和织女相会。中国人叫七月七日这一天"七夕"。他们也都在这一天和自己的家人和朋友一起庆祝情人节，希望家庭美满幸福。

Cóng qián yǒu yí gè piào liang de nǚ hái, míng jiào "zhī nǚ". Tā shì tiān shang yù huáng dà dì de dì qī gè nǚ ěr. Zhī nǚ měi tiān zhī zhe yún hé cǎi hóng, ràng tiān kōng gèng měi lì.

Yǒu yì tiān, zhī nǚ hé jié jie men dào rén jiān wán. Tā yù jiàn niú láng, hé tā xiāng ài bìng qiě jié hūn. Wáng mǔ niáng niang zhī dào yǐ hòu fēi cháng shēng qì. Wèi le chǔ fá tā men, tā bǎ zhī nǚ sòng dào yín hé běi biān, biàn chèng zhī nǚ xīng, bǎ niú láng sòng dào yín hé nán biān, biàn chéng niú láng xīng. Wáng mǔ niáng niang suī rán chǔ fá le niú láng hé zhī nǚ, dàn shì tā bù rěn xīn ràng nǚ ěr kàn bú dào zhàng fu. Suǒ yǐ měi nián qī yuè qī rì zhè yì tiān, jiù ràng tā men jiàn miàn yí cì.

Tā men de ài qíng gù shi gǎn dòng le tiān shang de què niǎo. Měi nián de qī yuè qī rì, què niǎo dā jiàn què qiáo, bāng zhù niú láng hé zhī nǚ xiāng huì. Zhōng guó rén jiào qī yuè qī rì zhè yì tiān "qī xī". Tā men yě dōu zài zhè yì tiān hé zì jǐ de jiā rén hé péng you yì qǐ qìng zhù qíng rén jié, xī wàng jiā tíng měi mǎn xìng fú.

Long ago there was a beautiful young woman known as the Weaving Maiden. The Weaving Maiden was the 7th daughter of the Emperor of Heaven and spent her days weaving clouds and rainbows to make the sky beautiful.

One day the Weaving Maiden made a trip to the earth with her sisters. While she was there she met and fell in love with a handsome Cowherd. The Cowherd persuaded her to stay on earth and marry him.

When the Queen Mother of the West found out what happened, she was furious! She punished the couple by sending the Weaving Maiden to live on a star called Vega and her husband to live on another star called Altair. Although the Queen Mother wished to punish the Weaving Maiden, she still loved her and realized how sad she was without her husband. So she allowed the two to meet once a year on the 7th day of the 7th month on the lunar calendar.

On this day the magpies, which were so touched by their story, form a bridge so that the husband and wife can be reunited. This day has become a day for people in China to celebrate with their loved ones and to express well wishes for happy marriages.

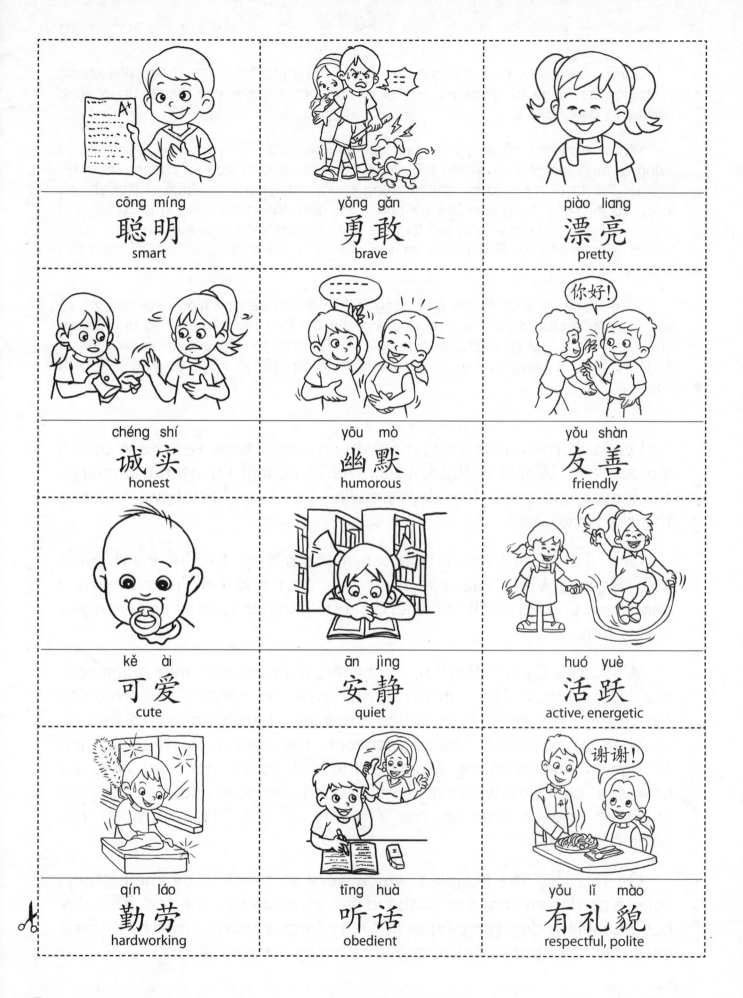

Game: Bumble Bee
游戏：小蜜蜂

Write 3 different adjectives that best describe you in either Chinese characters or pinyin. Then color and decorate the picture.

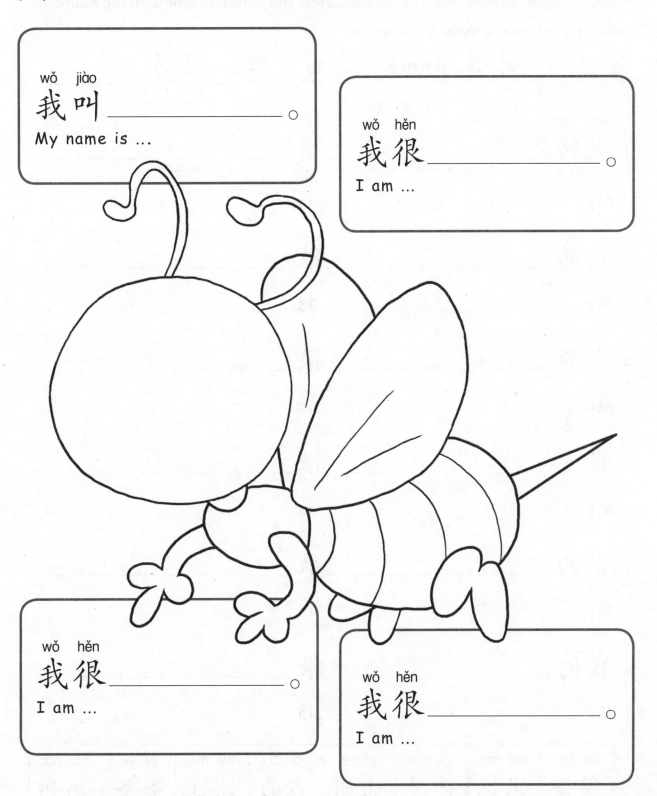

wǒ jiào
我 叫 _____ 。
My name is ...

wǒ hěn
我 很 _____ 。
I am ...

wǒ hěn
我 很 _____ 。
I am ...

wǒ hěn
我 很 _____ 。
I am ...

Writing Activity: Describe My Family Members
写一写：形容我的家人

Use the vocabulary list below on family members and the adjectives you have learned to fill in the blanks. If you are using a family member's name to complete the sentence, write the family member word in Chinese before the person's name as in the example.

Note: No need to add "是" before the adjectives.

我的 _____妹妹 Annie_____ 很_____聪明_____。

wǒ de   hěn

1. 我的 _____ 很_____。
         (family member)   (adjective)

   My _____ is _____.

2. 我的 _____ 很_____。

   My _____ is _____.

3. 我的 _____ 很_____。

   My _____ is _____.

4. 我的 _____ 很_____。

   My _____ is _____.

5. 我的 _____ 很_____。

   My _____ is _____.

6. 我的 _____ 很_____。

   My _____ is _____.

bà ba	mā ma	gē ge	jiě jie	dì di	mèi mei	yé ye	nǎi nai
爸爸	妈妈	哥哥	姐姐	弟弟	妹妹	爷爷	奶奶

Find the pinyin words listed below in the Word Search. Then write the meaning in English on the lines provided.

```
c a c h s o k q n y w c z p i q v c a e x d f h o
p l b z g s h j t o j r l x b c k c y f k o o b j
q b n n f t u u i n g v i m n p h p w h y n t w p
w h n b r c q t l g g u z u a e i s p u a v q i i
e y e l w r e s h g a z v a n a c r x s k i z f i
t g a i a b d r k a l v n g o i p h e h l x p m x
c o n g m i n g k n p j s l y o u l i m a o p h i
y o u s h a n k e a i h i q z q h y f y a l z i m
a m d k x z t n g n i a i x v s o v k e a s v u h
d c h t j n s j g y n n e r s u l s f p u d d o w
r v u m n p x s i g l t u m m q w o y q h x l i h
j a a v s f k w j a y t y o a t n n g d g l z m e
l c a z b q x m o z f w o z g r s m b o n v z h v
t v j a z u z l y k o z u k p q i b p o i x p u o
i g p w c p e y j a h j h z b i l a t z t z e p q
```

tīng huà	yōu mò	piào liang	chéng shí
_____	_____	_____	_____
yǒu lǐ mào	yǒu shàn	kě ài	ān jìng
_____	_____	_____	_____
huó yuè	qín láo	cōng míng	yǒng gǎn
_____	_____	_____	_____

名字：_____   _____ 月 _____ 日

Refer to the vocabulary words on p. 156 and write the correct pinyin words on the lines provided. Then use them to complete the puzzle.

Across: pinyin   **Down:**   pinyin

1. pretty   _____   7. obedient   _____

2. honest   _____   8. hardworking   _____

3. respectful   _____   9. active   _____

4. smart   _____   10. humorous   _____

5. cute   _____   11. friendly   _____

6. quiet   _____   12. brave   _____

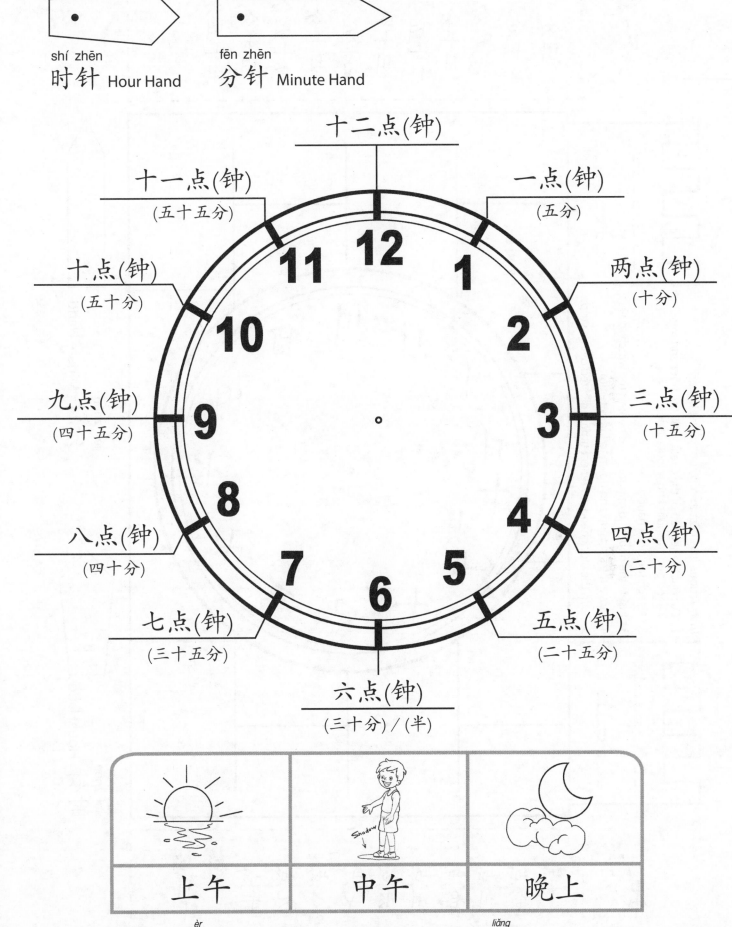

shí zhēn
时针 Hour Hand

fēn zhēn
分针 Minute Hand

十二点(钟)

一点(钟)
(五分)

十一点(钟)
(五十五分)

两点(钟)
(十分)

十点(钟)
(五十分)

三点(钟)
(十五分)

九点(钟)
(四十五分)

四点(钟)
(二十分)

八点(钟)
(四十分)

五点(钟)
(二十五分)

七点(钟)
(三十五分)

六点(钟)
(三十分) / (半)

上午	中午	晚上

èr   liǎng
Note: *When "二" becomes a measure word, it is substituted with "两".*

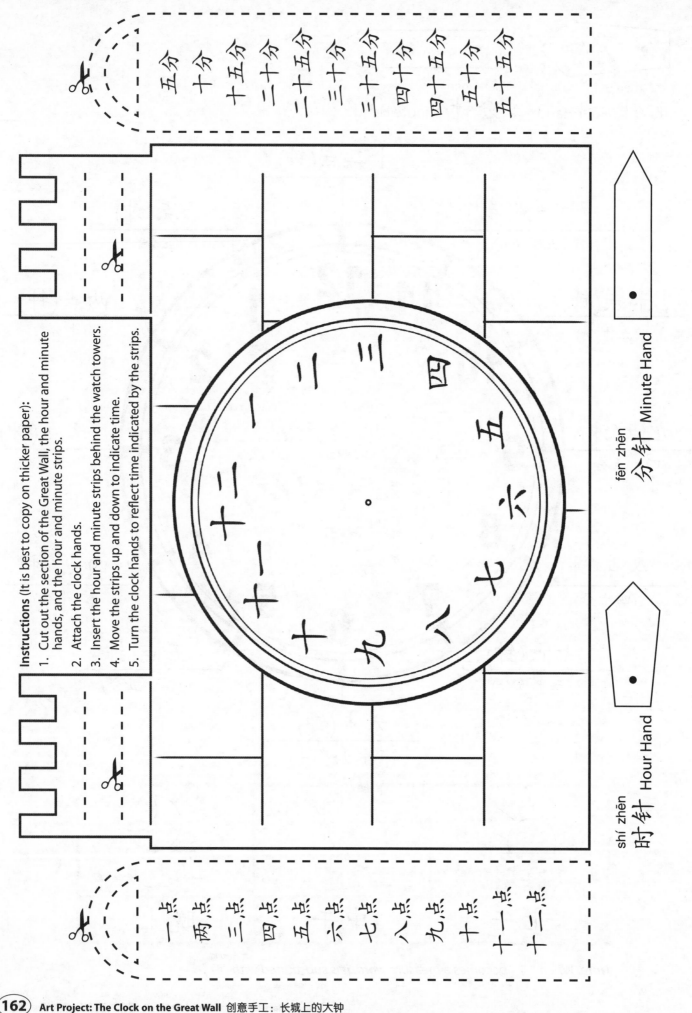

Instructions (It is best to copy on thicker paper):

1. Cut out the section of the Great Wall, the hour and minute hands, and the hour and minute strips.
2. Attach the clock hands.
3. Insert the hour and minute strips behind the watch towers.
4. Move the strips up and down to indicate time.
5. Turn the clock hands to reflect time indicated by the strips.

五分
十分
十五分
二十分
二十五分
三十分
三十五分
四十分
四十五分
五十分
五十五分

十二　一　二　三　四
十一　　　　　　五
十　九　八　七　六

一点
两点
三点
四点
五点
六点
七点
八点
九点
十点
十一点
十二点

fēn zhēn
分针 Minute Hand

shí zhēn
时针 Hour Hand

yī diǎn (zhōng) 一点(钟)	liǎng diǎn (zhōng) 两点(钟)	sān diǎn (zhōng) 三点(钟)
sì diǎn (zhōng) 四点(钟)	wǔ diǎn (zhōng) 五点(钟)	liù diǎn (zhōng) 六点(钟)
qī diǎn (zhōng) 七点(钟)	bā diǎn (zhōng) 八点(钟)	jiǔ diǎn (zhōng) 九点(钟)
shí diǎn (zhōng) 十点(钟)	shí yī diǎn (zhōng) 十一点(钟)	shí èr diǎn (zhōng) 十二点(钟)

Note: When making copies of this card game, make sure that pp.163-164 are copied back-to-back each other.

Card Game: Wolf, Wolf, What Time Is It? 卡片游戏：老狼，老狼，几点钟？

Song: What Time Is It Now?
儿歌：现在几点钟？

Melody: London Bridge Is Falling Down

xiàn zài xiàn zài / jǐ diǎn zhōng
现 在 现 在 几 点 钟？
What time is it now?

jǐ diǎn zhōng / jǐ diǎn zhōng
几 点 钟， 几 点 钟？
What time, what time?

xiàn zài xiàn zài / jǐ diǎn zhōng
现 在 现 在 几 点 钟？
What time is it now?

qǐng nǐ / gào su wǒ
请 你 告 诉 我。
Please tell me.

Draw: Telling Time ❶
画一画：现在几点(钟)？ ●

Draw the hour hand to indicate the time shown.

sān diǎn (zhōng)
三点(钟)

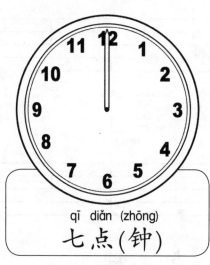

qī diǎn (zhōng)
七点(钟)

shí èr diǎn (zhōng)
十二点(钟)

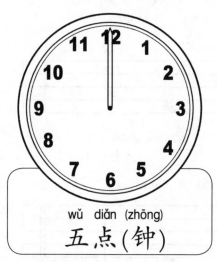

wǔ diǎn (zhōng)
五点(钟)

bā diǎn (zhōng)
八点(钟)

shí diǎn (zhōng)
十点(钟)

jiǔ diǎn (zhōng)
九点(钟)

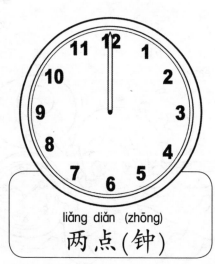

liǎng diǎn (zhōng)
两点(钟)

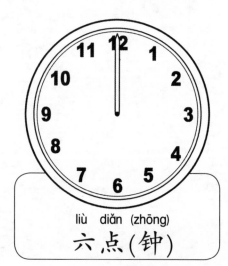

liù diǎn (zhōng)
六点(钟)

Fill in the Blanks: Telling Time ❷
填一填：现在几点(钟)？ ⊜

Write the time shown on each of the clocks.

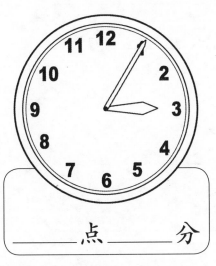

_____点_____分

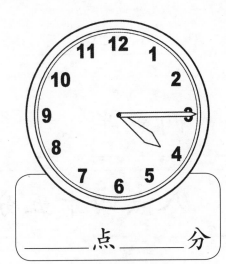

_____点_____分

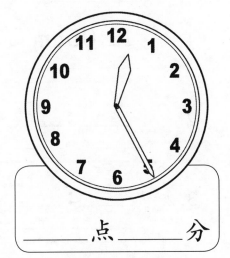

_____点_____分

_____点_____分

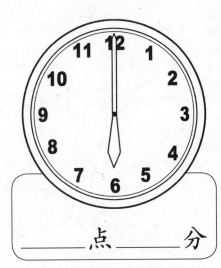

_____点_____分

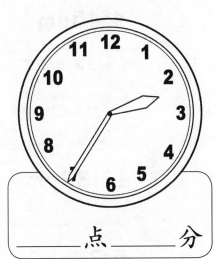

_____点_____分

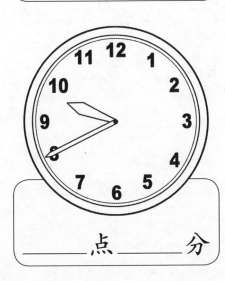

_____点_____分

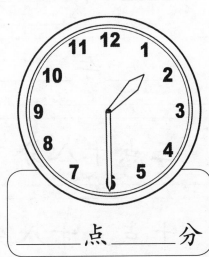

_____点_____分

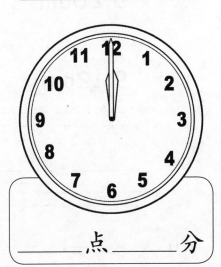

_____点_____分

Fill in the Blanks: Telling Time ❸
填一填：现在几点(钟)？ ❸

Translate the following times.

1. 12:05am ＿＿午＿＿＿点＿＿＿分

2. ＿＿＿：＿＿＿ 两点半

3. ＿＿＿：＿＿＿ 八点四十五分

4. 4:45pm ＿＿午＿＿＿点＿＿＿分

5. ＿＿＿：＿＿＿ 一点五十三分

6. 12:37pm ＿＿午＿＿＿点＿＿＿分

7. 5:20am ＿＿午＿＿＿点＿＿＿分

8. 9:12pm ＿＿午＿＿＿点＿＿＿分

9. ＿＿＿：＿＿＿ 三点十八分

10. ＿＿＿：＿＿＿ 十点五十八分

wǒ de yì tiān
我 的 一 天
My Daily Schedule

活动

名字：_____

一

wǒ   qǐ chuáng
我 _____ 起床。
   (time)

二

wǒ   chī zǎo cān
我 _____ 吃早餐。
   (time)

三

wǒ   shàng xué
我 _____ 上学。
   (time)

四

wǒ   chī wǔ cān
我 _____ 吃午餐。
   (time)

五

wǒ   wán yóu xì
我 _____ 玩游戏。
   (time)

六

wǒ _____ fàng xué
我 _____ 放学。
(time)

七

wǒ _____ chī diǎn xīn
我 _____ 吃点心。
(time)

八

wǒ _____ zuò gōng kè
我 _____ 做功课。
(time)

九

wǒ _____ chī wǎn cān
我 _____ 吃晚餐。
(time)

十

wǒ _____ xǐ zǎo
我 _____ 洗澡。
(time)

十一

wǒ _____ shuì jiào
我 _____ 睡觉。
(time)

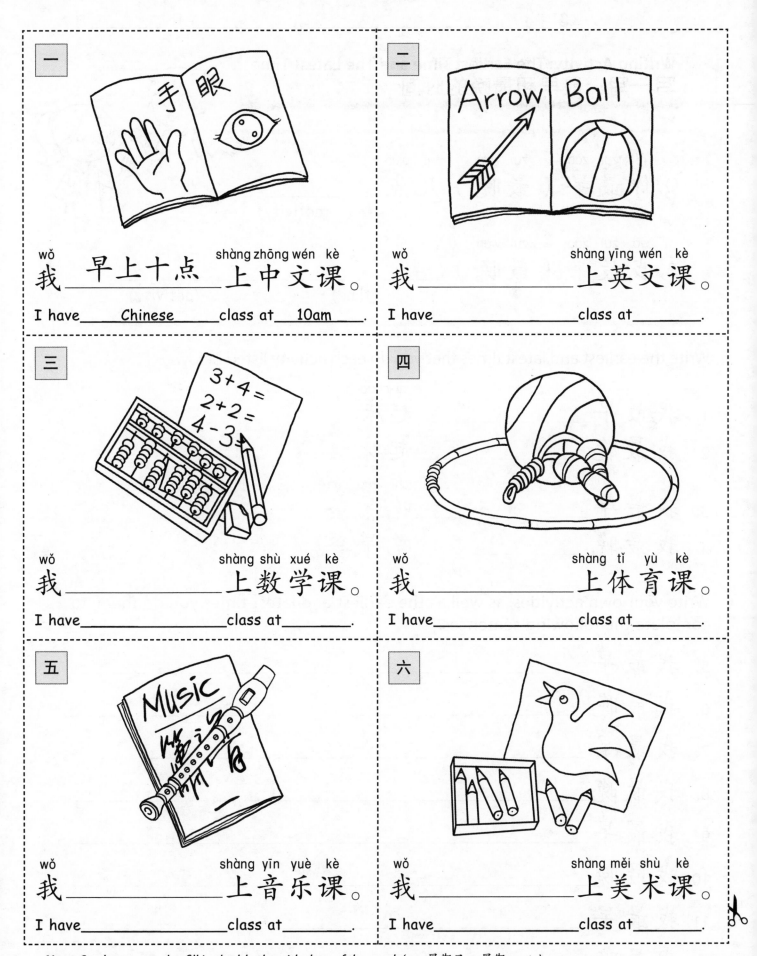

一

wǒ　　　　　　　　　　shàng zhōng wén　kè
我 ___早上十点___ 上 中 文 课。
I have ___Chinese___ class at ___10am___.

二

wǒ　　　　　　　　　　shàng yīng wén　kè
我 _____ 上 英 文 课。
I have _____ class at_____.

三

wǒ　　　　　　　　　　shàng shù xué　kè
我 _____ 上 数 学 课。
I have _____ class at_____.

四

wǒ　　　　　　　　　　shàng tǐ　yù　kè
我 _____ 上 体 育 课。
I have _____ class at_____.

五

wǒ　　　　　　　　　　shàng yīn yuè　kè
我 _____ 上 音 乐 课。
I have _____ class at_____.

六

wǒ　　　　　　　　　　shàng měi shù　kè
我 _____ 上 美 术 课。
I have _____ class at_____.

Note: Students may also fill in the blanks with days of the week (eg. 星期日、星期一 etc).

名字：_____   ____月____日

Writing Activity: The Earliest Time and The Latest Time
写一写：最早和最晚的时间

Q 你 最早（最晚）几点_____？
　　nǐ zuì zǎo　　zuì wǎn　　jǐ diǎn
　　　　　　　　　　　　　　　　　　　　(activity)

A 我 最早（最晚）_____ _____。
　　wǒ zuì zǎo　　zuì wǎn
　　　　　　　　　　　　　　(time)　　　　　(activity)

Write the earliest and latest times that you do each activity listed below.

1. 我最早_____起床。
　　　　　　　　　　qǐ chuáng

2. 我最晚_____起床。

3. 我最早_____吃早餐。
　　　　　　　　　　chī zǎo cān

4. 我最晚_____吃早餐。

Write your own activities, as well as the earliest and latest times you do them, to complete the following sentences.

5. 我最早_____ _____。

6. 我最晚_____ _____。

7. 我最早_____ _____。

8. 我最晚_____ _____。

9. 我最早_____ _____。

10. 我最晚_____ _____。

11. 我最早_____ _____。

12. 我最晚_____ _____。

名字：＿＿＿＿＿＿＿＿＿＿＿＿＿＿ ＿＿＿月＿＿＿日

Word Search: Daily Activities
找一找：日常活动

Find the Chinese characters listed below in the word search. Then fill in the blanks with the correct English meanings.

学	睡	放	课	洗	吃	起	早	放
早	做	学	床	做	功	课	上	睡
午	晚	觉	上	文	学	床	中	澡
学	澡	餐	餐	午	吃	学	文	功
洗	起	觉	吃	餐	晚	床	课	澡
起	餐	上	放	澡	睡	放	做	起
澡	吃	起	文	觉	功	餐	文	学
上	床	晚	课	上	课	早	上	餐
功	中	觉	餐	洗	上	吃	早	午

shàng xué
1. 上学：＿＿＿＿＿＿

chī wǎn cān
2. 吃晚餐：＿＿＿＿＿＿

shàng zhōng wén kè
3. 上中文课：＿＿＿＿＿＿

chī wǔ cān
4. 吃午餐：＿＿＿＿＿＿

fàng xué
5. 放学：＿＿＿＿＿＿

shuì jiào
6. 睡觉：＿＿＿＿＿＿

xǐ zǎo
7. 洗澡：＿＿＿＿＿＿

qǐ chuáng
8. 起床：＿＿＿＿＿＿

zuò gōng kè
9. 做功课：＿＿＿＿＿＿

chī zǎo cān
10. 吃早餐：＿＿＿＿＿＿

Reading: The First Emperor — Qin Shihuang
读一读：第一位皇帝——秦始皇

　　始皇帝生于大约两千两百年以前。他结束战国七雄，**统一**中国，建立**秦**朝。所以他叫自己"秦始皇帝"，简称"秦始皇"。

　　秦始皇统一了**文字**、**钱币**和**度量**的工具。但是他最大的成就是建造**万里长城**。在他之前，中国北方已有很多分散的长城用来抵抗**蒙古**人的入侵。秦始皇把这些长城连接并加长，成为后来的万里长城。

　　秦始皇拥有很大的权力。他相信自己死后会继续拥有权力。所以他命令全国工匠制作成千上万个真人尺寸的**兵马俑**，埋藏在他的皇陵四周。1974年这些埋在地下的兵马俑被几个**西安**的农民发现。这就是著名的兵马俑奇迹。

　　虽然秦始皇的成就不容怀疑，**但是**人们认为他也有**过失**。例如他强迫人民建造长城和皇陵，对不服从的人非常残暴。他也严厉控制人们的思想，维护中央政府的权威。你认为秦始皇是功大于过，还是过大于功呢？

Shǐ huáng dì shēng yú dà yuē liǎng qiān liǎng bǎi nián yǐ qián. Tā jié shù zhàn guó qī xióng, tǒng yī zhōng guó, jiàn lì qín cháo. Suǒ yǐ tā jiào zì jǐ "qín shǐ huáng dì", jiǎn chēng "qín shǐ huáng".

Qín shǐ huáng tǒng yī le wén zì, qián bì, hé dù liàng de gōng jù. Dàn shì tā zuì dà de chéng jiù shì jiàn zào wàn lǐ cháng chéng. Zài tā zhī qián, zhōng guó běi fāng yǐ yǒu hěn duō fēn sàn de cháng chéng yòng lái dǐ kàng měng gǔ rén de rù qīn. Qín shǐ huáng bǎ zhè xiē cháng chéng lián jiē bìng jiā cháng, chéng wéi hòu lái de wàn lǐ cháng chéng.

Qín shǐ huáng yōng yǒu hěn dà de quán lì. Tā xiāng xìn zì jǐ sǐ hòu huì jì xù yōng yǒu quán lì. Suǒ yǐ tā mìng lìng quán guó gōng jiàng zhì zuò chéng qiān shàng wàn gè zhēn rén chǐ cùn de bīng mǎ yǒng, mái zàng zài tā de huáng líng sì zhōu. Yī jiǔ qī sì nián zhè xiē mái zài dì xià de bīng mǎ yǒng bèi jǐ gè xī ān de nóng mín fā xiàn. Zhè jiù shì zhù míng de bīng mǎ yǒng qí jī.

Suī rán qín shǐ huáng de chéng jiù bù róng huái yí, dàn shì rén men rèn wéi tā yě yǒu guò shī. Lì rú tā qiáng pò rén mín jiàn zào cháng chéng hé huáng líng, duì bù fú cóng de rén fēi cháng cán bào. Tā yě yán lì kòng zhì rén men de sī xiǎng, wéi hù zhōng yāng zhèng fǔ de quán wēi. Nǐ rèn wéi qín shǐ huáng shì gōng dà yú guò, hái shì guò dà yú gōng ne?

Qin Shihuang was born approximately 2,200 years ago. He was responsible for unifying seven warring states into one central government. He established the Qin Dynasty from which China got its name.

Qin Shihuang was the first emperor to standardize the Chinese writing system, currency and measuring units. But Emperor Qin's greatest achievement was his contribution to building the Great Wall. Before he came to power, there were several separate walls built to defend the Han people from the Mongols in the north who tried to invade. Under his rule these separate walls were connected and extended to make what we know today as the Great Wall of China.

Qin Shihuang was an emperor with great power. He believed that he would continue his reign of power after his death. For this purpose he had an enormous tomb with thousands of human size clay soldiers and horses built for him. In 1974 this underground tomb was discovered by farmers in Xi'an. It is known as the Terra Cotta Army.

Although no one can dispute his great achievements, many people think that Emperor Qin made certain mistakes too. For example, he forced his people to build the Great Wall and the imperial tomb, and was very cruel to those who disobeyed him. Also, he controlled people's mind so as to defend the authority of the central government. Do you think his achievements outweigh his mistakes?

Quiz: Facts about Emperor Qin Shihuang
考考你：秦始皇

Fill in the blanks using the words provided.

qín 秦	suī rán 虽然	dàn shì 但是	wén zì 文字
tǒng yī 统一	bīng mǎ yǒng 兵马俑	dù liàng 度量	xī ān 西安
qián bì 钱币	guò shī 过失	měng gǔ 蒙古	wàn lǐ cháng chéng 万里长城

1. 秦始皇结束战国七雄，＿＿＿＿＿＿中国，建立
＿＿＿＿＿＿朝。

2. 秦始皇连接旧长城，修建成今天的＿＿＿＿＿＿。

3. 建长城是为了抵抗北方的＿＿＿＿＿人。

4. 秦始皇统一了＿＿＿＿＿＿、＿＿＿＿＿＿和＿＿＿＿＿＿
的工具。

5. 秦始皇命令工匠制作真人尺寸的＿＿＿＿＿＿。

6. 这些埋在地下的兵马俑后来在＿＿＿＿＿＿被农民
发现。

7. ＿＿＿＿＿＿秦始皇有很多伟大的成就，＿＿＿＿＿＿
人们认为他也有＿＿＿＿＿＿。

Essay Writing: Emperor Qin Shihuang
写短文：秦始皇

Do you think Qin Shihuang (The First Emperor) is a good or bad emperor? Do you think his achievements outweigh his cruelty? Write a short essay to state your opinion and explain why or why not.

(100 characters are recommended for advanced students. Beginner students may write in pinyin or English)

....

....

....

....

....

....

....

....

....

....

....

Let's Talk!
说一说

Sentence patterns:

1. 又……又……；很……，可是……有点儿……

2. 你几点＿＿＿＿？

Dialogue 1

(A) nǐ de gē ge gè xìng zěn me yàng
你的哥哥个性怎么样？

(B) wǒ de gē ge yòu cōng míng yòu huó yuè
我的哥哥又聪明又活跃。

(A) nǐ de dì di gè xìng zěn me yàng
你的弟弟个性怎么样？

(B) wǒ de dì di yòu tīng huà yòu yǒu lǐ mào
我的弟弟又听话又有礼貌。

(A) nà nǐ de mèi mei ne
那你的妹妹呢？

(B) wǒ de mèi mei hěn kě ài kě shì tā yǒu diǎnr ān jìng
我的妹妹很可爱，可是她有点儿安静。

Dialogue 2

(A) nǐ jǐ diǎn shàng xué
你几点上学？

(B) wǒ zǎo shàng bā diǎn zhōng shàng xué
我早上八点(钟)上学。

(A) nǐ jǐ diǎn chī wǔ cān
你几点吃午餐？

(B) wǒ zhōng wǔ shí èr diǎn zhōng chī wǔ cān
我中午十二点(钟)吃午餐。

(A) nǐ jǐ diǎn zuò gōng kè
你几点做功课？

(B) wǒ xià wǔ wǔ diǎn zhōng zuò gōng kè
我下午五点(钟)做功课。

Let's Write!
写一写

nǐ you	你	你		
wǒ I, me	我	我		
tā he, him	他	他		
men we, us, they, them	们	们		
míng name	名	名		
zì word	字	字		

三月
March

huā 花木
mù 木
lán 兰

• March 三月

年 ○ _____

xīng qī rì 星 期 日	xīng qī yī 星 期 一	xīng qī èr 星 期 二	xīng qī sān 星 期 三	xīng qī sì 星 期 四	xīng qī wǔ 星 期 五	xīng qī liù 星 期 六

名字：＿＿＿＿＿＿＿＿＿＿＿　＿＿＿＿月＿＿＿＿日

1. jīn tiān shì
   今天是＿＿＿＿ yuè 月＿＿＿＿ rì 日。

2. míng tiān shì
   明天是＿＿＿＿ yuè 月＿＿＿＿ rì 日。

3. zuó tiān shì
   昨天是＿＿＿＿ yuè 月＿＿＿＿ rì 日。

4. jīn tiān shì xīng qī
   今天是星期＿＿＿＿＿＿＿。

5. sān yuè yǒu
   三月有＿＿＿＿＿＿＿＿＿＿ tiān 天。

6. sān yuè zhōng tè bié de rì zi shì
   三月中特别的日子是＿＿＿＿＿＿＿＿＿＿＿。

7. fù nǚ jié shì
   妇女节是＿＿＿＿＿＿＿ yuè 月＿＿＿＿＿＿＿ rì 日。

8. sān yuè de dì yí gè xīng qī wǔ shì
   三月的第一个星期五是＿＿ yuè 月＿＿＿ rì 日。

9. sān yuè de zuì hòu yí gè xīng qī yī shì
   三月的最后一个星期一是＿＿ yuè 月＿＿＿ rì 日。

10. ＿＿＿＿＿＿＿＿＿ de shēng rì shì 的生日是＿＿ yuè 月＿＿＿ rì 日。
    (a person's name)

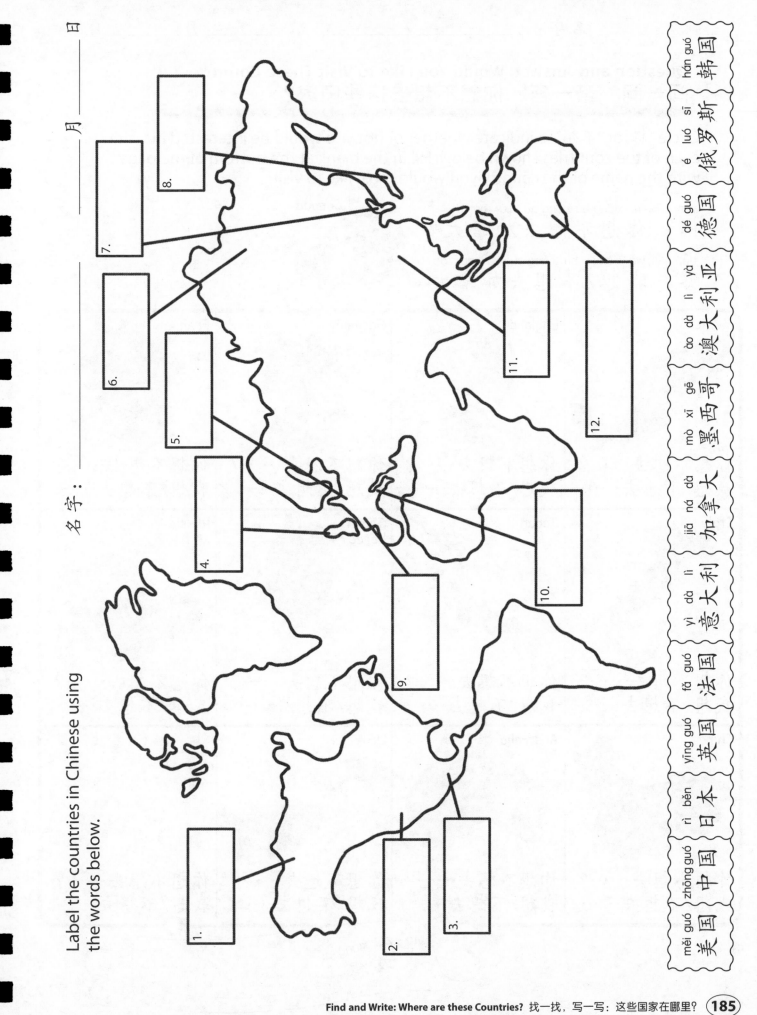

名字 : ＿＿＿＿＿＿＿＿

＿＿＿＿ 月 ＿＿＿＿ 日

Label the countries in Chinese using the words below.

hán guó 韩国	é luó sī 俄罗斯	dé guó 德国	ào dà lì yà 澳大利亚	mò xī gē 墨西哥	jiā ná dà 加拿大	yì dà lì 意大利	fǎ guó 法国	yīng guó 英国	rì běn 日本	zhōng guó 中国	měi guó 美国

Question and Answer: Would You Like to Visit These Countries?
问一问，答一答：你想不想去这些国家？

Circle "想" or "不想" to indicate whether or not you would be interested in visiting each of the countries shown below. Fill in the blank at the bottom of the page with the name of the country you would most like to visit.

Canada

wèn   nǐ xiǎng bù xiǎng qù jiā ná dà
问：你想不想去加拿大？

dá   wǒ xiǎng bù xiǎng qù jiā ná dà
答：我想/不想去加拿大。

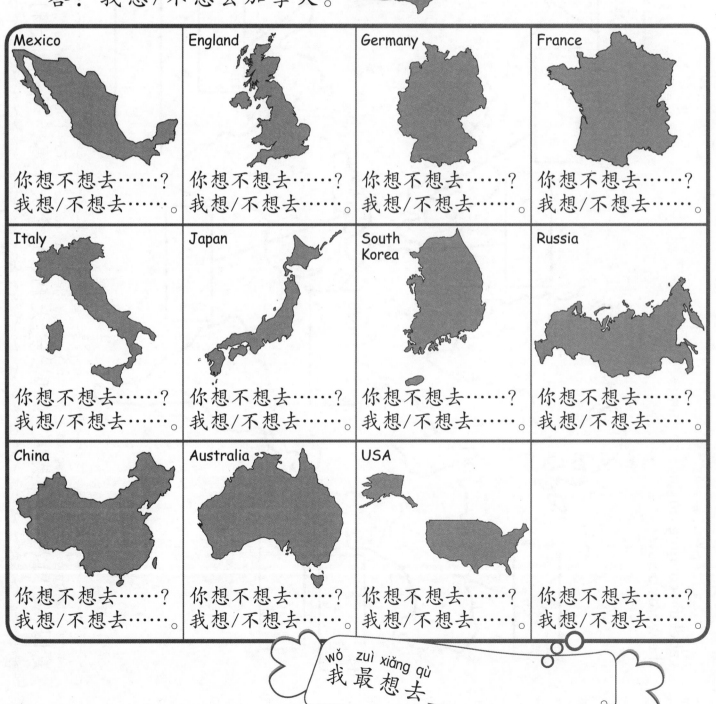

Mexico	England	Germany	France
你想不想去……？ 我想/不想去……。	你想不想去……？ 我想/不想去……。	你想不想去……？ 我想/不想去……。	你想不想去……？ 我想/不想去……。
Italy	Japan	South Korea	Russia
你想不想去……？ 我想/不想去……。	你想不想去……？ 我想/不想去……。	你想不想去……？ 我想/不想去……。	你想不想去……？ 我想/不想去……。
China	Australia	USA	
你想不想去……？ 我想/不想去……。	你想不想去……？ 我想/不想去……。	你想不想去……？ 我想/不想去……。	你想不想去……？ 我想/不想去……。

wǒ zuì xiǎng qù
我最想去＿＿＿＿＿＿＿＿。

Greeting: Say HELLO in Different Languages
打招呼：你好！

Practice saying "hello" in the different languages below.

fǎ wén
法文
(French)

xī bān yá wén
西班牙文
(Spanish)

(pronounced chow)
yì dà lì wén
意大利文
(Italian)

dé wén
德文
(German)

zhōng wén
中文
(Chinese)

é wén
俄文
(Russian)

rì wén
日文
(Japanese)

(pronounced ahn-yan-ha-say-yo)
hán wén
韩文
(Korean)

yīng wén
英文
(English)

shǒu yǔ
手语
American Sign Language

Word Search: Countries around the World
找一找：世界各国

美	英	大	中	加	本	中	英	本
利	大	德	本	意	国	大	加	日
中	西	利	国	拿	澳	意	本	澳
加	美	亚	日	亚	韩	国	大	法
拿	国	加	歌	意	拿	利	加	中
俄	意	西	利	国	亚	美	拿	英
日	罗	意	英	日	澳	本	大	墨
利	大	斯	大	韩	法	国	西	拿
美	中	加	英	利	意	哥	日	大

Find these words in the puzzle above and fill in the blanks with pinyin or English.

1. 美国：＿＿＿＿＿＿＿

2. 中国：＿＿＿＿＿＿＿

3. 意大利：＿＿＿＿＿＿＿

4. 法国：＿＿＿＿＿＿＿

5. 俄罗斯：＿＿＿＿＿＿＿

6. 日本：＿＿＿＿＿＿＿

7. 德国：＿＿＿＿＿＿＿

8. 加拿大：＿＿＿＿＿＿＿

9. 韩国：＿＿＿＿＿＿＿

10. 英国：＿＿＿＿＿＿＿

11. 墨西哥：＿＿＿＿＿＿＿

12. 澳大利亚：＿＿＿＿＿＿＿

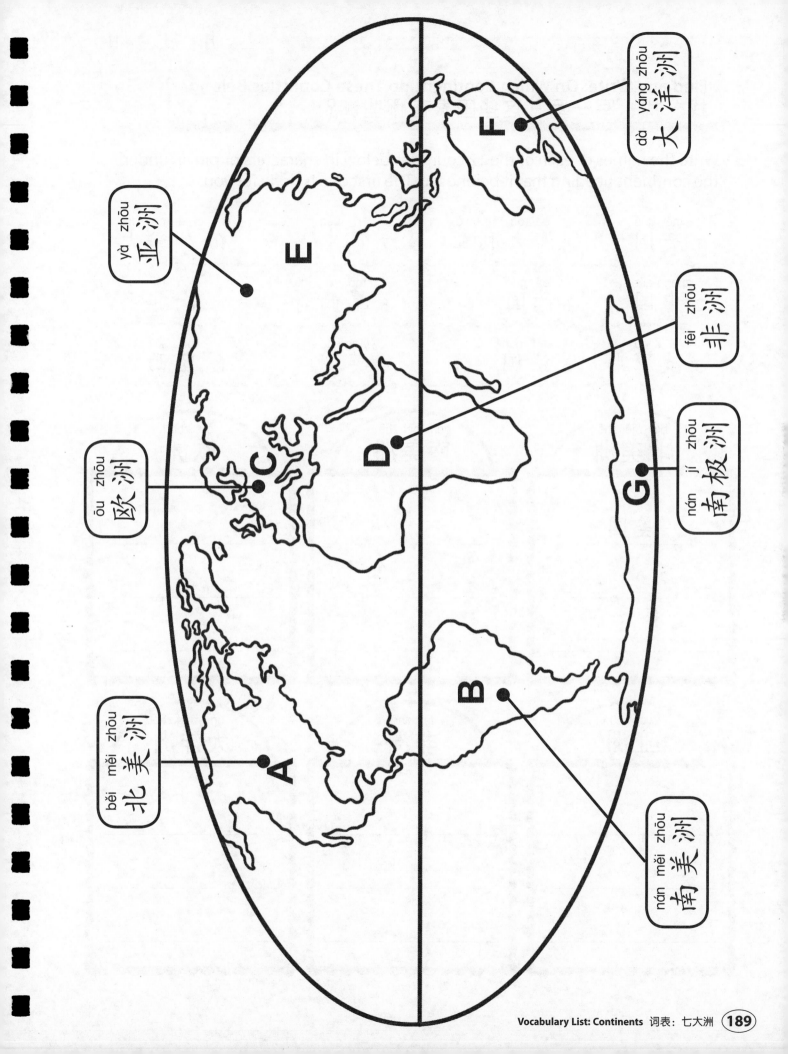

dà yáng zhōu
大洋洲

yà zhōu
亚洲

fēi zhōu
非洲

nán jí zhōu
南极洲

ōu zhōu
欧洲

běi měi zhōu
北美洲

nán měi zhōu
南美洲

F

E

D

C

G

A

B

Find and Write: On Which Continent do These Countries Belong?
找一找，写一写：这些国家在哪些洲？

Write the names of each of the 12 countries below in characters or pinyin under the continent heading that it belongs to. The first one is done for you.

měi guó 1. 美国	ào dà lì yà 4. 澳大利亚	rì běn 7. 日本	jiā ná dà 10. 加拿大
zhōng guó 2. 中国	dé guó 5. 德国	mò xī gē 8. 墨西哥	nán fēi 11. 南非
é luó sī 3. 俄罗斯	fǎ guó 6. 法国	yīng guó 9. 英国	bā xī 12. 巴西

běi měi zhōu
北美洲

美国
＿＿＿＿＿＿＿＿＿＿

＿＿＿＿＿＿＿＿＿＿

＿＿＿＿＿＿＿＿＿＿

nán měi zhōu
南美洲

＿＿＿＿＿＿＿＿＿＿

＿＿＿＿＿＿＿＿＿＿

＿＿＿＿＿＿＿＿＿＿

ōu zhōu
欧洲

＿＿＿＿＿＿＿＿＿＿

＿＿＿＿＿＿＿＿＿＿

＿＿＿＿＿＿＿＿＿＿

yà zhōu
亚洲

＿＿＿＿＿＿＿＿＿＿

＿＿＿＿＿＿＿＿＿＿

＿＿＿＿＿＿＿＿＿＿

fēi zhōu
非洲

＿＿＿＿＿＿＿＿＿＿

＿＿＿＿＿＿＿＿＿＿

＿＿＿＿＿＿＿＿＿＿

dà yáng zhōu
大洋洲

＿＿＿＿＿＿＿＿＿＿

＿＿＿＿＿＿＿＿＿＿

＿＿＿＿＿＿＿＿＿＿

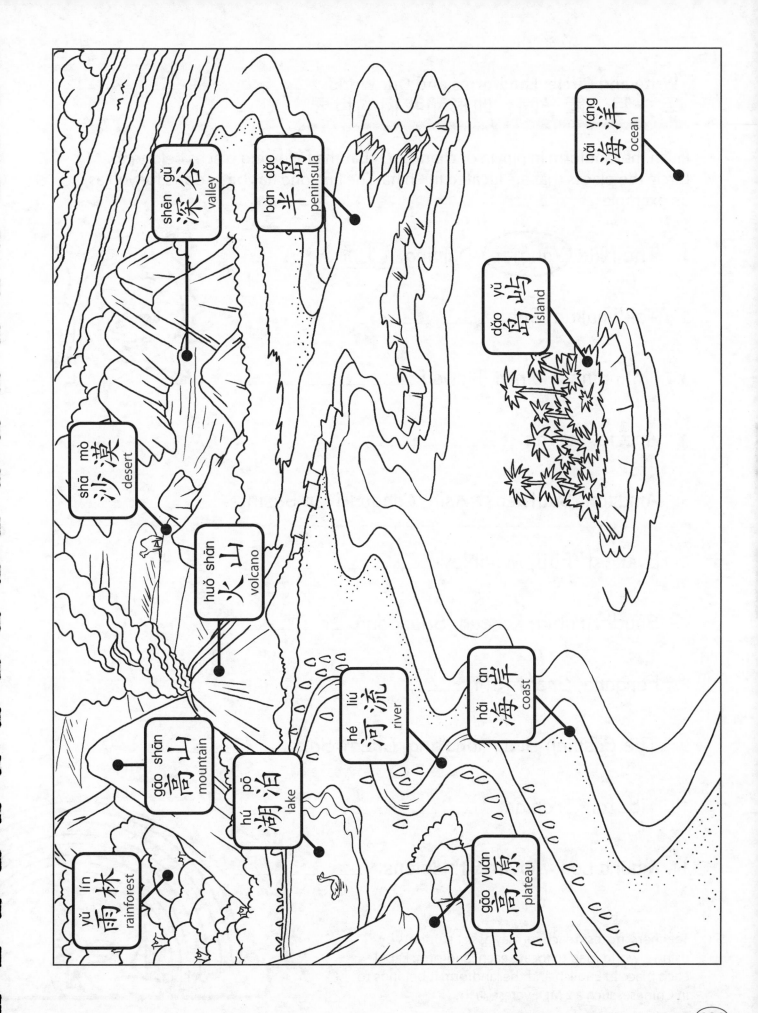

名字：_____ _____月_____日

Write and Circle: Landforms and Our World
写一写，圈一圈：地形和我们的世界

Fill in the landform in pinyin or characters that the following places belong to. Circle the places that are located in China. The first one has been done for you as an example.

1. The Nile, (Yangtze), Darling: 河流

2. Taklimakan, Gobi: _____

3. Philippine, Hainan, Hawaii: _____

4. Arctic, Pacific: _____

5. Amazon, Southeast Asia, Congo River Basin: _____

6. Everest, Fuji, Mckinley: _____

7. Saudi Arabia, Korean, Shandong: _____

8. Fergana, Great Rift: _____

9. The Caspian Sea, Dongting, Great Salt: _____

10. Tibetan, Iranian: _____

11. Mauna Loa, Mount St. Helens: _____

Teachers' notes: Teachers may assist students by using a world map to locate each landform. Label each place in English and the landform it belongs to in Chinese, such as: Mt. Everest 高山.

名字：_____   _____月_____日

Crossword Puzzle: Landforms
填字谜：地形

Use the clues below to complete this crossword puzzle.

Across:

2. Lava and steam come from its top.
5. The land beside a sea or ocean.
7. A tall, dense jungle that gets a lot of rain.
9. An elevated tableland that is flat on top.
11. A large, natural stream of water that flows.
12. It is surrounded by water on three of its sides.

Down:

1. A dry region that has less than 10 inches of rain annually.
3. A hollow depression surrounded by hills and mountains.
4. A large body of water completely surrounded by land.
5. A large body of saltwater that separates continents.
6. A body of land that is surrounded by water on all sides.
8. It is the tallest landform on Earth.

名字：＿＿＿＿＿＿＿＿＿＿＿＿＿＿　＿＿＿＿月＿＿＿＿日

Map Exercise: Locate Places on a World Map Grid
看地图：环绕地球找一找

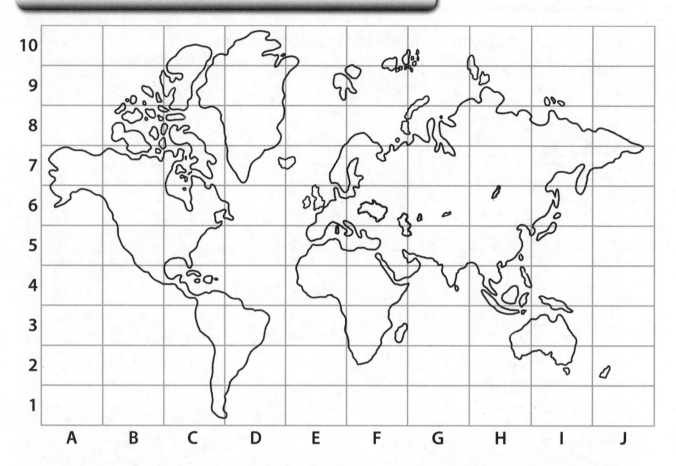

Use the world map grid above to locate the following places in the table below. Then write the landform in characters that these places belong to. The first one has been done for you as an example.

	Name of Place	Grid Location	Landform
1	Pacific Ocean	A3	海洋
2	Gobi Desert		
3	Taiwan		
4	Amazon		
5	Qomolangma		
6	South Korea		
7	Yangtze		
8	Mount St. Helens		
9	Tibet		
10	Great Salt		

xué xiào 学校	tú shū guǎn 图书馆	gōng ān jú 公安局
yī yuàn 医院	yóu jú 邮局	gòu wù zhōng xīn 购物中心
xiāo fáng jú 消防局	gōng yuán 公园	chāo jí shì chǎng 超级市场
yín háng 银行	diàn yǐng yuàn 电影院	cān guǎn 餐馆

Note: *In some areas, "police station" is also known as* "警察局". *(jǐng chá jú)*

名字：_____ _____月_____日

Find and Write: Where Can You Find Me?
找一找，写一写：你在哪里可以找到我？

Use pinyin or characters to write the name of a community place where you might find each of the objects below. There may be more than one choice for each item. (Refer to p. 16)

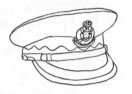

1. ....

2. ....

3. ....

4. ....

5. ....

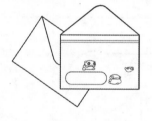

6. ....

7. ....

8. ....

Advanced Search

Q　在_____里，你还看到什么？
　　　　zài　　　　　　　　lǐ　　nǐ hái kàn dào shén me
　　　　　　(place)

A　在_____里，我还_____。
　　　　zài　　　　　　　　lǐ　　wǒ hái

196

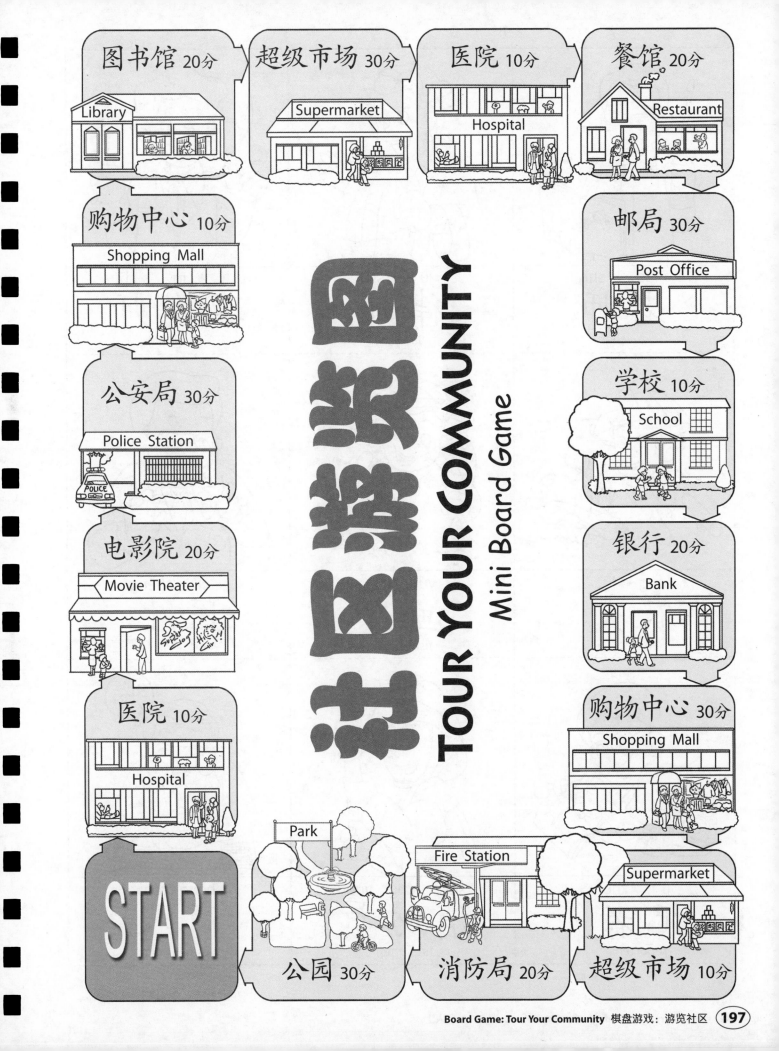

图书馆 20分
Library

超级市场 30分
Supermarket

医院 10分
Hospital

餐馆 20分
Restaurant

购物中心 10分
Shopping Mall

邮局 30分
Post Office

公安局 30分
Police Station

学校 10分
School

电影院 20分
Movie Theater

银行 20分
Bank

医院 10分
Hospital

购物中心 30分
Shopping Mall

社区游览图

TOUR YOUR COMMUNITY
Mini Board Game

START

Park
公园 30分

Fire Station
消防局 20分

Supermarket
超级市场 10分

lǎo shī
老师
teacher

lù shī
律师
lawyer

lǐ fà shī
理发师
barber

nóng fū
农夫
farmer

yú fū
渔夫
fisherman

yī shēng
医生
doctor

jì zhě
记者
reporter

xiāo fáng yuán
消防员
firefighter

shāng rén
商人
businessman

yá yī
牙医
dentist

kē xué jiā
科学家
scientist

yóu chāi
邮差
mail carrier

jǐng chá
警察
policeman

xiào zhǎng
校长
principal

hù shì
护士
nurse

chú shī
厨师
chef

shòu yī
兽医
veterinarian

jiàn zhù shī
建筑师
architect

名字：_____ ____月____日

Unscramble Fun: Community Helpers
拼拼乐：社会人士

Rearrange the letters to make the pinyin words for Community Helpers in Chinese.

1. _____ _____ 老师

2. _____ _____ 医生

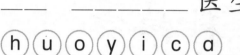

3. _____ _____ 邮差

4. ____ ____ _____ 理发师

architect

5. _____ _____ _____ 建筑师

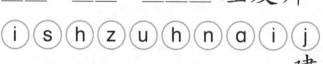

6. ____ _____ 律师

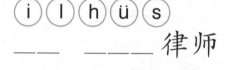

7. ____ _____ 护士

8. _____ _____ 农夫

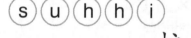

9. _____ _____ 警察

10. _____ _____ _____ 消防员

11. _____ 商人

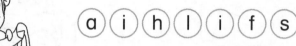

Unscramble Fun: Community Helpers

Guess and Write: Who Am I?
猜一猜，写一写：我是谁？

Read the clues to figure out the correct Community Helper. Write your answers in characters or pinyin in the blanks provided.

1. I help to build houses. 我是一个＿＿＿＿＿。

2. I grow food for people. 我是一个＿＿＿＿＿。

3. I patrol the roads. 我是一个＿＿＿＿＿。

4. I help the doctor to keep you well. 我是一个＿＿＿＿＿。

5. I help you learn as much as you can. 我是一个＿＿＿＿＿。

6. I bring you letters. 我是一个＿＿＿＿＿。

7. I help you get better when you are sick or injured. 我是一个＿＿＿＿＿。

8. I put out fires and rescue people. 我是一个＿＿＿＿＿。

9. I interview witnesses and tell people what is happening around them. 我是一个＿＿＿＿＿。

10. I help to keep your teeth healthy. 我是一个＿＿＿＿＿。

11. I make meals in a restaurant. 我是一个＿＿＿＿＿。

12. I catch and sell fish to fish markets. 我是一个＿＿＿＿＿。

Word Search: My Community
找一找：我的社区

Find each of the following Community Place words in the word search puzzle and write the meaning of each place in English.

```
a  s  u  a  i  y  c  y  u  u  i  g  u  n
g  o  n  g  a  n  j  u  g  a  g  g  a  z
g  n  a  h  c  i  h  s  i  j  o  a  h  c
h  a  n  a  g  x  d  u  j  y  w  u  a  e
t  u  s  h  u  g  u  a  n  x  y  y  y  y
x  y  g  n  y  n  g  e  n  x  h  h  i  u
u  g  o  a  x  o  t  a  x  n  a  n  y  o
g  n  j  u  g  h  i  a  y  i  h  u  u  u
j  i  a  g  j  z  x  s  x  a  a  h  a  a
y  y  n  n  a  u  y  g  n  o  g  o  n  a
x  n  s  a  a  w  i  g  f  n  j  g  n  u
a  a  g  c  a  u  n  y  y  u  n  i  n  n
c  i  i  g  i  o  n  i  o  o  u  c  f  h
c  d  o  u  j  g  n  a  f  o  a  i  x  a
```

1. xué xiào：_____

2. gōng ān jú：_____

3. yī yuàn：_____

4. yóu jú：_____

5. diàn yǐng yuàn：_____

6. xiāo fáng jú：_____

7. tú shū guǎn：_____

8. gōng yuán：_____

9. chāo jí shì chǎng：_____

10. gòu wù zhōng xīn：_____

11. yín háng：_____

12. cān guǎn：_____

Word Search: Community Helpers
找一找：社会人士

Use the clues below to complete this crossword puzzle in pinyin.

Across:

6. delivers letters

8. head of a school

9. helps sick people

10. helps students learn or teaches in a school

Down:

1. stops crimes

2. puts out fire and saves people

3. helps sick animals

4. Albert Einstein was one

5. helps keep teeth healthy or fixes teeth

7. cooks in a restaurant

Wǔ   Zétiān
武则天
Wu Zetian

Wáng   Wēiwēi
王薇薇
Vera Wang

Huā   Mùlán
花木兰
Hua Mulan

Tán   Ēnměi
谭恩美
Amy Tan

Guān   Yǐngshān
关颖珊
Michelle Kwan

Zōng   Yùhuá
宗毓华
Connie Chung

Zhào   Xiǎolán
赵小兰
Elaine Chao

Gǒng   Lì
巩俐
Gong Li

A brave girl who took her father's place in the army.

Fashion Designer

The Empress who claimed herself to be "the first female emperor" about 1,000 years ago in China.

Television Journalist

World Champion Figure Skater

Writer

A famous actress

Former US Secretary of Labor

She was born
in a wealthy
family in
ancient China.

Her first talent
was ice-skating.
She later began a
career in designing
wedding dresses.

She posed
as a man to fight
for her people.

She wrote
"The Moon Lady"
and "Sagwa,
The Chinese
Siamese Cat".

She wears
a dragon necklace
every time she is
in a competition.

She has worked
on television
networks NBC,
CBS and ABC.

She was born
in Taiwan and
moved to the US
at the age of 8.

She won many
acting awards.

Online Search: Famous Chinese Women
网上搜索：著名华人女性

Name: ....

Birth Year: ....

Birth Place: ....

Field of Contribution: ....

Photo /
picture
here

Three important facts:
(such as: her profile, her major accomplishments, her obstacles, the reason she is famous, etc.)

1. ....

   ....

2. ....

   ....

3. ....

   ....

What impresses you the most about her?

....

....

....

....

....

shù 树	cǎo 草	huār 花儿
yè zi 叶子	xiǎo niǎo 小鸟	hú dié 蝴蝶
mì fēng 蜜蜂	qīng wā 青蛙	fēng zheng 风筝
máo mao chóng 毛毛虫	cǎi hóng 彩虹	tài yáng 太阳

Circle and Color: Spring
圈一圈，涂一涂：春天

Circle the correct word for each picture. Then color the picture.

	yè zi 叶子 tài yáng 太阳 huār 花儿		shù 树 yè zi 叶子 huār 花儿
	cǎo 草 huār 花儿 hú dié 蝴蝶		xiǎo niǎo 小鸟 máo mao chóng 毛毛虫 qīng wā 青蛙
	cǎi hóng 彩虹 mì fēng 蜜蜂 xiǎo niǎo 小鸟		máo mao chóng 毛毛虫 mì fēng 蜜蜂 hú dié 蝴蝶
	tài yáng 太阳 cǎo 草 cǎi hóng 彩虹		cǎo 草 huār 花儿 yè zi 叶子
	fēng zheng 风筝 tài yáng 太阳 yè zi 叶子		xiǎo niǎo 小鸟 hú dié 蝴蝶 qīng wā 青蛙

Color and Write: What Is This?
涂一涂，写一写：这是什么？

Complete the pictures below and color them. Then fill in the blanks in Chinese and read them aloud.

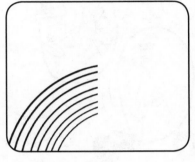

zhè shì
1. 这是_____。

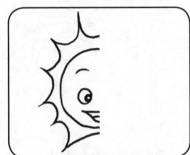

2. 这是_____。

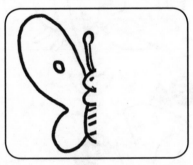

3. 这是_____。

4. 这是_____。

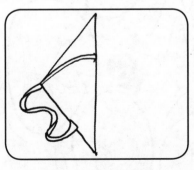

5. 这是_____。

6. 这是_____。

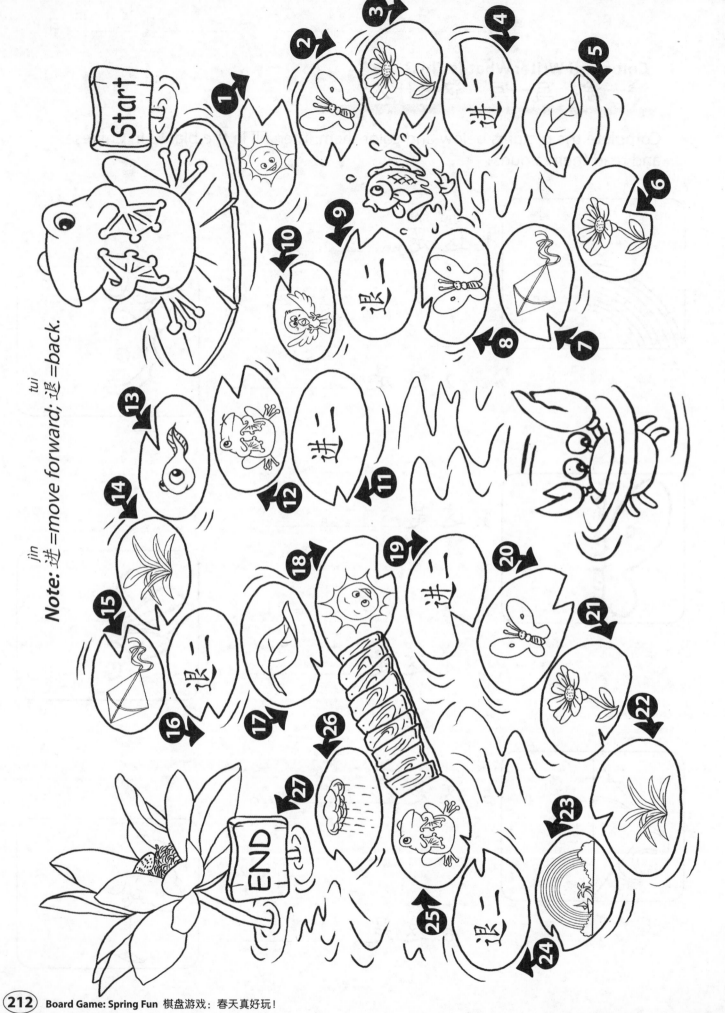

Note: 进 =move forward; 退 =back.

春天来了，
Chūn tiān lái le,
(Spring is coming.)

白花开，红花开，
Bái huā kāi, hóng huā kāi,
(The white flowers are blooming; the red flowers are blooming too.)

蝴蝶、蜜蜂，
都飞来。
Hú dié, mì fēng, dōu fēi lái.
(The butterflies and the bees are flying all over.)

春天来了，
Chūn tiān lái le,
(Spring is coming.)

花开了，
Huā kāi le,
(The flowers are blooming.)

草绿了，
Cǎo lù le,
(The grass is green.)

真美丽！
Zhēn měi lì
(It's very pretty.)

chūn tiān zhēn měi lì
春 天 真 美 丽 !

wǒ kàn dào
我看到……
I see...

wǒ tīng dào
我听到……
I listen...

wǒ chī dào
我吃到……
I eat...

wǒ wén dào
我闻到……
I smell...

wǒ mō dào
我摸到……
I touch...

名字：＿＿＿＿＿＿＿＿＿＿＿＿＿＿＿＿＿ ＿＿＿月＿＿＿日

Art Project: Paper Cuts
创意手工：剪纸

xiǎo niǎo
1. 小鸟

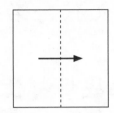

Step 1: Fold in half

Step 2: Draw and cut

Step 3: Open

xiǎo niǎo
2. 小鸟

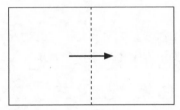

Step 1: Fold in half

Step 2: Draw and cut

Step 3: Open

huār
3. 花儿

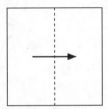

Step 1: Fold in half

Step 2: Draw and cut

Step 3: Open

huār
4. 花儿

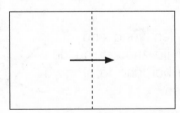

Step 1: Fold in half

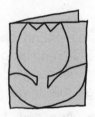

Step 2: Draw and cut

Step 3: Open

hú dié
5. 蝴蝶

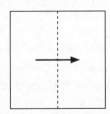

Step 1: Fold in half

Step 2: Draw and cut

Step 3: Open

Teachers' notes: Teachers may prepare a tracer for each pattern to assist students.

Reading: Hua Mulan
读一读：花木兰

很久以前，中国北方有一个女孩，名叫花木兰。她从小学习骑马和武术。

有一天，皇帝命令她的父亲上战场打仗，抵抗敌人。可是他又老又病，不能去打仗。于是，木兰打扮成男人，代替她的父亲去打仗。

木兰很勇敢，在战场上奋勇杀敌。最后，她终于打败了敌人，并回家照顾她的父母。后来，木兰军中的朋友来拜访她，惊讶地发现木兰竟然是个美丽的女人。

花木兰从此成了勇敢的女英雄。

Hěn jiǔ yǐ qián, zhōng guó běi fāng yǒu yí gè nǚ hái, míng jiào Huā Mùlán. Tā cóng xiǎo xué xí qí mǎ hé wǔ shù.

Yǒu yì tiān, huáng dì mìng lìng tā de fù qīn shàng zhàn chǎng dǎ zhàng, dǐ kàng dí rén. Kě shì tā yòu lǎo yòu bìng, bù néng qù dǎ zhàng. Yú shì, Huā Mùlán dǎ ban chéng nán rén, dài tì tā de fù qīn qù dǎ zhàng.

Mùlán hěn yǒng gǎn, zài zhàn chǎng shang fèn yǒng shā dí. Zuì hōu, tā zhōng yú dǎ bài le dí rén, bìng huí jiā zhào gù tā de fù mǔ. Hòu lái, Mùlán jūn zhōng de péng you lái bài fǎng tā, jīng yà de fā xiān Mùlán jìng rán shì gè měi lì de nǚ rén.

Huā Mùlán cóng cǐ chéng le yǒng gǎn de nǚ yīng xióng.

Long ago, in northern China, there lived a girl named Hua Mulan. When she was young, she learned how to ride horses and practice martial arts.

One day the emperor ordered her father to join the army to fight China's enemies. But her father was old and sick and was unable to fight. So Mulan dressed up as a young man to take her father's place in the army. Because she was so brave, Mulan succeeded in defeating the enemy and returned home to her parents.

Afterwards, Mulan's comrades were all very surprised to discover that she was, in fact, a beautiful woman. Hua Mulan has become a female idol of courage and honor.

名字： _____   ____月____日

Quiz: Hua Mulan
考考你：花木兰

Cut the following strips and rearrange them in sequence order.

✂ -

zuì hòu,   tā zhōng yú dǎ bài le dí rén,   bìng huí jiā zhào gù tā de
最后，她终于打败了敌人，并回家照顾她的
fù mǔ.
父母。

✂ -

tā cóng xiǎo xué xí qí mǎ hé wǔ shù
她从小学习骑马和武术。

✂ -

Huā Mùlán cóng cǐ chéng le yǒng gǎn de nǚ yīng xióng
花木兰从此成了勇敢的女英雄。

✂ -

Mùlán dǎ ban chéng nán rén   dài tì tā de fù qīn qù dǎ zhàng
木兰打扮成男人，代替她的父亲去打仗。

✂ -

hěn jiǔ yǐ qián   zhōng guó běi fāng yōu yí gè nǚ hái   míng jiào Huā Mùlán
很久以前，中国北方有一个女孩，名叫 花木兰。

✂ -

yǒu yì tiān   huáng dì mìng lìng tā de fù qīn shàng zhàn chǎng dǎ zhàng   dǐ kàng
有一天，皇帝命令她的父亲上战场打仗，抵抗
dí rén
敌人。

Huā　　Mùlán

花木兰
Hua Mulan

名字：＿＿＿＿＿＿＿＿＿＿＿

hěn jiǔ yǐ qián,　zhōng guó běi fāng yǒu
很久以前，中国北方有

yí gè nǔ hái　míng jiào Huā　Mùlán
一个女孩，名叫花木兰。

tā cóng xiǎo xué xí qí mǎ
她从小学习骑马

hé wǔ shù
和武术。

一

Long ago in China, there was a girl

named＿＿＿＿＿＿＿＿＿.

When she was young, she learned

h＿＿＿＿＿＿＿ riding and martial arts.

yǒu yì tiān, huáng dì mìng lìng tā
有一天，皇帝命令她

de fù qīn shàng zhàn chǎng dǎ zhàng
的父亲上战场打仗，

dǐ kàng dí rén kě shì tā yòu lǎo
抵抗敌人。可是他又老

yòu bìng bù néng qù dǎ zhàng
又病，不能去打仗。

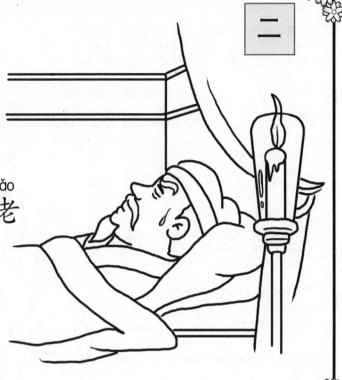

One day, her f_____ had to

join the army to fight for the country.

But he was too o_____ and sick.

yú shì Mùlán dǎ ban chéng
于是，木兰打扮成

nán rén dài tì tā de fù qīn
男人，代替她的父亲

qù dǎ zhàng
去打仗。

Mulan dressed like a young m_____

and took her father's place in the army.

yīn wèi Mùlán hěn yǒng gǎn
因为木兰很勇敢,

suǒ yǐ tā zhōng yú dǎ bài
所以,她终于打败

le dí rén bìng huí jiā
了敌人,并回家

zhào gù tā de fù mǔ
照顾她的父母。

Mulan was very b_____ .

She won the war and went

back home to take care of

her p_____ .

Mùlán jūn zhōng de péng you dōu hěn jīng
木兰军中的朋友都很惊

yà Mùlán jìng rán shì gè měi lì de
讶木兰竟然是个美丽的

nǚ rén. Huā Mùlán cóng cǐ chéng le
女人。花木兰从此成了

yǒng gǎn de nǚ yīng xióng.
勇敢的女英雄。

All her army friends were surprised

to find out that Mulan was a beautiful

_____ .

名字：＿＿＿＿＿＿＿＿＿＿ ＿＿＿月＿＿＿日

Let's Talk!
说一说

Dialogue 1

A 你去学校做什么？
nǐ qù xué xiào zuò shén me

B 我去学校上学。
wǒ qù xué xiào shàng xué

A 你去图书馆做什么？
nǐ qù tú shū guǎn zuò shén me

B 我去图书馆借书和还书。
wǒ qù tú shū guǎn jiè shū hé huán shū

A 你去超级市场做什么？
nǐ qù chāo jí shì chǎng zuò shén me

B 我去超级市场买牛奶和面包。
wǒ qù chāo jí shì chǎng mǎi niú nǎi hé miàn bāo

A 你去公园做什么？
nǐ qù gōng yuán zuò shén me

B 我去公园＿＿＿＿＿＿。
wǒ qù gōng yuán

Dialogue 2

A 你爸爸是做什么的？
nǐ bà ba shì zuò shén me de

B 我爸爸是牙医。
wǒ bà ba shì yá yī

A 你妈妈是做什么的？
nǐ mā ma shì zuò shén me de

B 我妈妈是老师。
wǒ mā ma shì lǎo shī

A 你舅舅是做什么的？
nǐ jiù jiu shì zuò shén me de

B 我舅舅是＿＿＿＿＿＿。
wǒ jiù jiu shì

Dialogue 3

A 春天里，你看到什么？
chūn tiān lǐ nǐ kàn dào shén me

B 我看到花和草。
wǒ kàn dào huā hé cǎo

A 你听到什么？
nǐ tīng dào shén me

B 我听到蜜蜂和小鸟叫。
wǒ tīng dào mì fēng hé xiǎo niǎo jiào

A 你喜欢春天吗？为什么？
nǐ xǐ huan chūn tiān ma wèi shén me

B 我＿＿＿＿＿＿。
wǒ

(221)

名字： _____ _____月_____日

Let's Write!
写一写

huā  flower	花	花		
guó  country	国	国		
zhú 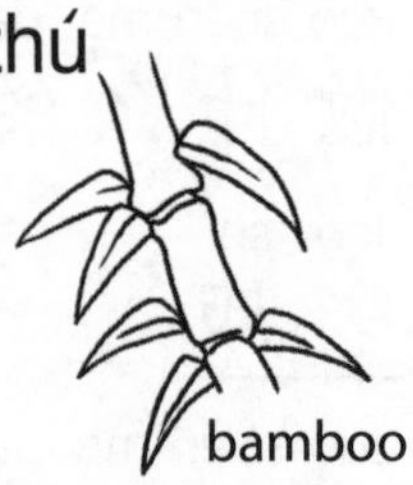 bamboo	竹	竹		
yú  fish	鱼	鱼		
péng  friend	朋	朋		
yǒu  friend	友	友		

四月
April

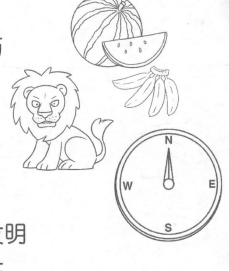

míng 明

fā 发

de 的

guó 国

zhōng 中

April 四月

年 〇

xīng qī rì 星期日	xīng qī yī 星期一	xīng qī èr 星期二	xīng qī sān 星期三	xīng qī sì 星期四	xīng qī wǔ 星期五	xīng qī liù 星期六

What's Happening in April?
四月知多少？

jīn tiān shì　　　　　　yuè　　　　　rì
1. 今天是＿＿＿＿月＿＿＿＿日。

míng tiān shì　　　　　　yuè　　　　　rì
2. 明天是＿＿＿＿月＿＿＿＿日。

hòu tiān shì　　　　　　yuè　　　　　rì
3. 后天是＿＿＿＿月＿＿＿＿日。

zuó tiān shì xīng qī
4. 昨天是星期＿＿＿＿＿＿。

qián tiān shì xīng qī
5. 前天是星期＿＿＿＿＿＿。

sì yuè yǒu　　　　　　　　gè xīng qī liù
6. 四月有＿＿＿＿＿＿＿＿个星期六。

sì yuè zhōng tè bié de rì zi shì
7. 四月中特别的日子是＿＿＿＿＿＿＿＿＿＿＿＿。

sì yuè de dì sān gè xīng qī rì shì　　　　　yuè　　　　rì
8. 四月的第三个星期日是＿＿月＿＿＿日。

sì yuè de zuì hòu yí gè xīng qī liù shì　　　　yuè　　　　rì
9. 四月的最后一个星期六是＿＿月＿＿＿日。

de shēng rì shì　　　　　　yuè　　　　rì
10. ＿＿＿＿＿＿＿＿＿的生日是＿＿月＿＿＿日。
　　(a person's name)

hēi sè
黑色

bái sè
白色

hóng sè
红色

lǜ sè
绿色

huáng sè
黄色

lán sè
蓝色

zōng sè
棕色

chéng sè
橙色

zǐ sè
紫色

zōng sè　　　*kā fēi sè*　*chéng sè*　　　*jú zi sè*
Note: *In certain areas, "棕色" is also known as "咖啡色", and "橙色" is also known as "桔子色".*

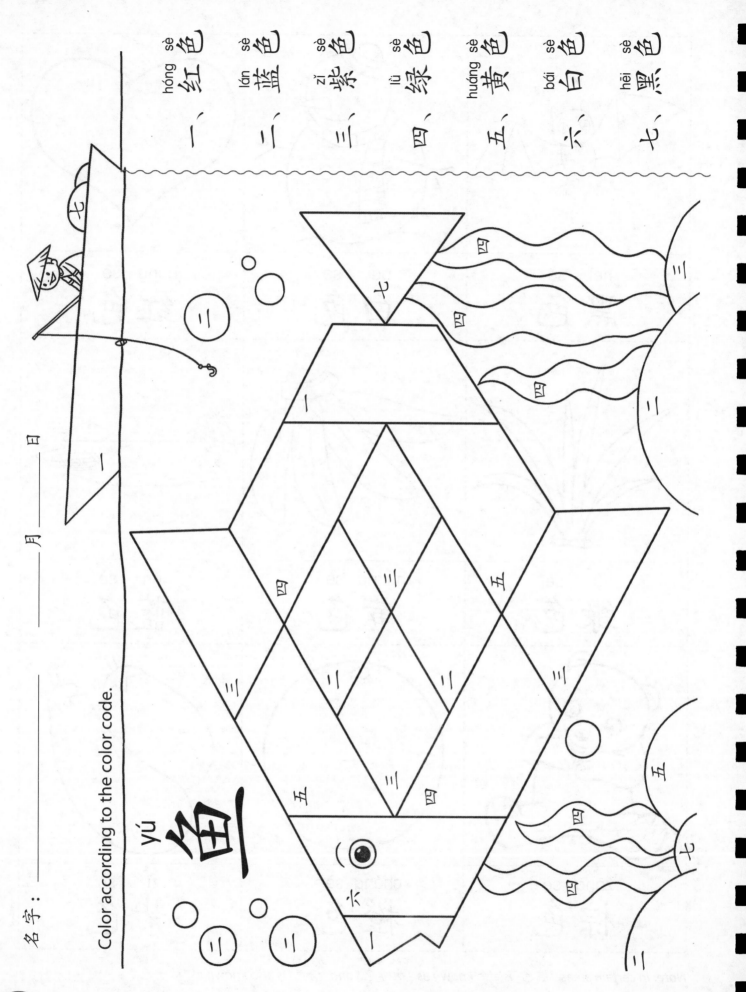

Color according to the color code.

yú
鱼

hóng sè 红色 一
lán sè 蓝色 二
zǐ sè 紫色 三
lù sè 绿色 四
huáng sè 黄色 五
bái sè 白色 六
hēi sè 黑色 七

名字：

月 日

Coloring Activity: Pagoda
涂颜色：宝塔

Match the numbers on the pagoda with the Chinese numbers to figure out the color code. Then color each level of the pagoda accordingly.

一	二	三	四	五
1	2	3	4	5

六	七	八	九	十
6	7	8	9	10

一： hóng sè 红色

二： zǐ sè 紫色

三： huáng sè 黄色

四： chéng sè 橙色

五： hēi sè 黑色

六： lán sè 蓝色

七： bái sè 白色

八： zōng sè 棕色

九： lǜ sè 绿色

Coloring Activity: The Bunny's House
涂颜色：兔子的家

The bunny wants to paint his house. Please help him pick 5 paint colors. Color each bucket with your choice and label them in pinyin below. Then color the house for the bunny.

＿＿＿＿ sè ＿＿＿＿ sè ＿＿＿＿ sè ＿＿＿＿ sè ＿＿＿＿ sè

Write, Draw, Color: My Color Wheel
写一写，画一画，涂一涂：我的彩色轮盘

Fill in the color words to complete each sentence in the color wheel about yourself.

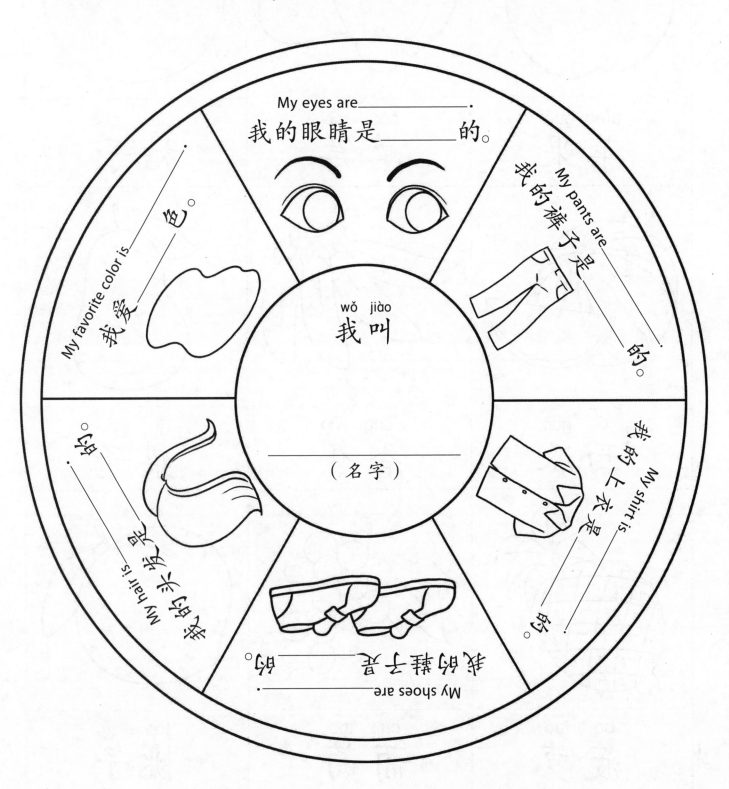

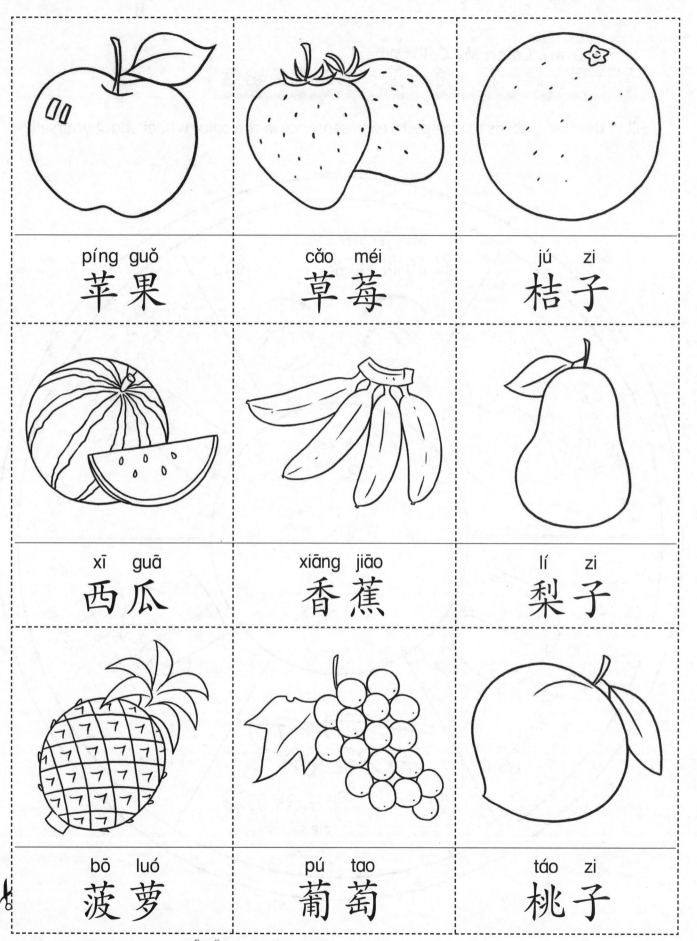

| píng guǒ | cǎo méi | jú zi |
| 苹果 | 草莓 | 桔子 |

| xī guā | xiāng jiāo | lí zi |
| 西瓜 | 香蕉 | 梨子 |

| bō luó | pú tao | táo zi |
| 菠萝 | 葡萄 | 桃子 |

Note: "Pineapple" *is also called* 凤梨 (fèng lí) *in some areas.*

I

三

二

wǒ ài bú ài chī
我爱/不爱吃 _____

我爱/不爱吃 _____

我爱/不爱吃 _____

wǒ chī shuǐ guǒ
我爱吃水果
I Love to Eat Fruit

名字：_____

五

我爱／不爱吃 ————○

七

我爱／不爱吃 ————○

四

我爱／不爱吃 ————○

六

我爱／不爱吃 ————○

Writing Activity: Colors of Fruits
写一写：水果的颜色

Write down the names of fruits under the correct color groups.
You can write in characters or pinyin.

hóng sè de shuǐ guǒ
红色的水果
_____

_____

zōng sè de shuǐ guǒ
棕色的水果
_____

_____

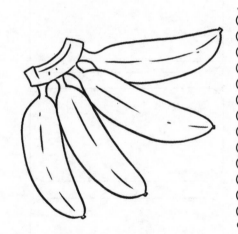

lǜ sè de shuǐ guǒ
绿色的水果
_____

_____

huáng sè de shuǐ guǒ
黄色的水果
_____

_____

zǐ sè de shuǐ guǒ
紫色的水果
_____

_____

名字：_____ _____月_____日

Ask your family members or
classmates about their favorite fruit.
Record your findings below.

ní ài chī shén me shuǐ guǒ
Ⓠ 你爱吃什么水果？

wǒ
Ⓐ 我爱吃_____。

名字 Name	水果 Fruit	Picture

ài chī
1. _____ 爱吃 _____

2. _____ 爱吃 _____

3. _____ 爱吃 _____

4. _____ 爱吃 _____

5. _____ 爱吃 _____

6. _____ 爱吃 _____

名字：＿＿＿＿＿＿＿＿＿＿＿＿＿ ＿＿＿＿月＿＿＿＿日

Write and Draw: My Very Hungry Caterpillar
写一写，画一画：毛毛虫好饿哦！

Write your answers in characters or pinyin on the lines provided and draw a picture for each at the end of the tail.

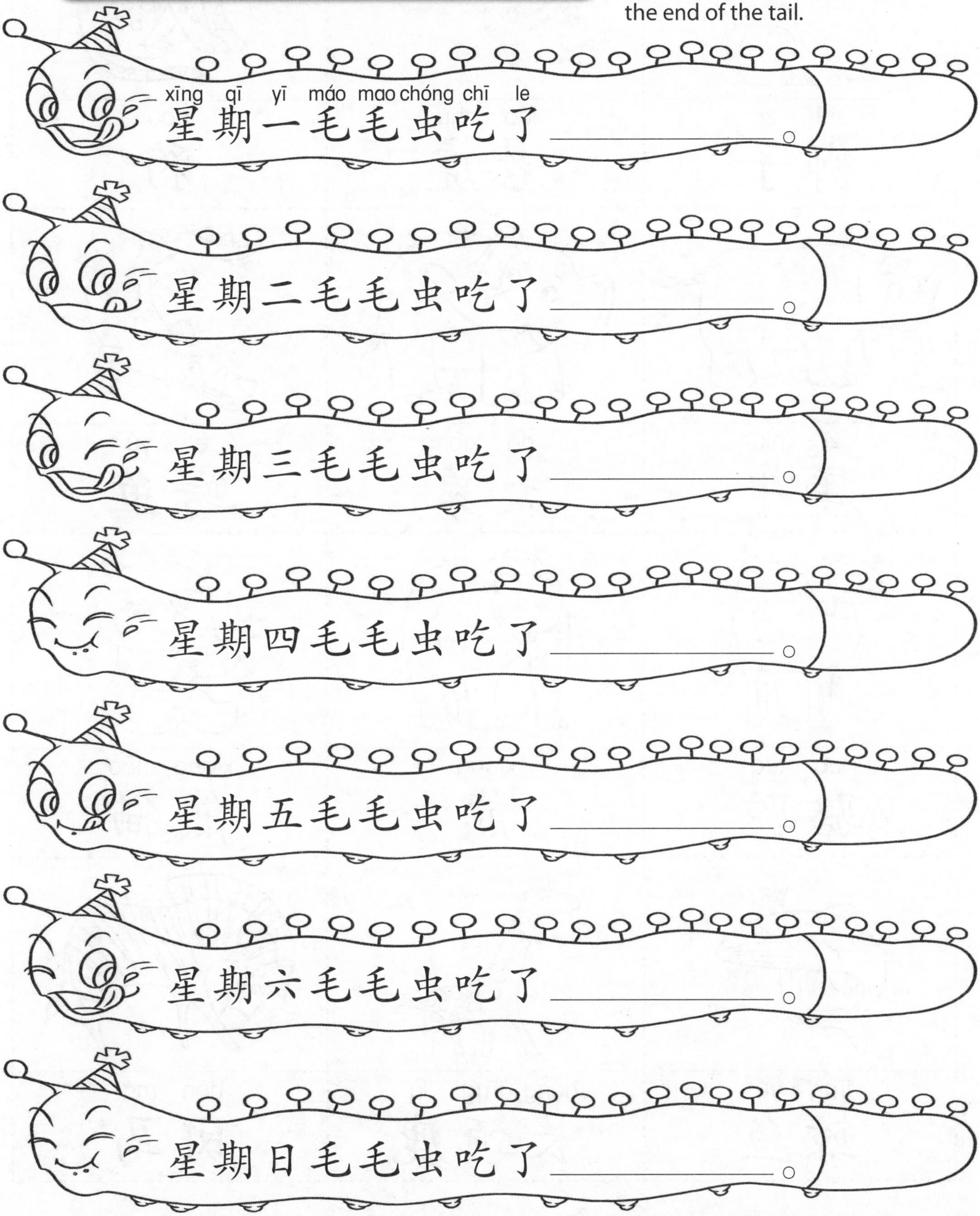

xīng qī yī máo mao chóng chī le
星期一毛毛虫吃了＿＿＿＿＿＿＿＿＿。

星期二毛毛虫吃了＿＿＿＿＿＿＿＿＿。

星期三毛毛虫吃了＿＿＿＿＿＿＿＿＿。

星期四毛毛虫吃了＿＿＿＿＿＿＿＿＿。

星期五毛毛虫吃了＿＿＿＿＿＿＿＿＿。

星期六毛毛虫吃了＿＿＿＿＿＿＿＿＿。

星期日毛毛虫吃了＿＿＿＿＿＿＿＿＿。

Note: Students should choose a different fruit for the caterpillar to eat on each day of the week.

237

shī zi	lǎo hǔ	bào
狮子	老虎	豹
xī niú	dà xiàng	è yú
犀牛	大象	鳄鱼
luò tuo	xióng	xióng māo
骆驼	熊	熊猫
jīng yú	cháng jǐng lù	bān mǎ
鲸鱼	长颈鹿	斑马

sōng shǔ
松鼠

cāng shǔ
仓鼠
hamster

yú
鱼

tù zi
兔子

wū guī
乌龟

mì fēng
蜜蜂

mǔ jī
母鸡

māo
猫

gǒu
狗

mǔ niú
母牛

niǎo
鸟

māo tóu yīng
猫头鹰

Make a Guess: Who's Talking?
猜一猜：谁在说话？

What animal makes that sound? Write the animal that makes each sound in pinyin or characters. Then choose the sound each animal makes in Chinese from the word bank and write it on the space provided.

	Name of Animal	Sound in Chinese
1. meow, meow	＿＿＿＿＿＿＿＿	＿＿＿＿＿＿＿＿
2. baa, baa	＿＿＿＿＿＿＿＿	＿＿＿＿＿＿＿＿
3. neigh, neigh	＿＿＿＿＿＿＿＿	＿＿＿＿＿＿＿＿
4. oink, oink	＿＿＿＿＿＿＿＿	＿＿＿＿＿＿＿＿
5. woof, woof	＿＿＿＿＿＿＿＿	＿＿＿＿＿＿＿＿
6. quack, quack	＿＿＿＿＿＿＿＿	＿＿＿＿＿＿＿＿
7. moo, moo	＿＿＿＿＿＿＿＿	＿＿＿＿＿＿＿＿
8. cock-a-doodle-doo	＿＿＿＿＿＿＿＿	＿＿＿＿＿＿＿＿

miē miē	gā gā	wāng wāng	mōu mōu
咩咩	嘎嘎	汪汪	哞哞
wō wō	miāo miāo	gū lū	huī huī
喔喔	喵喵	咕噜	唉唉

Song: Old McDonald Had a Farm
儿歌：王老先生有块地

wáng lǎo xiān sheng yǒu kuài dì　　yī yā yī yā yo

（一）王老先生有块地，依呀依呀哟。

tā zài tián li yǎng xiǎo jī　　yī yā yī yā yo

他在田里养小鸡*，依呀依呀哟。

zhī zhī zhī　　zhī zhī zhī

吱吱吱**，吱吱吱，

zhī zhī zhī　　zhī zhī zhī　　zhī zhī zhī

吱吱吱，吱吱吱，吱吱吱，

wáng lǎo xiān sheng yǒu kuài dì　　yī yā yī yā yo

王老先生有块地，依呀依呀哟。

xiǎo gǒu　　wāng wāng wāng

（二）*小狗　**汪汪汪

xiǎo māo　　miāo miāo miāo

（三）*小猫　**喵喵喵

xiǎo zhū　　gū lū gū lū

（四）*小猪　**咕噜咕噜

241

名字：＿＿＿＿＿＿＿＿＿＿＿＿＿＿＿ ＿＿＿＿月＿＿＿＿日

Compare and Write: Which Animal Has...? Which Animal Can...?
比一比，写一写：谁有……？谁会……？

Refer to the animal Vocabulary Flash Cards on pages 238-239 to answer questions 1-5. Use the word bank to create your own questions and answers for 6-10. Add the word "和" if your answer includes more than one animal.

shéi yǒu liǎng zhī jiǎo
1. 谁有两只脚？
   ＿＿＿＿＿＿＿有两只脚。

   sì
2. 谁有四只脚？
   ＿＿＿＿＿＿＿有四只脚。

   wěi ba
3. 谁有尾巴？
   ＿＿＿＿＿＿＿有尾巴。

   huì yóu yǒng
4. 谁会游泳？
   ＿＿＿＿＿＿＿会游泳。

   fēi
5. 谁会飞？
   ＿＿＿＿＿＿＿会飞。

Make interesting questions to challenge your partner.

6. 谁有 / 会＿＿＿＿＿＿？
   (A) ＿＿＿＿＿＿＿＿＿。

7. 谁有 / 会＿＿＿＿＿＿？
   (A) ＿＿＿＿＿＿＿＿＿。

8. 谁有 / 会＿＿＿＿＿＿？
   (A) ＿＿＿＿＿＿＿＿＿。

9. 谁有 / 会＿＿＿＿＿＿？
   (A) ＿＿＿＿＿＿＿＿＿。

10. 谁有 / 会＿＿＿＿＿＿？
    (A) ＿＿＿＿＿＿＿＿＿。

zài lù shang shēng huó
在陆上生活

shuǐ li
在水里生活

★★★★★★

pǎo de kuài
跑得快

màn
跑得慢

★★★★★★

jiào
会叫

pá shù
会爬树

pǎo
会跑

kān mén
会看门

xià dàn
会下蛋

★★★★★★

zuì zhòng
最重

qīng
最轻

★★★★★★

méi jiǎo
没有脚

没有尾巴

chī cǎo
吃草

ròu
吃肉

Quiz: Where Can They Be Found?
考考你：它们住在哪儿？

Refer to Vocabulary Flash Cards: Animals on pages 238-239. List at least 2 animals that can be found in the following places.

shān shang
山上
mountain

_____

_____

sēn lín
森林
forest

狮子住在森林里。

_____

shuǐ li
水里
river / sea

_____

_____

nóng chǎng
农场
farm

_____

_____

tiān shang
天上
sky

_____

_____

dòng wù yuán
动物园
zoo

_____

_____

名字：_____ _____月_____日

Read and Write: Pet Show
认一认，写一写：宠物秀

Look at the picture and answer the question below.

nǐ xiǎng yào shén me chǒng wù
Q 你想要什么宠物？

wǒ
A 我想要_____。

Essay Writing: My Pet
写一写：我的宠物

同学们，假如你有一只宠物，请写一篇大约100字的短文描述一下你的宠物。它是什么动物，什么形状、大小、颜色？你从哪里得到它？它喜欢吃什么？喜欢做什么？你和宠物一起做些什么？

Paste your pet picture here

Reading: Qing Ming Jie (Tomb Sweeping Day)
读一读：清明节

　　清明节，又称扫墓节。它是一个中国传统的民俗节日。每年四月，全家大小到祖先坟上打扫，祭拜，请求祖先保佑全家平安。

　　中国人孝顺父母，尊敬老人。清明节是传承"家"的观念最实际，也是最有效的生活教育。

　　清明时节春暖花开，除了扫墓祭祖之外，它也是全家郊游踏青的好时节。很多放风筝的活动也在清明节前后举行。

Qīng míng jié, yòu chēng sǎo mù jié. Tā shì yí gè zhōng guó chuán tǒng de mín sú jié rì. Měi nián sì yuè, quán jiā dà xiǎo dào zǔ xiān fén shang dǎ sǎo, jì bài, qǐng qiú zǔ xiān bǎo yòu quán jiā píng ān.

Zhōng guó rén xiào shùn fù mǔ, zūn jìng lǎo rén. Qīng míng jié shì chuán chéng jiā de guān niàn zuì shí jì, yě shì zuì yǒu xiào de shēng huó jiào yù.

Qīng míng shí jié chūn nuǎn huā kāi, chú le sǎo mù jì zǔ zhī wài, tā yě shì quán jiā jiāo yóu tà qīng de hǎo shí jié. Hěn duō fàng fēng zheng de huó dòng yě zài qīng míng jié qián hòu jǔ xíng.

Qing Ming Jie literally means "Clear Bright Festival", and is commonly known as the Tomb Sweeping Day in English. This is a traditional holiday to honor one's ancestors. Falling on early April, it is a time for people to visit their family members' grave sites. They pay respect to their ancestors by sweeping and cleaning the tombstone and leaving flowers or other offerings at the grave.

Chinese people share a long tradition of worshipping their ancestors' spirits. By doing so, it is commonly believed that the ancestors will look after the family and help bring good luck and peace in the coming year. Participating in the Tomb Sweeping rituals ensures that this family value will be passed on to the next generation and also reinforces family relationships.

Although Qing Ming Jie is considered a solemn holiday, it is not necessarily a sad occasion. Many families look forward to this festival as a special time for their family to enjoy a nice spring day together outdoors. Some even take pleasure in the ancient Chinese invention of flying kites during this time.

Answer the following questions.

1. What are the other names for Qing Ming Jie?

_____

2. When is Qing Ming Jie?

_____

3. Where do people go on Qing Ming Jie?

_____

4. How do people show respect to their ancestors?

_____

5. Is Qing Ming Jie a sad holiday for Chinese people?
   If not, why?

_____

_____

Fill in the Blanks: Cloze
填一填：清明习俗

Fill in the blanks using words from the word bank.

家	四月	中国	父母	踏青
清明	平安	老人	风筝	祖先

＿＿＿＿＿＿节，又称扫墓节，是＿＿＿＿＿＿
(1)   (2)

传统的民俗节日。每年＿＿＿＿＿＿，全家大小
(3)

到＿＿＿＿＿＿坟上打扫，祭拜，请求祖先保佑
(4)

全家＿＿＿＿＿＿。中国人孝顺＿＿＿＿＿＿，尊敬
(5)   (6)

＿＿＿＿＿＿。清明节是传承"＿＿＿＿＿＿"的观
(7)   (8)

念最实际，也是最有效的生活教育。

清明节春暖花开，是全家郊游＿＿＿＿＿＿的
(9)

好时节。放＿＿＿＿＿＿的活动也是在清明节时前
(10)

后举行。

Tang Poem: Qingming
唐诗：清明

qīng míng
清明

dù mù
杜牧（唐）

清明时节雨纷纷， 　Qīng míng shí jié yǔ fēn fēn,

路上行人欲断魂。 　Lù shang xíng rén yù duàn hún.

借问酒家何处有？ 　Jiè wèn jiǔ jiā hé chù yǒu?

牧童遥指杏花村。 　Mù tóng yáo zhǐ xìng huā cūn.

A drizzling rain falls like tears on the Mourning Day;
The mourner's heart is going to break on his way.
Where can a food stand be found to take a rest?
The cowherd points to a village of "apricot flowers".

同学们，第249页的《清明》是唐朝晚期诗人杜牧所写的一首诗。你们可以把它改一改吗？

（改成每句四个字） （改成每句三个字）

（改成每句二个字） （改成每句一个字）

 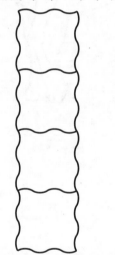

同学们，请把下面几个字放在正确的地方：

路上	清明	牧童
杏花村	行人	酒家

（人）：_____ 。

（地）：_____ _____。

（时间）：_____ 。

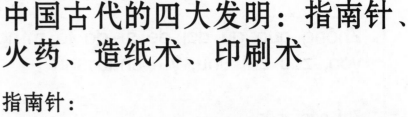

Reading: Four Great Inventions from Ancient China
读一读：中国古代四大发明

中国古代的四大发明：指南针、火药、造纸术、印刷术

指南针：

古时候，人们在海上只能依赖月亮和星星辨识方向。后来，约两千两百年前，中国人发明了指南针，将它用于航海。郑和利用指南针，前后七次成功地航行到东亚各国和印度洋附近，比1492年哥伦布发现新大陆更早。

火药：

火药是中国道士在制作药丸过程中无意间发明的。中国人最初用火药来制造鞭炮、烟火，后来还发展到军事用途。火药经由阿拉伯人传入欧洲以后，用途更广。不仅用来制造武器，更用来开山、造路、造桥等。

造纸术：

造纸术发明以前，中国人把字刻或写在牛骨、龟壳、竹片或树叶上。大约一千八百年前，蔡伦发明了轻薄的材料，适合书写又方便携带。造纸术的发明帮助古代资料的保存及传播，促进世界文明的发展。

印刷术：

中国人以前想要拥有一本书，必须一字一句地抄写。后来发明了雕版印刷术，虽然印刷速度加快，但内容不易更改。直到九百多年前，毕升发明了活字版印刷术，使得印刷变成书本又经济又省时。活字印刷术后来传遍全世界，大大地加快了世界各国的文化交流活动。

Reading: Four Great Inventions from Ancient China
读一读：中国古代四大发明

Zhōng guó gǔ dài de sì dà fā míng: zhǐ nán zhēn, huǒ yào, zào zhǐ shù, yìn shuā shù

Zhǐ nán zhēn:

Gǔ shí hou, rén men zài hǎi shang zhǐ néng yī lài yuè liang hé xīng xing biàn shí fāng xiàng. Hòu lái, yuē liǎng qiān liǎng bǎi nián qián, zhōng guó rén fā míng le zhǐ nán zhēn, jiāng tā yòng yú háng hǎi. Zhèng Hé lì yòng zhǐ nán zhēn, qián hòu qī cì chéng gōng de háng xíng dào dōng yà gè guó hé yìn dù yáng fù jìn, bǐ yī sì jiǔ èr nián Gē Lún Bù fā xiàn xīn dà lù gèng zǎo.

Huǒ yào:

Huǒ yào shì zhōng guó dào shi zài zhì zuò yào wán guò chéng zhōng wú yì jiān fā míng de. Zhōng guó rén zuì chū yòng huǒ yào lái zhì zào biān pào, yān huǒ. Hòu lái hái fā zhǎn dào jūn shì yòng tú. Huǒ yào jīng yóu ā lā bó rén chuán rù ōu zhōu yǐ hòu, yòng tú gèng guǎng. Bù jǐn yòng lái zhì zào wǔ qì, gèng yòng lái kāi shān, zào lù, zào qiáo děng.

Zào zhǐ shù:

Zào zhǐ shù fā míng yǐ qián, zhōng guó rén bǎ zì kè huò xiě zài niú gǔ, guī ké, zhú piàn huò shù yè shang. Dà yuē yì qiān bā bǎi nián qián, Cài Lún fā míng le qīng báo de cái liào, shì hé shū xiě yòu fāng biàn xié dài. Zào zhǐ shù de fā míng bāng zhù gǔ dài zī liào de bǎo cún jí chuán bō, cù jìn shì jiè wén míng de fā zhǎn.

Yìn shuā shù:

Zhōng guó rén yǐ qián xiǎng yào yōng yǒu yì běn shū, bì xū yí zì yí jù de chāo xiě. Hòu lái fā míng le diāo bǎn yìn shuā shù, suī rán yìn shuā sù dù jiā kuài, dàn nèi róng bú yì gēng gǎi. Zhí dào jiǔ bǎi duō nián qián, Bì Shēng fā míng le huó zì bǎn yìn shuā shù, shǐ de yìn shuā biàn chéng shū běn yòu jīng jì yòu shěng shí. Huó zì yìn shuā shù hòu lái chuán biàn quán shì jiè, dà dà de jiā kuài le shì jiè gè guó de wén huà jiāo liú huó dòng.

Reading: Four Great Inventions from Ancient China
读一读：中国古代四大发明

The compass, gunpowder, papermaking and printing are four great inventions of ancient China.

The Compass:

In ancient times all seafarers depended on the position of the sun and stars to show them direction. Then, about 2,200 years ago, in China they discovered that a magnet could indicate north and south and invented the first compass. Admiral Zheng, a Chinese explorer, used the compass to complete seven successful voyages around the Indian Ocean and Southeast Asia. This occurred much earlier than the voyage Columbus made to the New World in 1492.

Gunpowder:

Taoist chemists in China trying to make pills for immortality accidentally discovered the formula for making gunpowder! Its first use was for making firecrackers and fireworks. Soon after that it was used by the military to create gunpowder based weapons. When it reached Europe, gunpowder was used for weapons, but also started to be used to improve technology in the construction industry.

Papermaking:

The earliest writings from China were found on ox bones, shells, bamboo shoots and tree bark. Approximately 2,000 years ago, a Chinese official named Cai Lun invented a thin light paper that was suitable for writing. This new convenient and inexpensive writing material quickly became very popular.

The Chinese invention of papermaking has been a tremendous contribution to the promotion and development of civilizations worldwide.

Printing:

The earliest books written by man were hand written. Then block printing was invented and this technology allowed multiple copies of a document to be printed. But printing was still very time-consuming because the type had to be reset one character at a time for each document to be printed.

Around 900 years ago a man named Bi Sheng engraved Chinese characters on small pieces of clay to make movable type. This was the first invention for movable type printing. From China the invention of movable type printing has spread to many other countries where it has been modified and developed.

Quiz: Four Great Inventions from Ancient China
考考你：中国古代四大发明

Answer the following questions.

1. What are the four great inventions of ancient China?

2. How was gunpowder invented?

3. Name four uses for the invention of gunpowder.

4. Who made seven voyages to Southeast Asia and the Indian Ocean?

5. When was paper invented? Who invented it?

6. How did the invention of paper change civilization?

7. Who invented movable type printing?

8. How did movable type printing change civilization?

名字：_____　　　　　_____月_____日

Fill in the missing words or pictures.

名字：

日_____月_____

中国的发明

| chá 茶 | zhǐ nán zhēn 指南针 | suàn pán 算盘 | yān huǒ 烟火 |

zhǐ 纸 (paper)

(compass)

(fireworks)

(abacus)

mǐ fàn 米饭 (rice)

(tea)

Which invention do you think is the most useful?

fēng zheng 风筝 (kite)

tài yáng yǎn jìng 太阳眼镜 (sunglasses)

kuài zi 筷子 (chopsticks)

miàn tiáo 面条 (noodles)

bīng qí lín 冰淇淋 (ice-cream)

Crossword Puzzle: Chinese Inventions
填字谜：中国的发明

Fill in the puzzle based on the pictures below in English. You will discover the mystery invention after filling in the puzzle correctly. Draw it in the box below.

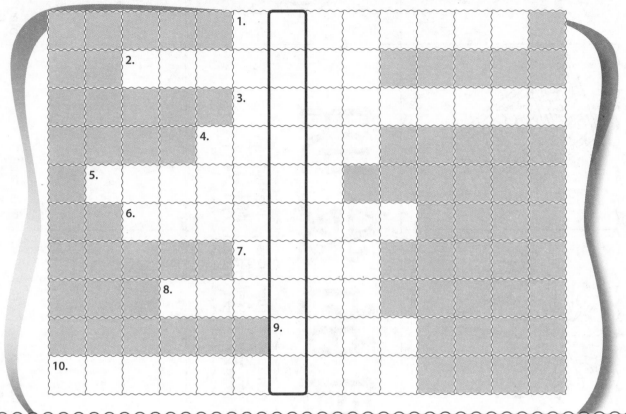

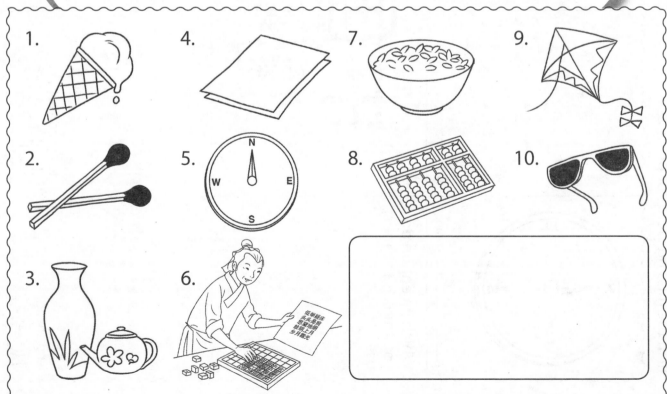

1.

2.

3.

4.

5.

6.

7.

8.

9.

10.

Word Search: Chinese Inventions
找一找：中国的发明

Find each of the following words in the word search.

p	r	i	t	c	k	s	w	e	u	k	h	g
w	n	a	i	b	s	d	i	f	m	g	l	u
a	o	n	c	u	m	b	r	e	l	l	a	n
i	p	r	i	n	t	i	n	g	c	b	n	p
t	l	e	r	i	r	k	l	m	o	r	t	o
i	g	s	c	a	n	i	k	p	m	e	e	w
n	m	o	r	o	b	k	c	r	p	s	r	d
k	i	t	e	e	l	l	k	e	a	l	n	e
p	n	e	o	i	l	b	e	p	s	l	b	r
e	p	a	s	t	a	o	r	e	s	r	a	t
i	s	k	c	i	t	s	p	o	h	c	n	s
h	g	k	p	a	p	r	o	i	r	w	s	a
n	o	o	d	l	e	s	k	w	e	t	e	p

1. rice
2. kite
3. gunpowder
4. compass
5. umbrella
6. tea
7. chopsticks
8. printing
9. wheelbarrow
10. noodles
11. lantern
12. silk

Guess and Write: Things that Came from China
猜一猜，写一写：中国的发明

Read the descriptions on the left. Guess what each invention is and write it down on the right.

Your guess:

1	2,500 years ago, people in China came up with a special tool to help them with math. It is the earliest kind of computer.	
2	1,900 years ago, the Chinese made it out of pulp taken from fishing nets, rags and plants.	
3	A Chinese man mixed some different chemicals together. They then began to spark and explode.	
4	It was invented by the Chinese about 1,000 years ago. It is a tool to help people find directions. Christopher Columbus used it on his trip to America in 1492.	
5	7,000 years ago, it was first grown and eaten in China. People in China still eat it every day.	
6	Chinese people began to drink it 5,000 years ago.	
7	It was invented in China 4,000 years ago. It was made from rice, milk, spices and snow. Most children like it.	
8	It was eaten in China 3,000 years ago. A lot of people think it was invented by the Italians.	
9	It is made of wood. People use it as a tool to eat.	
10	It was invented by the Chinese 500 years ago. It provides shade from the hot sun.	
11	It was invented 3,000 years ago. It comes in different shapes like butterflies, birds, and dragons. It flies in the sky.	

Let's Talk: Fruits and Animals
说一说：水果和动物

Dialogue 1

(A) nǐ ài chī shén me shuǐ guǒ
你爱吃什么水果？

(B) wǒ ài chī pú tao hé xiāng jiāo　nǐ ne
我爱吃葡萄和香蕉。你呢？

(A) wǒ ài chī píng guǒ　cǎo méi hé xī guā
我爱吃苹果、草莓和西瓜。

(B) ó　nǐ ài chī hóng sè de shuǐ guǒ
哦，你爱吃红色的水果，

duì bú duì
对不对？

Dialogue 2

(A) nǐ xǐ huan shén me chǒng wù
你喜欢什么宠物？

(B) wǒ xǐ huan gǒu
我喜欢狗。

(A) wèi shén me
为什么？

(B) yīn wèi gǒu hěn hǎo wán
因为狗很好玩。

tā huì bǎo hù wǒ
它会保护我，

hé wǒ zuò péng you
和我做朋友。

Dialogue 3

(A) nǐ xǐ huan dà dòng wù　hái shì xiǎo dòng wù
你喜欢大动物，还是小动物？

(B) wǒ xǐ huan dà dòng wù　xiàng shī zi hé lǎo hǔ　nǐ ne
我喜欢大动物，像狮子和老虎。你呢？

(A) wǒ xǐ huan xiǎo dòng wù　xiàng xiǎo māo　xiǎo gǒu　xiǎo tù zi
我喜欢小动物，像小猫、小狗、小兔子。

(B) wèi shén me
为什么？

(A) yīn wèi xiǎo dòng wù hěn kě ài　tā men kě yǐ zuò
因为小动物很可爱。它们可以做

wǒ de péng you
我的朋友。

(B) ng　yǒu dào lǐ
嗯，有道理！

Let's Write!
写一写

zuǒ				
(left)	左	左		
yòu				
(right)	右	右		
dōng				
N W→E S (east)	东	东		
xī				
N W←E S (west)	西	西		
nán				
N W E ↓S (south)	南	南		
běi				
N↑ W E S (north)	北	北		

五月
May

May Calendar	五月月历
Food	食物
Mother's Day	母亲节
Tea-Drinking	中国茶
Try It Out!	每月一练

Let's Talk!	说一说
Let's Write!	写一写

茶壶

茶叶

zhōng 中
guó 国
cài 菜

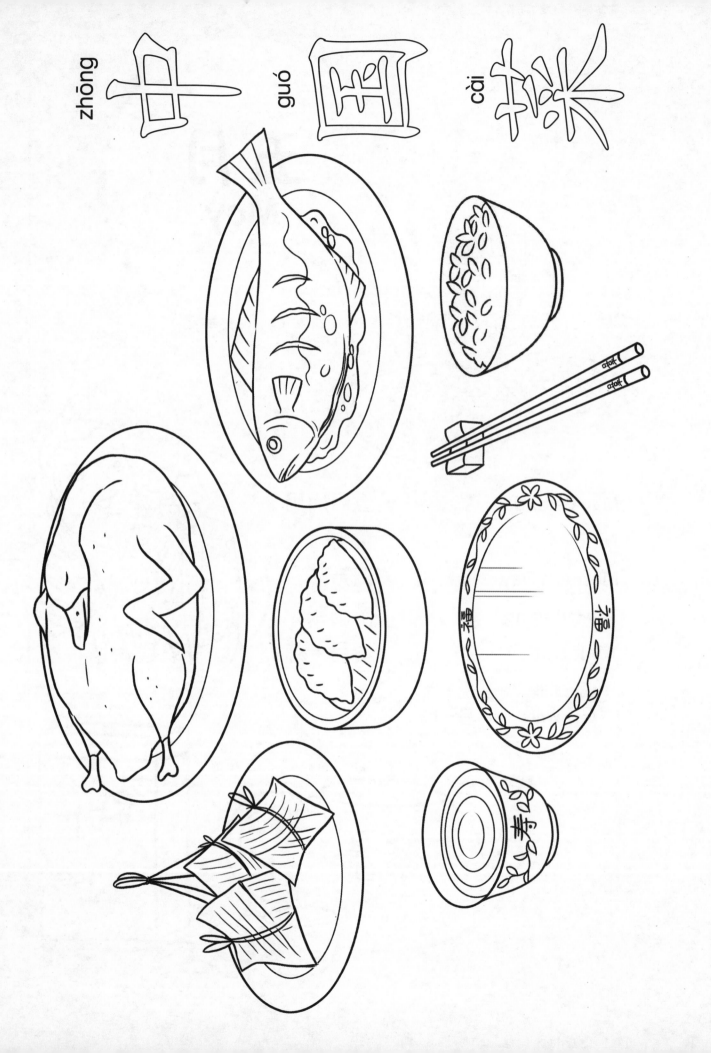

五月 · May

年 ○

xīng qī rì 星期日	xīng qī yī 星期一	xīng qī èr 星期二	xīng qī sān 星期三	xīng qī sì 星期四	xīng qī wǔ 星期五	xīng qī liù 星期六

What's Happening in May?
五月知多少?

jīn tiān shì　　　　　　yuè　　　　rì
1. 今天是_____月_____日。

míng tiān shì　　　　　　yuè　　　　rì
2. 明天是_____月_____日。

hòu tiān shì　　　　　　yuè　　　　rì
3. 后天是_____月_____日。

zuó tiān shì xīng qī
4. 昨天是星期_____。

qián tiān shì xīng qī
5. 前天是星期_____。

wǔ yuè yǒu　　　　　　　　gè xīng qī sān
6. 五月有_____个星期三。

wǔ yuè zhōng tè bié de rì zi shì
7. 五月中特别的日子是_____。

wǔ yuè shí rì de sān tiān qián shì　　　yuè　　　rì
8. 五月十日的三天前是____月_____日。

wǔ yuè èr shí èr rì de sān tiān hòu shì　　　yuè　　　rì
9. 五月二十二日的三天后是____月_____日。

　　　　　　　　de shēng rì shì　　　yuè　　　rì
10. _____的生日是____月_____日。
(a person's name)

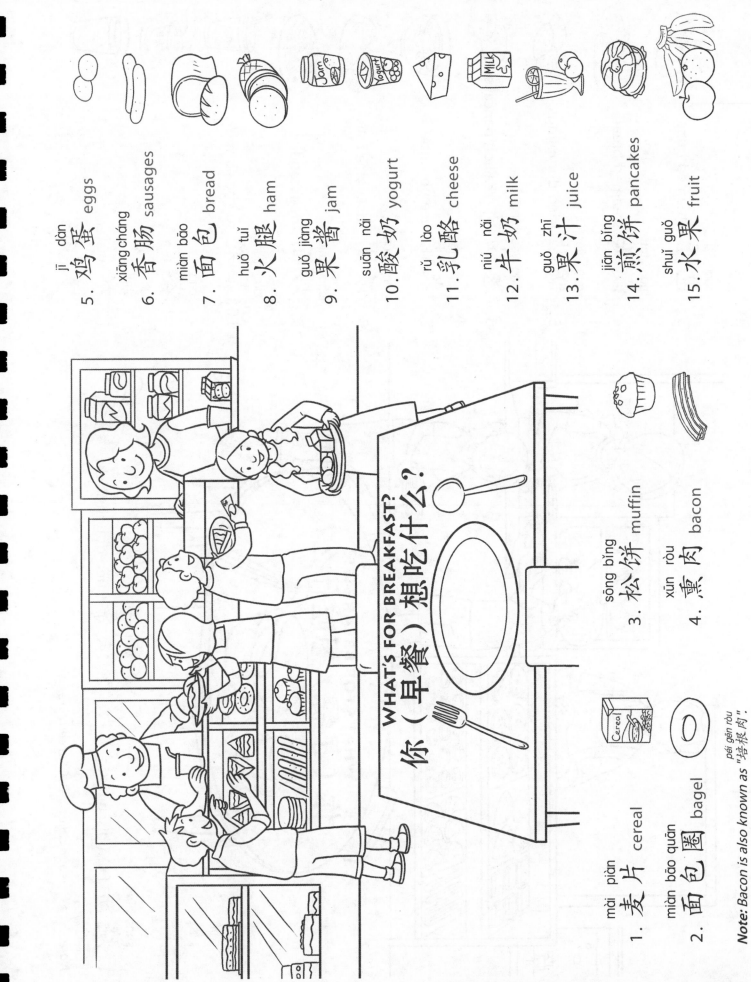

5. jī dàn 鸡蛋 eggs

6. xiāng cháng 香肠 sausages

7. miàn bāo 面包 bread

8. huǒ tuǐ 火腿 ham

9. guǒ jiàng 果酱 jam

10. suān nǎi 酸奶 yogurt

11. rǔ lào 乳酪 cheese

12. niú nǎi 牛奶 milk

13. guǒ zhī 果汁 juice

14. jiān bǐng 煎饼 pancakes

15. shuǐ guǒ 水果 fruit

WHAT'S FOR BREAKFAST?
你（早餐）想吃什么？

1. mài piàn 麦片 cereal

2. miàn bāo quān 面包圈 bagel

3. sōng bǐng 松饼 muffin

4. xūn ròu 熏肉 bacon

Note: Bacon is also known as "培根肉". péi gēn ròu

Vocabulary List: Western Style Breakfast 词表：西式早餐 **(265)**

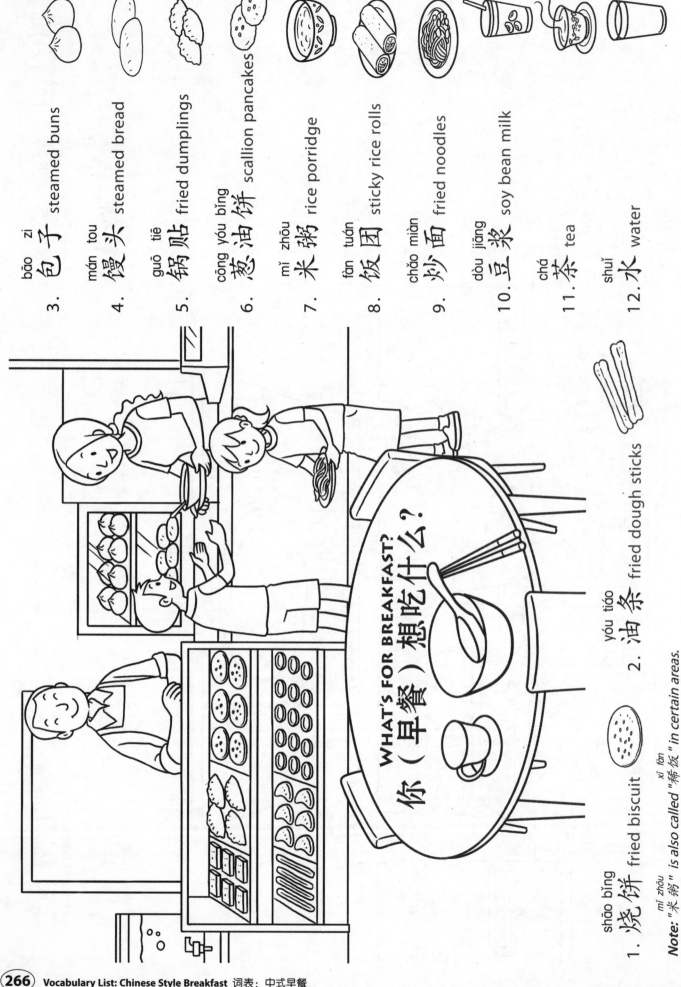

3. 包子 bāo zi steamed buns

4. 馒头 mán tou steamed bread

5. 锅贴 guō tiē fried dumplings

6. 葱油饼 cōng yóu bǐng scallion pancakes

7. 米粥 mǐ zhōu rice porridge

8. 饭团 fàn tuán sticky rice rolls

9. 炒面 chǎo miàn fried noodles

10. 豆浆 dòu jiāng soy bean milk

11. 茶 chá tea

12. 水 shuǐ water

WHAT'S FOR BREAKFAST?

你（早餐）想吃什么？

1. 烧饼 shāo bǐng fried biscuit

2. 油条 yóu tiáo fried dough sticks

Note: mǐ zhōu "米粥" is also called "稀饭" xī fàn "in certain areas.

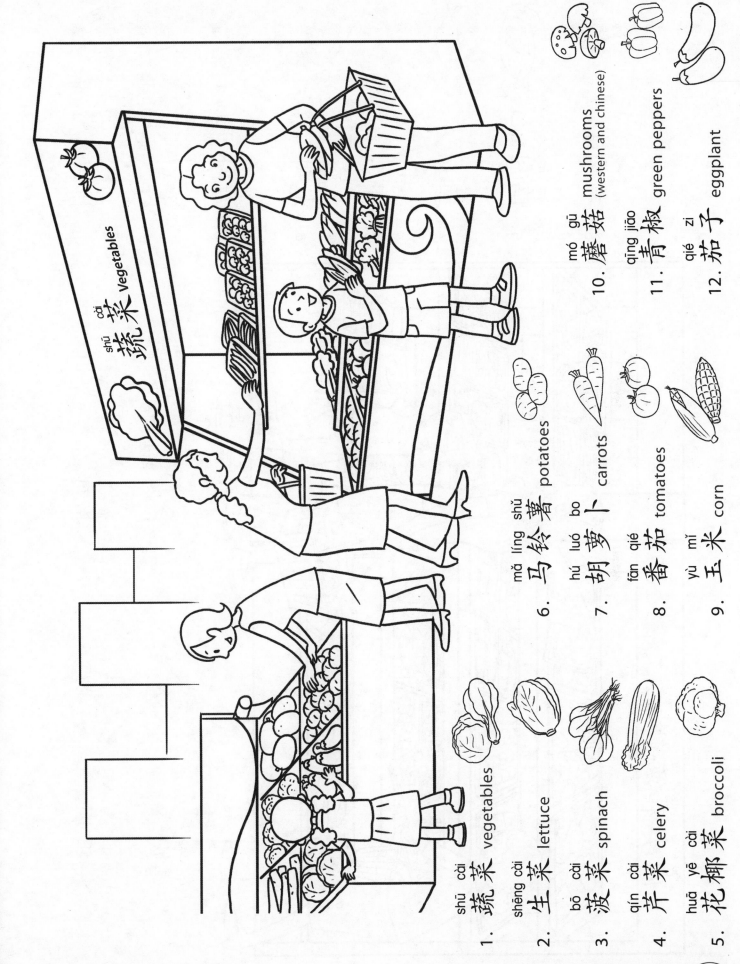

shū cài
1. 蔬菜 vegetables

shēng cài
2. 生菜 lettuce

bō cài
3. 菠菜 spinach

qín cài
4. 芹菜 celery

huā yē cài
5. 花椰菜 broccoli

mǎ líng shǔ
6. 马铃薯 potatoes

hú luó bo
7. 胡萝卜 carrots

fān qié
8. 番茄 tomatoes

yù mǐ
9. 玉米 corn

mó gū
10. 蘑菇 mushrooms (western and chinese)

qīng jiāo
11. 青椒 green peppers

qié zi
12. 茄子 eggplant

shū cài
蔬菜 vegetables

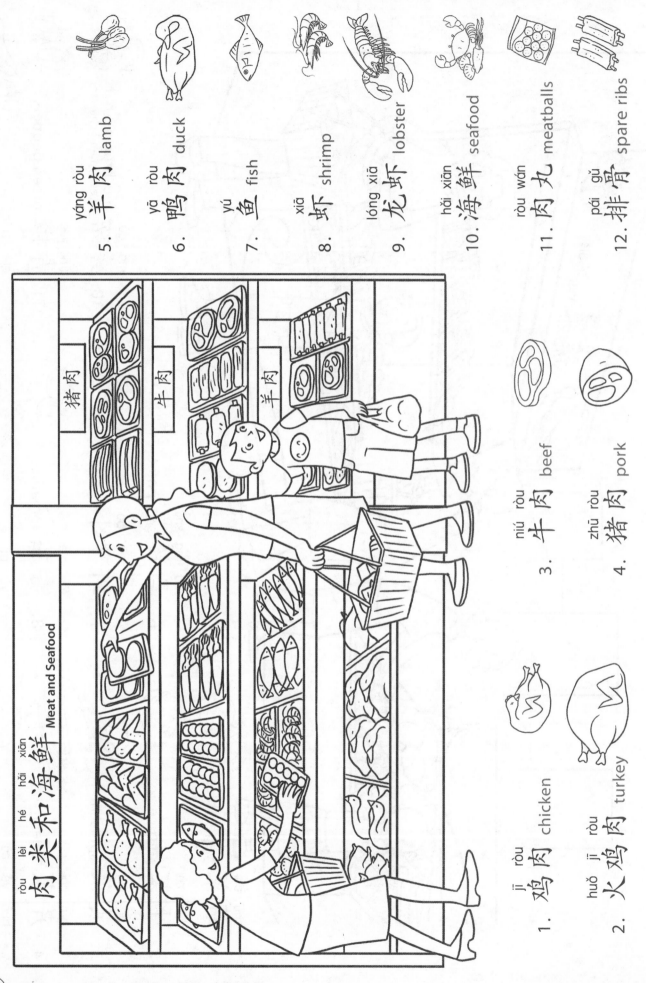

ròu lèi hé hǎi xiān
肉类和海鲜 Meat and Seafood

1. jī ròu 鸡肉 chicken
2. huǒ jī ròu 火鸡肉 turkey
3. niú ròu 牛肉 beef
4. zhū ròu 猪肉 pork

5. yáng ròu 羊肉 lamb
6. yā ròu 鸭肉 duck
7. yú 鱼 fish
8. xiā 虾 shrimp
9. lóng xiā 龙虾 lobster
10. hǎi xiān 海鲜 seafood
11. ròu wán 肉丸 meatballs
12. pái gǔ 排骨 spare ribs

Writing Activity: Supermarket Manager
写一写：超市经理

You are the supermarket manager. You need to label the vegetables in Chinese characters or pinyin. Select the right words from the tray below to label the vegetables.

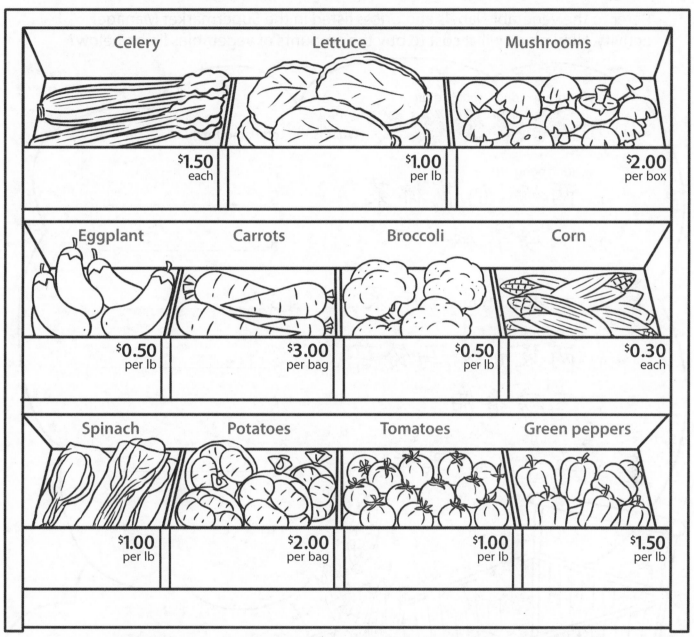

Celery
$1.50 each

Lettuce
$1.00 per lb

Mushrooms
$2.00 per box

Eggplant
$0.50 per lb

Carrots
$3.00 per bag

Broccoli
$0.50 per lb

Corn
$0.30 each

Spinach
$1.00 per lb

Potatoes
$2.00 per bag

Tomatoes
$1.00 per lb

Green peppers
$1.50 per lb

生菜 shēng cài   菠菜 bō cài   芹菜 qín cài

花椰菜 huā yē cài   马铃薯 mǎ líng shǔ   胡萝卜 hú luó bo

番茄 fān qié   玉米 yù mǐ   磨菇 mó gū   青椒 qīng jiāo   茄子 qié zi

Math: Food Shopping
算一算：买菜

Refer to the vegetable labels and prices listed in the Supermarket Manager activity. How much will it cost to buy the amounts of vegetables listed below?

yí gòng duō shǎo qián
一共多少钱？
(What is the total amount?)

liǎng bàng
1. 两磅（lb）花椰菜 $_____

2. 一磅青椒 $_____

bǎ
3. 一把（bunch）芹菜 $_____

dài
4. 两袋（bag）马铃薯 $_____

5. 三磅番茄 $_____

gè
6. 五个（ear）玉米 $_____

7. 一共多少钱？
The total is

$_____

chūn juǎn

春卷

spring rolls

chǎo fàn

炒饭

fried rice

chǎo miàn

炒面

fried noodles

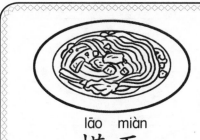

lāo miàn

捞面

lo mein

chǎo mǐ fěn

炒米粉

fried rice noodles

dàn huā tāng

蛋花汤

egg drop soup

hún tun tāng

馄饨汤

wonton soup

suān là tāng

酸辣汤

hot and sour soup

jī tāng

鸡汤

chicken soup

shū cài tāng

蔬菜汤

vegetable soup

diǎn xīn

点心

dim sum

dòu fu

豆腐

tofu

Writing Activity: Let's Go Shopping!
写一写：一起去买菜！

Today is your birthday. Your Mom will invite Grandpa, Grandma and some of your friends over for dinner. Your Mom asks you to go to the supermarket with her. She will make some Western food and Chinese food for the dinner. What are you going to buy? You need to first decide the dishes you would like your Mom to make.

What dishes would you like your Mom to make? Name 5 of them in Chinese and English.

我要妈妈
做……
(I would like Mom to make...)

	Chinese	English
1.	_____	_____
2.	_____	_____
3.	_____	_____
4.	_____	_____
5.	_____	_____

My Supermarket Shopping List for my Birthday Dinner.

Name 12 food items here.

wō yào mǎi
我要买：

	Chinese	English		Chinese	English
1.	_____	_____	7.	_____	_____
2.	_____	_____	8.	_____	_____
3.	_____	_____	9.	_____	_____
4.	_____	_____	10.	_____	_____
5.	_____	_____	11.	_____	_____
6.	_____	_____	12.	_____	_____

名字：＿＿＿＿＿＿＿＿＿＿＿＿ ＿＿＿月＿＿＿日

Integrated Activity: Ordering Food from a Chinese Menu
综合活动：点中国菜

Below is a menu from Everyday Restaurant. Review the items on the menu before proceeding to the next activity.

tiān tiān xiǎo guǎn
天天小馆
cài dān
菜单

yǐn liào
饮料：
Drinks

 shuǐ 水   chá 茶 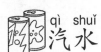 qì shuǐ 汽水   kě lè 可乐   guǒ zhī 果汁

xiǎo cài
小菜：
Appetizer

 huā shēng 花生   hǎi dài 海带   xūn yú 熏鱼  dòu fu gān 豆腐干

tāng
汤：
Soup

 dàn huā tāng 蛋花汤   hún tun tāng 馄饨汤   yù mǐ tāng 玉米汤

 suān là tāng 酸辣汤   shū cài tāng 蔬菜汤

zhǔ cài
主菜：
Main Course

 gài lán niú ròu 芥蓝牛肉 táng cù pái gǔ 糖醋排骨

zhī ma jī 芝麻鸡 táng cù yú 糖醋鱼

běi jīng yā 北京鸭 má pó dòu fu 麻婆豆腐

tián diǎn
甜点：
Dessert

 hóng dòu tāng 红豆汤  zhī ma tāng yuán 芝麻汤圆

 bīng qí lín 冰淇淋    shuǐ guǒ 水果

Integrated Activity: Ordering Food from a Chinese Menu ❶
综合活动: 点中国菜 ➊

Everyday Restaurant offers a special weekend dinner set for $10 a person.
It includes a drink, an appetizer, a soup, a main course and a dessert.
What would you like to order? Write down your order on the form below.

天天小馆
点菜单

gù kè míng zì
顾客名字: _____

yǐn liào
饮料: _____

xiǎo cài
小菜: _____

tāng
汤: _____

zhǔ cài
主菜: _____

tián diǎn
甜点: _____

Integrated Activity: Ordering Food from a Chinese Menu ❷
综合活动：点中国菜 ❷

Role play the following dialogue with a partner.

fú wù yuán　　　　qǐng wèn nǐ yào hē shén me
服务员：请问你要喝什么？
(What would you like to drink?)

gù kè　　　　　　　　　kě lè
顾客：我要喝可乐。

　　　　　　shén me xiǎo cài
服务员：你要什么小菜？
(What appetizer would you like?)

　　　　　　huā shēng
顾客：我要花生。

　　　　　　shén me tāng
服务员：你要什么汤？
(What kind of soup would you like?)

　　　　　　suān là tāng
顾客：我要酸辣汤。

　　　　　　shén me zhǔ cài
服务员：你要什么主菜？
(What main dish would you like?)

　　　　　　gài lán niú ròu
顾客：我要芥蓝牛肉。

　　　　　　shén me tián diǎn
服务员：你要什么甜点？
(What would you like for dessert?)

　　　　　　bīng qí lín
顾客：我要冰淇淋。

Decode the Word Search: Chinese Food
数字解码：中国菜的秘密

Use the Chinese Food Vocabulary List to complete this word puzzle. Each number in the chart below stands for a different letter of the alphabet. Once you decode the numbers, you will find out the pinyin of each food item. Fill in the pinyin, tones and English meaning in the space provided. The first one has been done for you.

1	2	3	4	5	6	7	8	9	10	11	12	13
d	m	s	h	v	z	a	j	p	y	e	u	i

14	15	16	17	18	19	20	21	22	23	24	25	26
g	t	q	b	x	k	f	w	n	c	r	l	o

Pinyin   **English**

1. j ī   t ā n g   chicken soup
    8 13   15 7 22 14

2. __ __ __   __ __ __   __ __ __ __
    3 4 12   23 7 13   15 7 22 14

3. __ __ __ __   __ __ __
    23 4 7 26   20 7 22

4. __ __ __ __   __ __ __
    1 13 7 22   18 13 22

5. __ __ __   __ __ __   __ __ __ __
    1 7 22   4 12 7   15 7 22 14

6. __ __ __   __ __
    1 26 12   20 12

7. __ __ __ __   __ __   __ __ __
    23 4 7 26   2 13   20 11 22

8. __ __ __ __   __ __ __ __
    23 4 12 22   8 12 7 22

9. __ __ __   __ __ __ __
    25 7 26   2 13 7 22

10. __ __ __   __ __ __   __ __ __ __
    4 12 22   15 12 22   15 7 22 14

名字：_____ _____月_____日

Read the food pyramid carefully and find out how many servings you will need everyday for each food item below.

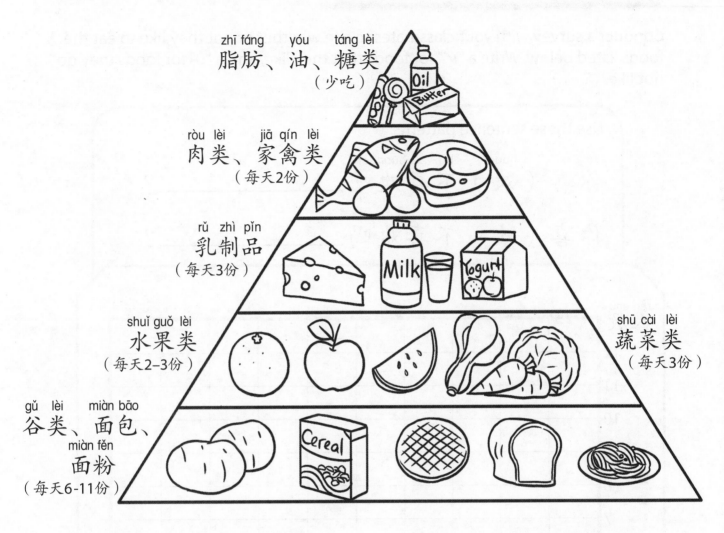

Food item	number of servings per day		Food item	number of servings per day
píng guǒ 1. 苹果	_____		chǎo miàn 6. 炒面	_____
niú ròu 2. 牛肉	_____		hú luó bo 7. 胡萝卜	_____
miàn bāo 3. 面包	_____		jī dàn 8. 鸡蛋	_____
yóu 4. 油	_____		rǔ lào 9. 乳酪	_____
niú nǎi 5. 牛奶	_____		mǎ líng shǔ 10.马铃薯	_____

名字：_____ _____月_____日

Survey: Favorite Food
问卷：爱吃的中国菜

Conduct a survey with your classmates to see whether or not they like to eat the foods listed below. Write a "✔" for foods that they like, and a "0" for foods they do not like.

Use these sentence patterns:

nǐ xǐ huan bù xǐ huan chī
你喜（欢）不喜欢吃_____？

hē
你喜（欢）不喜欢喝_____？

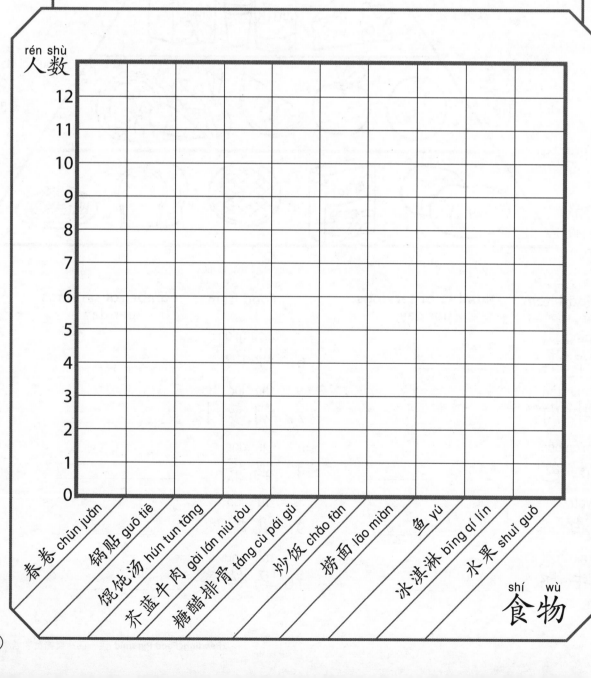

rén shù
人数

12
11
10
9
8
7
6
5
4
3
2
1
0

春卷 chūn juǎn
锅贴 guō tiē
馄饨汤 hún tun tāng
芥蓝牛肉 gài lán niú ròu
糖醋排骨 táng cù pái gǔ
炒饭 chǎo fàn
捞面 lāo miàn
鱼 yú
冰淇淋 bīng qí lín
水果 shuǐ guǒ

shí wù
食物

Write and Say: Favorite Food and Healthy Food
写一写，说一说：爱吃和健康的食物

Write 3 food items under each appropriate heading. You can write in characters or pinyin. Then practice saying sentences with this information using the sentence patterns provided.

说一说：
wǒ xǐ huan   bù xǐ huan chī
我喜欢 / 不喜欢吃……。

喜欢	不喜欢
like	dislike
_____	_____
_____	_____
_____	_____

说一说：
chī   hěn jiàn kāng   bú jiàn kāng
吃……很健康 / 不健康。

健康	不健康
healthy	unhealthy
_____	_____
_____	_____
_____	_____

说一说：
wǒ cháng cháng chī   bù cháng chī   cóng lái méi chī guò
我常常吃 / 不常吃 / 从来没吃过……。

常常吃	不常吃	从来没吃过
often eat	rarely eat	never eat
_____	_____	_____
_____	_____	_____
_____	_____	_____

Rap: Mom Is Cooking Dinner
说唱：妈妈做晚餐

mā ma zuò wǎn cān
妈妈做晚餐，
Mom is cooking dinner.

shén me cài　shén me fàn
什么菜？什么饭？
What kind of dishes?

ràng wǒ kàn yí kàn
让我看一看。
Let me take a look.

hú luǒ bo　niú ròu fàn
胡萝卜，牛肉饭；
Carrots and beef fried rice;

hái yǒu fān qié hé jī dàn
还有番茄和鸡蛋。
Also some tomatoes and eggs.

ā　chī de wǒ hǎo bǎo
啊！吃得我好饱。
Ah! Delicious food fills my tummy.

mā ma nǐ zhēn bàng　nǐ　zhēn　bàng
妈妈你真棒！你—真—棒！
Mom, you are terrific!

Reading: Tea-Drinking
读一读：中国茶

中国人常说："开门七件事：柴、米、油、盐、酱、醋、茶。"大部分中国人天天喝茶。喝茶是重要的中国文化之一。

中国人喝茶有很久的历史了。传说古代神农氏有一次坐在茶树下，一阵风把一些茶叶吹进了他的热水杯中。神农氏喝了茶水以后非常喜欢。这就是最早关于喝茶的故事。

中国人喝茶是用茶叶，而不是像西方人用茶包。茶叶是用茶树上的新鲜叶子做成的。泡茶时，把茶叶放进茶壶里，注入热水，加盖。几分钟以后，茶叶慢慢展开，茶色变黄，茶便可以喝了。

茶有很多种类。有绿茶、红茶和花茶等。绿茶是制作过程中不发酵的茶。龙井是绿茶之一。乌龙茶是半发酵的绿茶。普洱茶和铁观音是红茶。花茶中以茉莉花茶最普遍，又叫"香片"。

茶壶

茶叶

每天喝绿茶对身体有益。绿茶还被做成绿茶蛋糕、绿茶月饼等甜食。

Zhōng guó rén cháng shuō: "Kāi mén qī jiàn shì: chái, mǐ, yóu, yán, jiàng, cù, chá." Dà bù fèn zhōng guó rén tiān tiān hē chá. Hē chá shì zhòng yào de zhōng guó wén huà zhī yī.

Zhōng guó rén hē chá yǒu hěn jiǔ de lì shǐ le. Chuán shuō gǔ dài shén nóng shì yǒu yí cì zuò zài chá shù xià. Yí zhèn fēng bǎ yì xiē chá yè chuī jìn le tā de rè shuǐ bēi zhōng. Shén nóng shì hē le chá shuǐ yǐ hòu fēi cháng xǐ huan. Zhè jiù shì zuì zǎo guān yú hē chá de gù shi.

Zhōng guó rén hē chá shì yòng chá yè, ér bú shì xiàng xī fāng rén yòng chá bāo. Chā yè shì yòng shù shang de xīn xiān yè zi zuò chéng de. Pào chá shí, bǎ chá yè fàng jìn chá hú li, zhù rù rè shuǐ, jiā gài. Jǐ fēn zhōng yǐ hòu, chá yè màn man zhǎn kāi, chá sè biàn huáng, chá biàn kě yǐ hē le.

Chá yǒu hěn duō zhǒng lèi. Yǒu lù chá, hóng chá hé huā chá děng. Lù chá shì zhì zuò guò chéng zhōng bù fā jiào de chá. Lóng jǐng shì lù chá zhī yī. Wū lóng chá shì bàn fā jiào de lù chá. Pú ěr chá hé tiě guān yīn shì hóng chá. Huā chá zhōng yǐ mò lì huā chá zuì pǔ biàn, yòu jiào "xiāng piàn".

Měi tiān hē lù chá duì shēn tǐ yǒu yì. Lù chá hái bèi zuò chéng lù chá dàn gāo, lù chá yuè bǐng děng tián shí.

The Chinese have a saying: "Firewood, rice, oil, salt, sauce, vinegar and tea are the seven necessities to begin a day." Most of the Chinese drink tea every day. It is an important part of Chinese culture.

Chinese people have a long history of drinking tea. According to a legend, a man named King Shen Nong once sat under a tree waiting for his cup of hot water to cool down. A wind blew some tea leaves into his cup. After drinking the water, King Shen Nong liked the taste. This is the earliest story about tea-drinking.

Unlike the westerners drinking tea from tea bags, the Chinese make tea from tea leaves. Chinese tea is made from young, tender leaves of tea trees. To make a pot of tea, first put a spoonful of tea leaves in the teapot, then pour in boiling water and cover it with a lid. After a few minutes, the tea leaves are loose and open and the tea is ready to serve.

There are many kinds of tea such as: green teas, black teas and scented teas. Tea that has not been fermented during the process is called "green tea". An example of green tea is called Long Jing, which means "Dragon Well". Oolong Tea (Black Dragon) is semi-fermented green tea; Pu'er and Tie Guan Yin (Iron Goddess of Mercy) are black tea. Jasmine tea is one of the most popular among scented teas. It is also known as "Xiang Pian", which means "Fragrant Piece".

Scientists suggest that drinking tea daily is good for one's health. Tea is also used to make birthday cakes, moon cakes and other desserts.

名字：_____ _____月_____日

Quiz: Tea-Drinking
考考你：中国茶

Read the passage on Tea-drinking and answer the questions. You are encouraged to answer the questions in Chinese.

chuán shuō zhōng shéi fā xiàn le hē chá de fāng fǎ
1. 传说中谁发现了喝茶的方法？
According to a Chinese legend, who discovered how to make tea?

_____

zhōng guó rén měi tiān kāi mén qī jiàn shì shì shén me
2. 中国人每天开门七件事是什么？
What are the seven basic items needed for daily life?

_____

nǐ rú hé pào chá
3. 你如何泡茶？ （依顺序标示1,2,3）
How do you make a pot of tea? (Label 1,2,3 before the correct sentences.)

dào kāi shuǐ
_____倒开水

jiā gài
_____加盖

fàng chá yè
_____放茶叶

gè xiě chū yì zhǒng chá yè de míng chēng
4. 各写出一种茶叶的名称：
(Write the name for each type of tea in English.)

lù chá   hóng chá   huā chá
绿茶：   红茶：   花茶：

_____   _____   _____

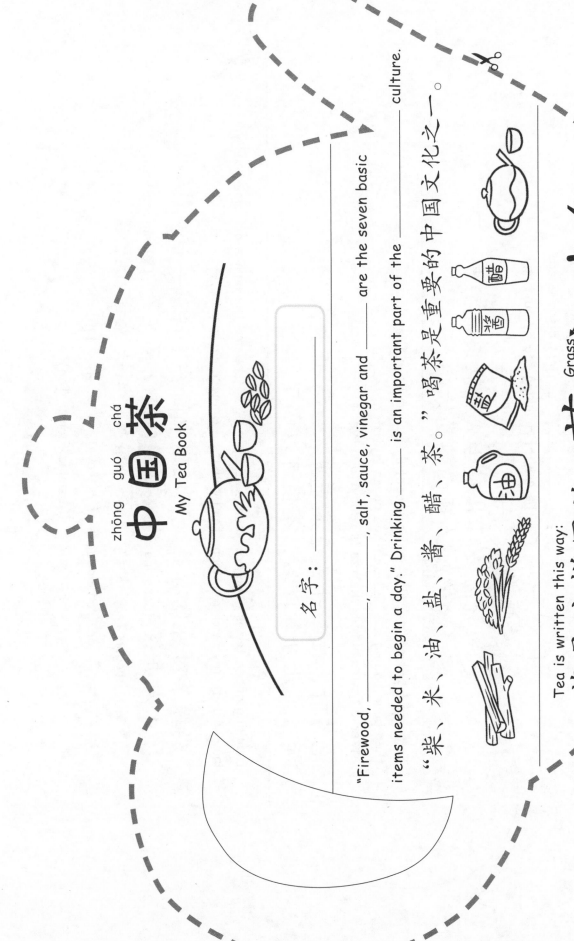

zhōng guó chá
中 国 茶
My Tea Book

名字：

"Firewood, _____, _____, salt, sauce, vinegar and _____ are the seven basic items needed to begin a day." Drinking _____ is an important part of the _____ culture.

"柴、米、油、盐、酱、醋、茶。"喝茶是重要的中国文化之一。

Tea is written this way:
茶是这样写的：
艹 Grass
人 Man
木 Tree
chá

According to the legend, King _____ first discovered _____ the way of drinking tea by putting _____ in _____ water.

传说古代神农氏最早发现喝茶的方法。

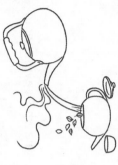

To make a pot of tea, first put a spoonful tea leaves in the _____ then pour boiling _____ and cover it with a _____. After a few minutes, the tea is ready to serve.

泡茶时，把茶叶放进茶壶里，注入开水，加盖。几分钟以后，茶便可以喝了。

Drinking green tea is good for your _____. Here are the names of some teas you may wish to try next time your family visits a Chinese restaurant.

喝绿茶对身体有益。下次到中国餐馆请试一试：
1. 龙井茶 (Longjing or Dragon Well Tea) 2. 乌龙茶 (Oolong or Black Dragon Tea) 3. 普洱茶 (Pu'er Tea) 4. 铁观音 (Tie Guan Yin or Iron Goddess of Mercy Tea) 5. 茉莉花茶 (Jasmine Flower Tea)

Dialogue 1

妈妈 (mā ma)：小弟，晚饭想 (xiǎo dì，wǎn fàn xiǎng) 吃什么？(chī shén me)

小弟 (xiǎo dì)：我想吃 (wǒ xiǎng chī) 排骨和芥蓝鸡。(pái gǔ hé gài lán jī)

妈妈 (mā ma)：想喝什么汤？(xiǎng hē shén me tāng)

小弟 (xiǎo dì)：我想喝蛋花汤。(wǒ xiǎng hē dàn huā tāng)

Dialogue 2

妈妈 (mā ma)：小妹，明天早餐 (xiǎo mèi，míng tiān zǎo cān) 想吃什么？(xiǎng chī shén me)

小妹 (xiǎo mèi)：我想吃 (wǒ xiǎng chī) 面包、火腿和蛋。(miàn bāo，huǒ tuǐ hé dàn)

妈妈 (mā ma)：想喝什么？(xiǎng hē shén me)

小妹 (xiǎo mèi)：我想喝牛奶。(wǒ xiǎng hē niú nǎi)

Dialogue 3

哥哥 (gē ge)：妈妈，今天我学了食物金字塔。(mā ma，jīn tiān wǒ xué le shí wù jīn zì tǎ)

妈妈 (mā ma)：真的吗？很有趣吧？给我说说看。(zhēn de ma　hěn yǒu qù ba　gěi wǒ shuō shuō kàn)

哥哥 (gē ge)：老师说多吃青菜和水果才会健康。(lǎo shī shuō duō chī qīng cài hé shuǐ guǒ cái huì jiàn kāng)

妈妈 (mā ma)：对啊！但是肉类和谷类食物也很重要的。(duì a　dàn shì ròu lèi hé gǔ lèi shí wù yě hěn zhòng yào de)

哥哥 (gē ge)：老师说每种食物都要吃，(lǎo shī shuō měi zhǒng shí wù dōu yào chī) 只是不要吃太多就好。(zhǐ shì bú yào chī tài duō jiù hǎo)

妈妈 (mā ma)：对对对，每样食物都要吃，还要多运动，(duì duì duì　měi yàng shí wù dōu yào chī　hái yào duō yùn dòng) 身体就会健康！(shēn tǐ jiù huì jiàn kāng)

Let's Write!
写一写

chūn spring	春	春		
xià summer	夏	夏		
qiū autumn	秋	秋		
dōng winter	冬	冬		
fēng wind	风	风		
yǔ rain	雨	雨		

六 月
June

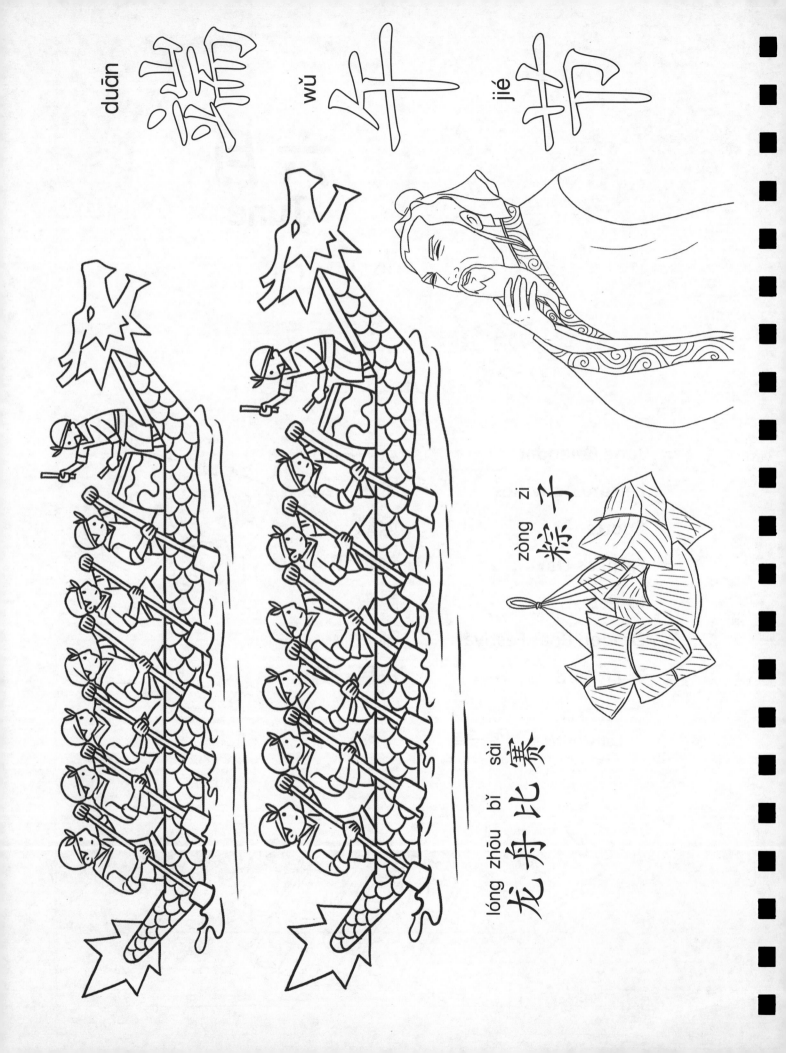

duān 端

wǔ 午

jié 节

zòng zi 粽子

lóng zhōu bǐ sài 龙舟比赛

June 六月

年 ○

xīng qī liù 星 期 六	xīng qī wǔ 星 期 五	xīng qī sì 星 期 四	xīng qī sān 星 期 三	xīng qī èr 星 期 二	xīng qī yī 星 期 一	xīng qī rì 星 期 日

What's Happening in June?
六月知多少？

jīn tiān shì   yuè   rì
1. 今天是_____月_____日。

míng tiān shì   yuè   rì
2. 明天是_____月_____日。

hòu tiān shì   yuè   rì
3. 后天是_____月_____日。

zuó tiān shì xīng qī
4. 昨天是星期_____。

qián tiān shì xīng qī
5. 前天是星期_____。

liù yuè yí gòng yǒu   tiān
6. 六月一共有_____天。

liù yuè zhōng tè bié de rì zi shì
7. 六月中特别的日子是_____。

liù yuè shí rì de sì tiān qián shì   yuè   rì
8. 六月十日的四天前是_____月_____日。

liù yuè shí wǔ rì de shī tiān hòu shì   yuè   rì
9. 六月十五日的十天后是_____月_____日。

de shēng rì shì   yuè   rì
10. _____的生日是_____月_____日。
_____(a person's name)

| kàn shū | xià qí | huà huà |
| 看书 | 下棋 | 画画 |

| kàn diàn shì | dǎ diàn wán | shàng wǎng |
| 看电视 | 打电玩 | 上网
surf the web |

| wán yuè qì | kàn diàn yǐng | yùn dòng |
| 玩乐器 | 看电影 | 运动
play sports |

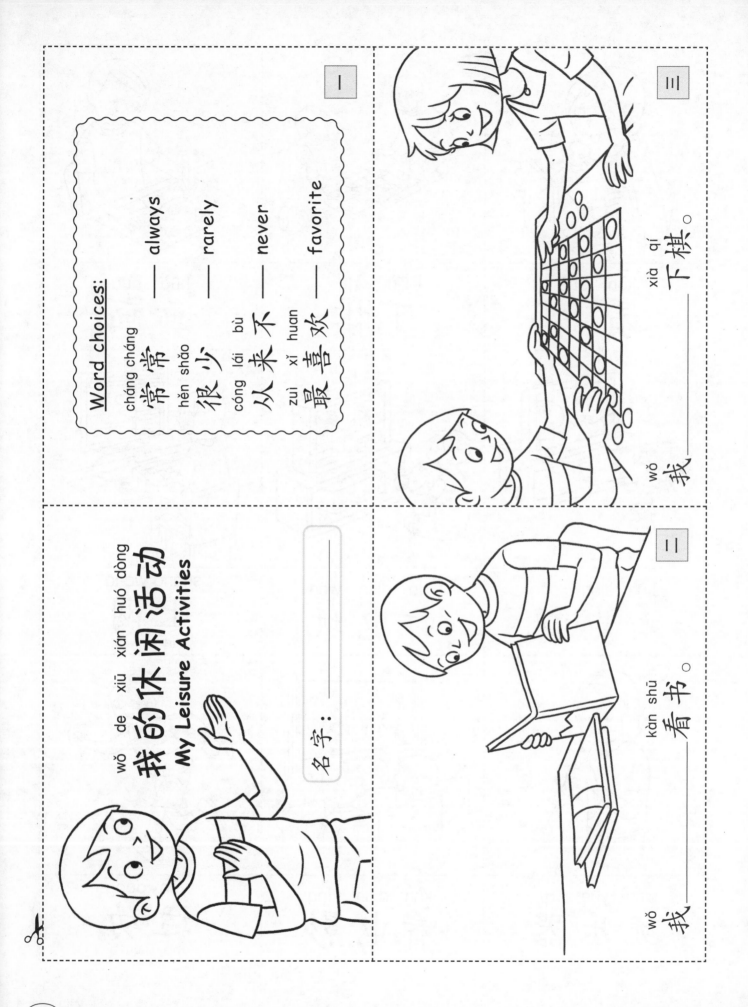

Word choices:

cháng cháng
常 常 —— always

hěn shǎo
很 少 —— rarely

cóng lái bù
从 来 不 —— never

zuì xǐ huan
最 喜欢 —— favorite

1

wǒ de xiū xián huó dòng
我的休闲活动
My Leisure Activities

míng zì:
名字:_____

三

xià qí
下棋。

wǒ
我_____

二

kàn shū
看 书。

wǒ
我_____

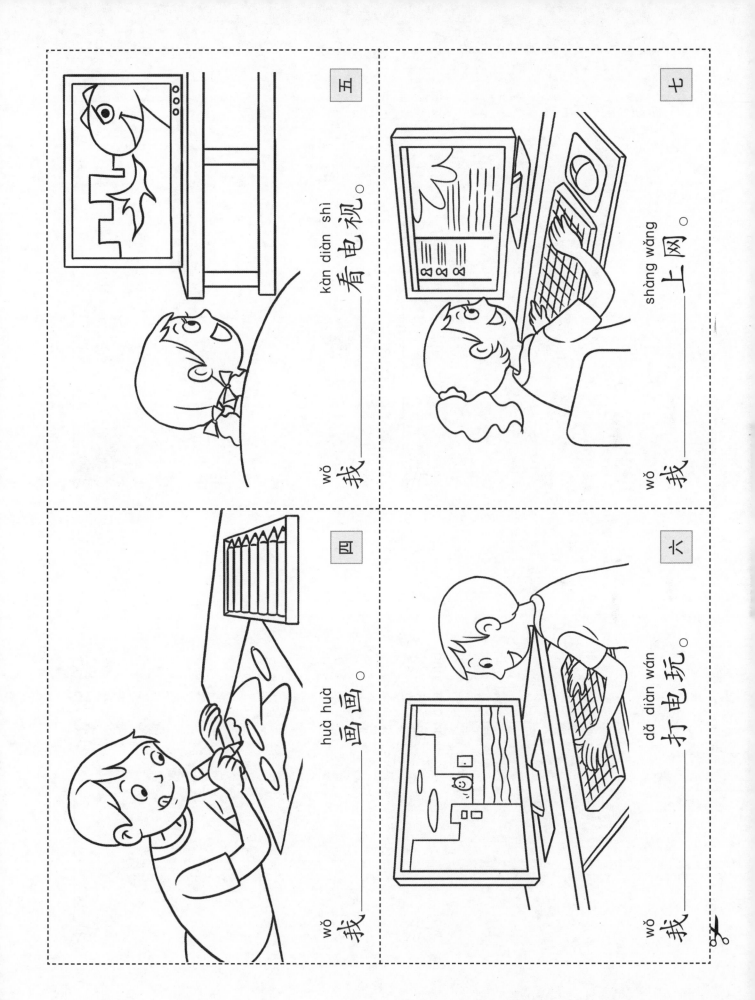

五
kàn diàn shì
看 电 视。
wǒ
我 _____

七
shàng wǎng
上 网。
wǒ
我 _____

四
huà huà
画 画。
wǒ
我 _____

六
dǎ diàn wán
打 电 玩。
wǒ
我 _____

九

我 wǒ ＿＿＿＿＿ 运动 yùn dòng 。

八

我 wǒ ＿＿＿＿＿ 看电影 kàn diàn yǐng 。

十一

我 wǒ ＿＿＿＿＿ 。

十

我 wǒ ＿＿＿＿＿ 玩乐器 wán yuè qì 。

名字：_____ _____月_____日

白云 悠悠，　阳光 柔和，

青山 绿水 一片 锦 绣。

走！走！走走走！我们小手 拉小手，

走！走！走走走！一同去郊 游。

dǎ bàng qiú
(打)棒球

dǎ lán qiú
(打)篮球

dǎ gǎn lǎn qiú
(打)橄榄球

dǎ pái qiú
(打)排球

tī zú qiú
(踢)足球

dǎ pīng pāng qiú
(打)乒乓球

dǎ wǎng qiú
(打)网球

dǎ bīng qiú
(打)冰球

dǎ bǎo líng qiú
(打)保龄球

bīng qiú　　bīng shang qū gùn qiú　　dǎ
Note: The full name of "冰球" is "冰上曲棍球"。"打" means "to play".

yóu yǒng	qí chē	liàn tǐ cāo
游泳	骑车	(练)体操

dǎ yǔ máo qiú	pǎo bù	dǎ lěi qiú
(打)羽毛球	跑步	(打)垒球

xué wǔ shù	huá xuě	liū bīng
(学)武术	滑雪	溜冰

Write and Draw: My Favorite Sport
写一写，画一画：我最喜欢的运动

wǒ zuì xǐ huan
我最喜欢_____。
My favorite sport is

wǒ zuì xiǎng qù xué
我最想去学_____。
I would like to learn

Pick 5 of your favorite sports to complete this chant.

wǒ xǐ huan
我喜欢 (verb) (name of sport)

1. ＿＿＿ (name of sport) ，我喜欢 ＿＿＿ ：

2. ＿＿＿ ，我喜欢 ＿＿＿ ：

3. ＿＿＿ ，我喜欢 ＿＿＿ ：

4. ＿＿＿ ，我喜欢 ＿＿＿ ：

5. ＿＿＿ ，我喜欢 ＿＿＿ ：

lái lái lái　yì qǐ wán
来 来 来，一起玩！
Come, come, come. Let's play!

名字：＿＿＿＿＿＿＿＿＿＿＿＿　＿＿月＿＿日

Art Project: My Weekly Schedule on Sports
创意手工：运动时间表

Instructions:

1. Cut out Wheels A and B.
2. Place Wheel A on top of Wheel B and attach them in the center with a paper fastener.
3. Turn Wheel B to match an activity for each day of the week and practice reading with a partner.

A

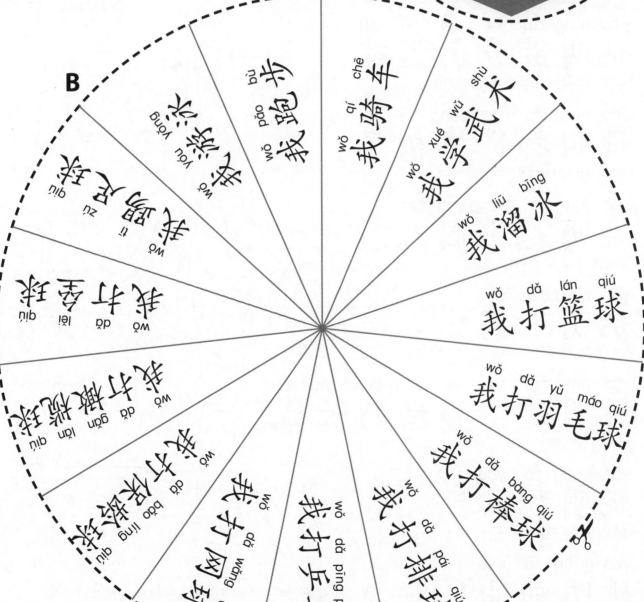

B

Reading: Yao Ming
读一读：姚明加油！

Read the following sentences.

yáo míng shì yùn dòng yuán
姚明是运动员。
Yao Ming is an athlete.

yáo míng shì lán qiú yùn dòng yuán
姚明是NBA篮球运动员。
Yao Ming is an NBA basketball player.

yáo míng zuì ài dǎ lán qiú
姚明最爱打篮球。
Yao Ming loves to play basketball.

yáo míng dǎ de bàng jí le
姚明打得棒极了。
Yao Ming plays extremely well.

yáo míng shì zhōng guó rén
姚明是中国人。
Yao Ming is Chinese.

yáo míng hěn gāo
姚明很高。
Yao Ming is very tall.

yáo míng shì yí dòng de cháng chéng
姚明是"移动的长城"。
He is a "Moving Great Wall".

yáo míng jiā yóu
姚明加油！
Go! Go! Yao Ming!

yáo míng jiā yóu
姚明加油！
Go! Go! Yao Ming!

Note: Students can replace Yao Ming's name and basketball with other names and sports using this reading as a model.

Art Project: No.1 Dad Badge/Gold Medal
创意手工："爸爸第一名"徽章

bà   bā
爸爸

dì   yī   míng
第一名！

No.1 Dad

ér zi nǚ ér
儿子/女儿
(son)   (daughter)

_____
(Your name)

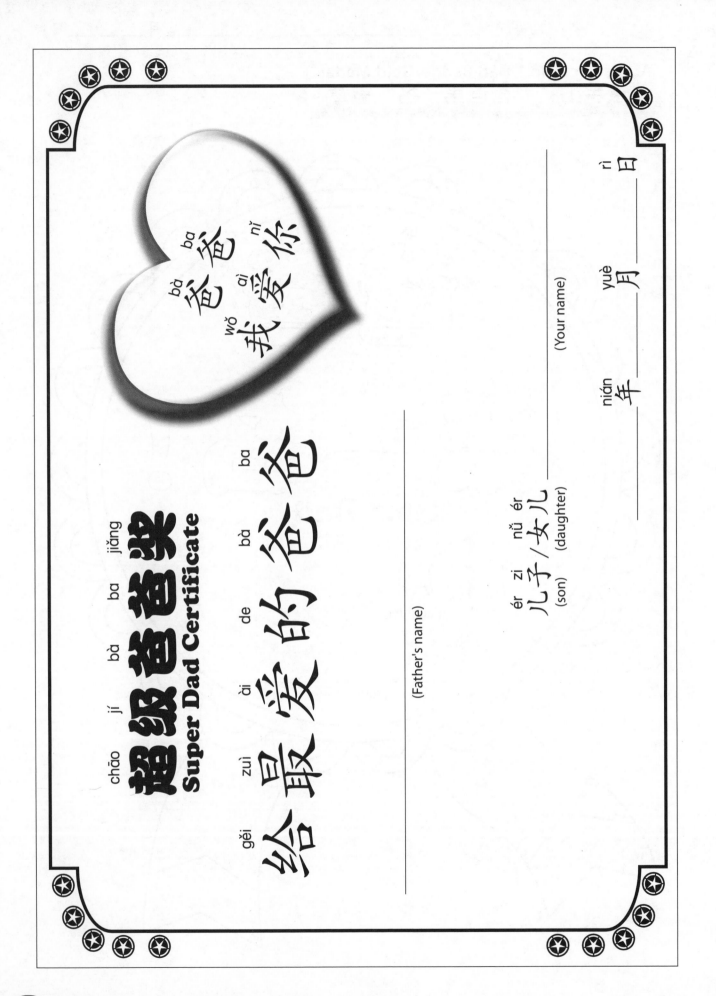

超级爸爸奖
chāo jí bà ba jiǎng
Super Dad Certificate

给 最 爱 的 爸 爸
gěi zuì ài de bà ba

爸爸 我 爱 你
bà ba wǒ ài nǐ

_____ (Father's name)

儿子 / 女儿
ér zi nǚ ér
(son) (daughter)

_____ (Your name)

_____年_____月_____日
nián yuè rì

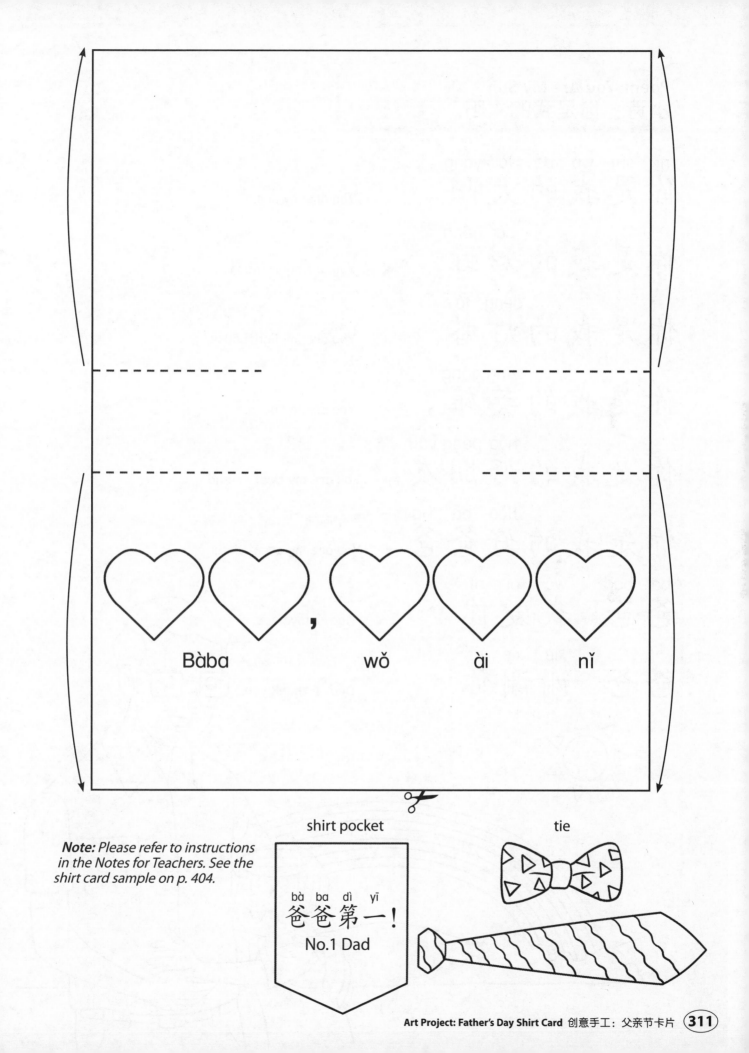

Bàba , wǒ ài nǐ

Note: *Please refer to instructions in the Notes for Teachers. See the shirt card sample on p. 404.*

shirt pocket

tie

bà ba dì yī
爸爸第一！
No.1 Dad

Poem: You Are My Sun
小诗：你是我的太阳

nǐ shì wǒ de tài yáng
你是我的太阳。 You are my sun.

cǎi hóng
你是我的彩虹。 You are my rainbow.

dēng tǎ
你是我的灯塔。 You are my lighthouse.

yīng xióng
你是我的英雄。 You are my hero.

hǎo péng yǒu
你是我的好朋友。 You are my best friend.

hǎo bà ba
你是我的好爸爸。 You are my great dad.

bà ba, wǒ ài nǐ
爸爸，我爱你。 Dad, I love you.

xiè xie nǐ
爸爸，谢谢你。 Dad, I thank you.

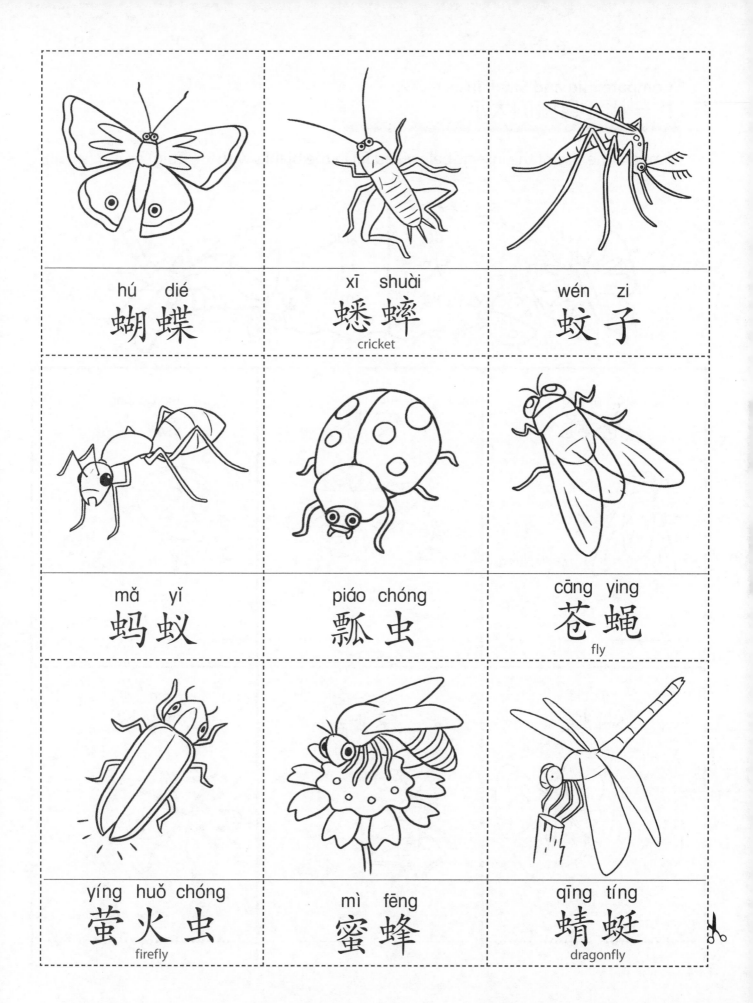

hú dié
蝴蝶

xī shuài
蟋蟀
cricket

wén zi
蚊子

mǎ yǐ
蚂蚁

piáo chóng
瓢虫

cāng ying
苍蝇
fly

yíng huǒ chóng
萤火虫
firefly

mì fēng
蜜蜂

qīng tíng
蜻蜓
dragonfly

Compare: Big and Small Insects
比一比：昆虫的大小

Compare the size of the insects below and fill in the blanks with "大" (big) or "小" (small).

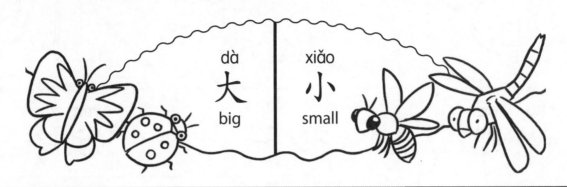

| dà 大 big | xiǎo 小 small |

| cāng ying 苍蝇 | mì fēng 蜜蜂 | piáo chóng 瓢虫 |

_____ _____

· ·

_____ _____

| hú dié 蝴蝶 | xī shuài 蟋蟀 | mǎ yǐ 蚂蚁 |

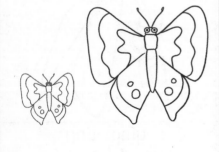

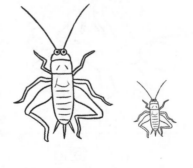

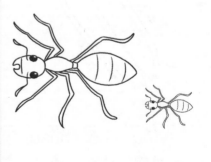

· ·

· ·

名字：_____   _____月_____日

Activity A: Use the dialogue below to find out which insects your classmates like. Record their answers by making a "✔" for each positive response in the table below.

nǐ   xǐ huan shén me   kūn chóng
Ⓐ 你喜欢什么昆虫？
What is your favorite insect?

wǒ   xǐ huan
Ⓑ 我喜欢_____。
My favorite insect is

Activity B: Let's Catch

游戏：你能捉几只昆虫？ **Game:** How many insects can you catch?

wǒ zhuō le   zhī kūn chóng
我捉了_____只昆虫。 **I caught**_____ **insects.**

hú dié 蝴蝶 butterfly											
xī shuài 蟋蟀 cricket											
wén zi 蚊子 mosquito											
mǎ yǐ 蚂蚁 ant											
piáo chóng 瓢虫 ladybug											
cāng ying 苍蝇 fly											
yíng huǒ chóng 萤火虫 firefly											
mì fēng 蜜蜂 bee											
qīng tíng 蜻蜓 dragonfly											

一人　二人　三人　四人　五人　六人　七人　八人　九人　十人

Note: For Activity B, see instructions in Notes for Teachers.

名字：_____ _____月_____日

Write and Color: Body Parts of Insects
写一写，涂一涂：昆虫的身体部位

Fill in the blanks for the parts of the insect's body with the words below.

tuǐ	tóu	yǎn jing	dù zi	chù jiǎo	xiōng bù
腿	头	眼睛	肚子	触角	胸部
leg	head	eye	abdomen	antenna	thorax

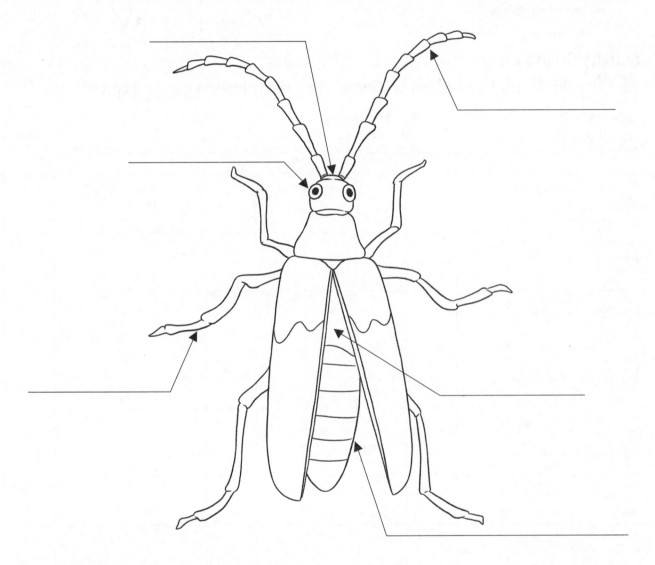

Color the different body parts of the insect as indicated below:

1.	tuǐ 腿	：	hēi sè 黑色	3.	tóu 头	：	huáng sè 黄色	5. xiōng bù 胸部 ： lǜ sè 绿色
2.	yǎn jing 眼睛	：	hóng sè 红色	4.	dù zi 肚子	：	lán sè 蓝色	6. chù jiǎo 触角 ： zǐ sè 紫色

Fill in the Blanks: Are You Afraid Of These Insects?
填一填：你怕不怕这些昆虫？

Fill in the blanks with "怕" or "不怕" to indicate whether or not you are afraid of each of the insects below using pinyin or characters.

^{pà} ^{bú pà}

| pà
怕
afraid of | bú pà
不怕
not afraid of |

1. 我 _____ hú dié
蝴蝶。

5. 我 _____ mì fēng
蜜蜂。

2. 我 _____ wén zi
蚊子。

6. 我 _____ mǎ yǐ
蚂蚁。

3. 我 _____ qīng tíng
蜻蜓。

7. 我 _____ xī shuài
蟋蟀。

4. 我 _____ piáo chóng
瓢虫。

8. 我 _____ cāng ying
苍蝇。

Reading: Story of the Silkworm
读一读：蚕丝的故事

传说五千多年以前，中国有一位"黄帝"。他和妻子西陵氏住在一个大皇宫里。宫里有一个美丽的花园，种了很多桑树。

西陵氏喜欢早晨在花园散步，然后在桑树下休息喝茶。

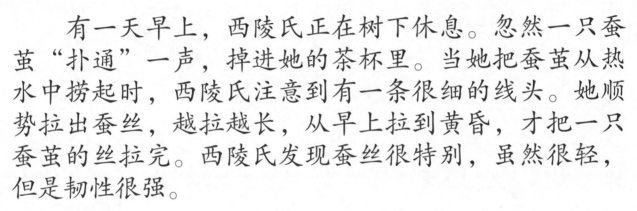

有一天早上，西陵氏正在树下休息。忽然一只蚕茧"扑通"一声，掉进她的茶杯里。当她把蚕茧从热水中捞起时，西陵氏注意到有一条很细的线头。她顺势拉出蚕丝，越拉越长，从早上拉到黄昏，才把一只蚕茧的丝拉完。西陵氏发现蚕丝很特别，虽然很轻，但是韧性很强。

她开始寻找更多蚕茧进行抽丝及纺纱。后来，她开始大量养蚕并做成彩色的丝绸衣服和扇子等。由于丝绸非常珍贵，很多外国人都到中国来买，因此形成了一条著名的"丝路"。西陵氏因发明蚕丝的制作方法，被尊称为"嫘祖"。

Chuán shuō wǔ qiān duō nián yǐ qián, zhōng guó yǒu yí wèi "Huáng Dì". Tā hé qī zi Xī Líng Shì zhù zài yí gè dà huáng gōng li. Gōng li yǒu yí gè měi lì de huā yuán, zhòng le hěn duō sāng shù.

Xī Líng Shì xǐ huan zǎo chén zài huā yuán sàn bù, rán hòu zài sāng shù xià xiū xi hē chá.

Yǒu yì tiān zǎo shang, Xī Líng Shì zhèng zài shù xia xiū xi. Hū rán yì zhī cán jiǎn "pū tōng" yì shēng, diào jìn tā de chá bēi li. Dāng tā bǎ cán jiǎn cóng rè shuǐ zhōng lāo qǐ shí, Xī Líng Shì zhù yì dào yǒu yì tiáo hěn xì de xiàn tóu. Tā shùn shì lā chū cán sī, yuè lā yuè cháng, cóng zǎo shang lā dào huáng hūn, cái bǎ yì zhī cán jiǎn de sī lā wán. Xī Líng Shì fā xiàn cán sī hěn tè bié, suī rán hěn qīng, dàn shì rèn xìng hěn qiáng.

Tā kāi shǐ xún zhǎo gèng duō cán jiǎn jìn xíng chōu sī jí fǎng shā. Hòu lái, tā kāi shǐ dà liàng yǎng cán bìng zuò chéng cǎi sè de sī chóu yī fu hé shàn zi děng. Yóu yú sī chóu fēi cháng zhēn guì, hěn duō wài guó rén dōu dào zhōng guó lái mǎi, yīn cǐ xíng chéng le yì tiáo zhù míng de "sī lù". Xī Líng Shì yīn fā míng cán sī de zhì zuò fāng fǎ, bèi zhūn chēng wéi "léi zǔ".

According to a Chinese legend, Huang Di, known as the Yellow Emperor, ruled China about five thousand years ago. He and his wife Xi Ling Shi lived together in an enormous palace with beautiful gardens. The palace gardens were full of mulberry trees.

Empress Xi Ling Shi loved to take long walks in the palace garden every morning. Afterwards, her servants would often bring her tea and cakes to enjoy while she rested in the shade of the mulberry trees.

On one such day, a cocoon fell from a mulberry tree right into the Empress' hot tea. As she started to remove the cocoon from her tea, the Empress noticed a fine white string from around the cocoon begin to unravel. She continued to pull the string from morning to evening until the entire covering of the cocoon was unwound. Empress Xi Ling Shi realized that this string was special, in that it was very light and yet very strong.

Excited by this amazing discovery, Empress Xi Ling Shi called on her servants to find more cocoons, unwind the strands, and join them together into a single fiber. Later, Empress Xi Ling Shi began to raise silkworms to produce silk for making colorful silk clothing, fans, and other items. The silk was so special that many foreigners traveled to China to get it through a route known as the "Silk Road".

Quiz: Story of the Silkworm
考考你：蚕丝的故事

Fill in the blanks using the words provided.

yī fu 衣服	huáng dì 黄帝	cán jiǎn 蚕茧	sī lù 丝路	léi zǔ 嫘祖
sī chóu 丝绸	shàn zi 扇子	sāng shù 桑树	xī líng shì 西陵氏	wǔ qiān duō nián 五千多年

zhōng guó chuán shuō zhōng zuì zǎo de huáng dì shì
1. 中国传说中最早的皇帝是＿＿＿＿＿＿＿。

fā xiàn cán sī de rén shì
2. 发现蚕丝的人是＿＿＿＿＿＿＿。

xī líng shì yòu jiào
3. 西陵氏又叫＿＿＿＿＿＿＿。

cán chī de yè zi shì zhǎng zài　　　　　shang de
4. 蚕吃的叶子是长在＿＿＿＿＿＿＿上的。

hěn duō wài guó rén dào zhōng guó lái mǎi
5. 很多外国人到中国来买＿＿＿＿＿＿＿。

gǔ shí hou cóng wài guó dào zhōng guó mǎi sī chóu de lù jiào zuò
6. 古时候从外国到中国买丝绸的路叫做＿＿＿＿＿＿＿。

sī kě yǐ zuò chéng　　　　　hé
7. 丝可以做成＿＿＿＿＿＿和＿＿＿＿＿＿。

　　　　　yǐ qián　　zhōng guó rén jiù fā míng le sī
8. ＿＿＿＿＿＿＿以前，中国人就发明了丝。

sī shì cóng　　　　　qǔ chū lái de
9. 丝是从＿＿＿＿＿＿取出来的。

名字： _____   ____ 月 ____ 日

Number the pictures to show the correct order in the silk making process.

The Silk Making Process

shài gān cán jiǎn
晒干蚕茧 Drying cocoons

cán sī rǎn sè
蚕丝染色 Dyeing the silk

cǎi sāng yè
采桑叶 Gathering mulberries

yǎng cán
养蚕 Feeding the silkworms

fǎng shā zhī bù
纺纱织布 Weaving the silk into fabric

chōu sī
抽丝 Spinning silk from cocoons

Compare: Life Cycles of the Butterfly and the Silkworm Moth
比一比：蝴蝶和蚕蛾的生命周期

Compare the life cycles of butterfly and silkworm moth and write down their similarities and differences.

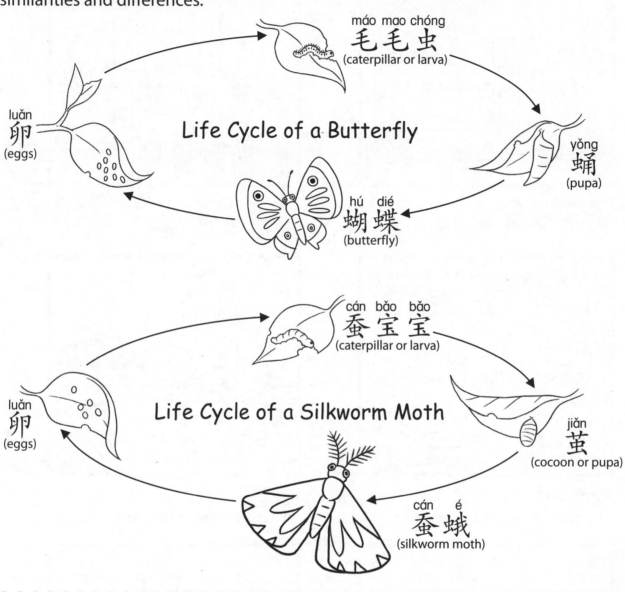

máo mao chóng
毛毛虫
(caterpillar or larva)

luǎn
卵
(eggs)

Life Cycle of a Butterfly

yǒng
蛹
(pupa)

hú dié
蝴蝶
(butterfly)

cán bǎo bǎo
蚕宝宝
(caterpillar or larva)

luǎn
卵
(eggs)

Life Cycle of a Silkworm Moth

jiǎn
茧
(cocoon or pupa)

cán é
蚕蛾
(silkworm moth)

xiāng tóng
相同 Similarities

_____

_____

_____

bù tóng
不同 Differences

_____

_____

_____

Reading: Dragon Boat Festival
读一读：端午节

从前中国有一个名叫屈原的**读书人**，他在朝廷做官。当时中国有很多**战乱**。于是屈原给皇帝提供**治理国家**的**建议**。但是皇帝不同意他的看法，并把他的官位**罢免**了。

从此屈原常常在家乡附近的江边行走，并开始写作诗赋。后来他写了《离骚》，并成为一位有名的诗人。

有一天，屈原掉进江中淹死了。为了保护这位伟大的诗人，人们沿着江水划龙船驱除邪怪，保护屈原。另外，人们还用竹叶包了很多"**粽子**"，把它们丢进江中给鱼吃，希望它们不要伤害屈原的身体。

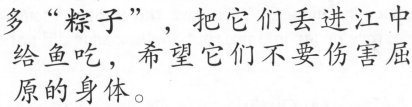

从此，每年到了农历五月五日屈原去世的这一天，中国人就举办**龙舟比赛**和包粽子来纪念这位**爱国诗人**。

323

Cóng qián zhōng guó yǒu yí gè míng jiào Qū Yuán de dú shū rén. Tā zài cháo tíng zuò guān. Dāng shí zhōng guó yǒu hěn duō zhàn luàn. Yú shì Qū Yuán gěi huáng dì tí gōng zhì lǐ guó jiā de jiàn yì. Dàn shì huáng dì bù tóng yì tā de kàn fǎ, bìng bǎ tā de guān wèi bà miǎn le.

Cóng cǐ Qū Yuán cháng cháng zài jiā xiāng fù jìn de jiāng biān xíng zǒu, bìng kāi shǐ xiě zuò shī fù. Hòu lái tā xiě le "lí sāo", bìng chéng wèi yí wèi yǒu míng de shī rén.

Yǒu yì tiān, Qū Yuán diào jìn jiāng zhōng yān sǐ le. Wèi le bǎo hù zhè wèi wěi dà de shī rén, rén men yán zhe jiāng shuǐ huá lóng chuán qū chú xié guài, bǎo hù Qū Yuán. Lìng wài, rén men hái yòng zhú yè bāo le hěn duō "zòng zi", bǎ tā men diū jìn jiāng zhōng gěi yú chī, xī wàng tā men bú yào shāng hài Qū Yuán de shēn tǐ.

Cóng cǐ, měi nián dào le nóng lì wǔ yuè wǔ rì Qū Yuán qù shì de zhè yì tiān, zhōng guó rén jiù jǔ bàn lóng zhōu bǐ sài hé bāo zòng zi lái jì niàn zhè wèi ài guó shī rén.

Long ago in China there lived a wise man named Qu Yuan. He worked as an advisor to the emperor at a time when there was a great deal of chaos in China. Qu Yuan gave the emperor some good ideas about how to restore order in China, but the emperor did not agree with his ideas and sent him away.

After that Qu Yuan spent his time taking long walks along the river by his home and began to write poetry. Before long, he wrote a famous poem "Li Sao" and became known as a great poet in China.

One day Qu Yuan fell into the river and drowned. To protect this great poet, people rowed boats decorated with carved dragons along the river trying to keep the evil spirits from hurting Qu Yuan. They also made bunches of rice dumplings wrapped with bamboo or reed leaves known as "zong zi". They threw zong zi into the river, hoping that the fish in the river would eat them instead of Qu Yuan's body.

From that day on, on the 5th day of the 5th lunar month, the death anniversary of Qu Yuan, people in China hold dragon boat races and eat zong zi in honor of this patriotic poet, Qu Yuan.

Match: Dragon Boat Festival
配一配：端午节

Match the words in Column A with the words in Column B:

(Column A)

龙舟比赛

爱国诗人

治理国家

不同意

战乱

读书人

罢免

粽子

从此

建议

(Column B)

remove from office

chaos and wars

dragon boat races

from this date on

suggest

rice dumplings wrapped with bamboo or reed leaves

is not agreeable

scholar

govern the country

Qu Yuan

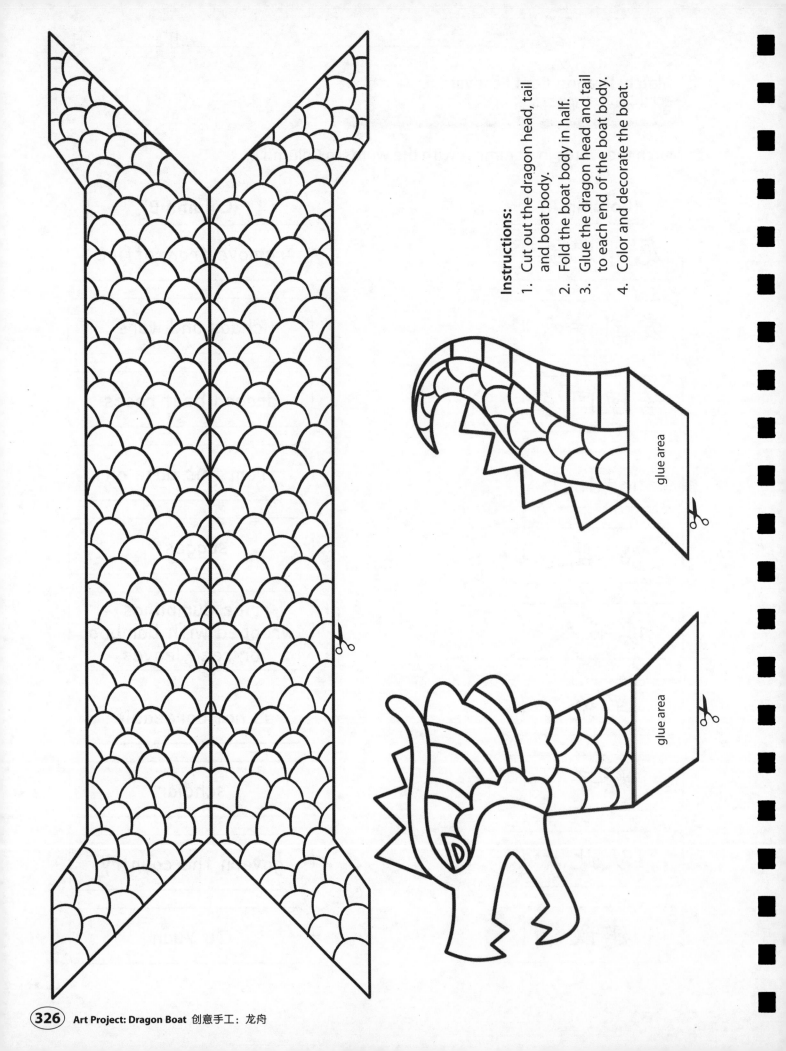

Instructions:

1. Cut out the dragon head, tail and boat body.
2. Fold the boat body in half.
3. Glue the dragon head and tail to each end of the boat body.
4. Color and decorate the boat.

glue area

glue area

Let's Talk: Hobbies and Sports
说一说：爱好和运动

Dialogue 1

(A) nǐ xǐ huan zuò shén me xiū xián huó dòng
你喜欢做什么休闲活动？

(B) wǒ xǐ huan pǎo bù   nǐ e
我喜欢跑步。你呢？

(A) wǒ xǐ huan dǎ qiú
我喜欢打球。

(B) wǒ yě xǐ huan dǎ qiú
我也喜欢打球。

(A) hǎo jí le   míng tiān wǒ men yì qǐ qù dǎ qiú   zěn me yàng
好极了。明天我们一起去打球，怎么样？

(B) hǎo a   míng tiān jiàn
好啊，明天见！

Dialogue 2

(A) nǐ zuì xǐ huan shén
你最喜欢什
me yùn dòng
么运动？

(B) wǒ zuì xǐ huan dǎ lán qiú
我最喜欢打篮球。

(A) nǐ zuì bù xǐ huan   tǎo yàn
你最不喜欢（讨厌）
shén me yùn dòng
什么运动？

(B) wǒ zuì bù xǐ huan   tǎo yàn
我最不喜欢（讨厌）

_____。

Dialogue 3

(A) xià tiān kě yǐ zuò shén me
夏天可以做什么
yùn dòng
运动？

(B) xià tiān kě yǐ
夏天可以

_____。

(A) dōng tiān kě yǐ zuò shén me
冬天可以做什么
yùn dòng
运动？

(B) dōng tiān kě yǐ
冬天可以

_____。

327

Let's Write!
写一写

jiāng big river	江	江		
hé river	河	河		
yù jade	玉	玉		
shí stone	石	石		
yī clothes	衣	衣		
dāo knife	刀	刀		

七 月
July

七月 · July

年

xīng qī rì 星期日	xīng qī yī 星期一	xīng qī èr 星期二	xīng qī sān 星期三	xīng qī sì 星期四	xīng qī wǔ 星期五	xīng qī liù 星期六

What's Happening in July?
七月知多少？

_{jīn tiān shì} _{yuè} _{rì}
1. 今天是 ＿＿＿＿＿ 月 ＿＿＿＿＿ 日。

_{míng tiān shì} _{yuè} _{rì}
2. 明天是 ＿＿＿＿＿ 月 ＿＿＿＿＿ 日。

_{hòu tiān shì} _{yuè} _{rì}
3. 后天是 ＿＿＿＿＿ 月 ＿＿＿＿＿ 日。

_{zuó tiān shì xīng qī}
4. 昨天是星期 ＿＿＿＿＿＿＿＿＿＿＿＿＿＿＿＿＿。

_{qián tiān shì xīng qī}
5. 前天是星期 ＿＿＿＿＿＿＿＿＿＿＿＿＿＿＿＿＿。

_{qī yuè yí gòng yǒu} _{tiān}
6. 七月一共有 ＿＿＿＿＿＿＿＿＿＿＿＿＿＿ 天。

_{qī yuè zhōng tè bié de rì zi shì}
7. 七月中特别的日子是 ＿＿＿＿＿＿＿＿＿＿＿＿＿。

_{qī yuè de tiān qì hěn}
8. 七月的天气很 ＿＿＿＿＿＿＿＿＿＿＿＿＿＿＿＿。

_{qī yuè shí wǔ rì de yì xīng qī hòu shì} _{yuè} _{rì}
9. 七月十五日的一星期后是 ＿＿＿ 月 ＿＿＿＿＿ 日。

_{de shēng rì shì} _{yuè} _{rì}
10. ＿＿＿＿＿＿＿＿＿＿＿＿＿ 的生日是 ＿＿＿ 月 ＿＿＿＿＿ 日。
(a person's name)

yān huǒ
烟火

měi guó
美国

guó qí
国旗

qī yuè sì rì
七月四日

zì yóu nǚ shén
自由女神

yóu xíng
游行
parade

rè gǒu
热狗

lǎo yīng
老鹰
eagle

yě cān
野餐
picnic

Match and Write: Independence Day
连一连，写一写：美国独立日

Draw a line to match the characters in Column A with those in Column B to make new words. Then write the pinyin and meaning for each.

Column A	Column B	pinyin	meaning
1. 美 •	• 狗 →	_____	_____
2. 自由 •	• 旗 →	_____	_____
3. 烟 •	• 鹰 →	_____	_____
4. 热 •	• 四日 →	_____	_____
5. 老 •	• 国 →	_____	_____
6. 国 •	• 女神 →	_____	_____
7. 七月 •	• 行 →	_____	_____
8. 野 •	• 餐 →	_____	_____
9. 游 •	• 火 →	_____	_____

Word Search: Independence Day
找一找：美国独立日

Find and circle each of the words listed below the puzzle, then write the English meaning for each word in the space provided.

o	u	c	g	x	y	n	o	g	i	a	q	u
m	e	i	g	u	o	i	m	e	r	u	l	y
y	q	x	o	h	o	n	y	t	i	a	a	h
g	a	m	y	q	c	q	x	r	e	g	o	u
n	i	o	t	g	r	t	i	u	o	r	y	r
h	r	y	u	o	a	s	h	q	a	r	i	g
g	y	o	i	q	e	x	u	i	g	a	n	e
a	r	u	t	u	b	r	n	g	y	u	g	g
n	g	x	y	i	m	h	s	r	i	h	o	r
u	o	i	a	e	a	g	t	u	s	n	c	a
t	q	n	g	a	c	x	q	r	y	a	u	x
h	t	g	y	o	n	a	o	g	r	y	m	i
g	i	s	u	i	g	q	n	r	y	o	s	h

1. lǎo yīng ＿＿＿＿＿＿＿＿＿

2. guō qí ＿＿＿＿＿＿＿＿＿

3. yān huǒ ＿＿＿＿＿＿＿＿＿

4. qī yuè sì rì ＿＿＿＿＿＿＿

5. rè gǒu ＿＿＿＿＿＿＿＿＿

6. yě cān ＿＿＿＿＿＿＿＿＿

7. měi guó ＿＿＿＿＿＿＿＿＿

8. yóu xíng ＿＿＿＿＿＿＿＿＿

Coloring: National Day around the World
涂颜色：世界各国的国庆节

Color the flags below and write the dates of each country's national day in Chinese. Draw your own country flag in the empty box and fill in the date of your country's national day in Chinese.

_____月_____日   _____月_____日

_____月_____日   _____月_____日

(Draw a flag of your choice.)

_____月_____日   _____月_____日

Note: Students are encouraged to do online search for this activity. Refer to the answers in Notes for Teachers on p. 61.

Write, Draw, Color: My Country's National Day
写一写，画一画，涂一涂：我的国庆节

Fill in the blanks in Chinese characters and in English.

nǐ hǎo   wǒ jiào
1. 你好。我叫_____。

Hello. My name is _____.

wǒ zhù zài
2. 我住在_____。 (name of country)

I live in _____.

wǒ de guó qìng jié shì   yuè   rì
3. 我的国庆节是_____月_____日。

My country's national day is on _____.

wǒ de guó qí de yán sè yǒu   sè
4. 我的国旗的颜色有_____色。

The colors of my country's flag are _____.

Draw and color your country's flag below.

京剧是中国优美的艺术形式之一。京剧中有四种重要角色——生：男主角；旦：女主角；净：英雄及武士角色；丑：动作表情引人发笑的角色。

京剧中的角色各有不同的服装、脸谱和表演动作。

红色代表忠实，黄色代表狂野，绿色代表勇敢，蓝色代表英勇，白色代表阴险，黑色代表正直，金银色代表神灵和鬼怪。

京剧结合了说、唱、表演和武打的艺术。表演时以中国传统乐器伴奏。

Jīng jù shì zhōng guó yōu měi de yì shù xíng shì zhī yī. Jīng jù zhōng yǒu sì zhǒng zhòng yào jué sè — shēng: nán zhǔ jué; dàn: nǚ zhǔ jué; jìng: yīng xióng jí wǔ shì jué sè; chǒu: dòng zuò biǎo qíng yǐn rén fā xiào de jué sè.

Jīng jù zhōng de jué sè gè yǒu bù tóng de fú zhuāng, liǎn pǔ hé biǎo yǎn dòng zuò.

Hóng sè dài biǎo zhōng shí, huáng sè dài biǎo kuáng yě, lù sè dài biǎo yǒng gǎn, lán sè dài biǎo yīng yǒng, bái sè dài biǎo yīn xiǎn, hēi sè dài biǎo zhèng zhí, jīn yín sè dài biǎo shén líng hé guǐ guài.

Jīng jù jié hé le shuō, chàng, biǎo yǎn hé wǔ dǎ de yì shù. Biǎo yǎn shí yǐ zhōng guó chuán tǒng yuè qì bàn zòu.

Peking Opera is a popular art form in China. There are four main roles: Sheng (leading male roles), Dan (leading female roles), Jing (heroes and warriors), and Chou (clown-like roles).

The performers all have their special costumes, make-up and movements. Audience members can easily identify the good or evil characters on stage by the colors and designs on their painted faces. Here is a general explanation of what the colors represent:

- Red: loyal, honest
- Yellow: wild, angry
- Green: brave, stable
- Blue: fearless
- White: dangerous, tricky
- Black: moral, just
- Gold/Silver: for gods and ghosts

Peking Opera combines recital, singing, acting and acrobatic fighting. It is also accompanied by traditional musical instruments.

sheng

生

dàn

旦

chǒu

丑

sūn wù kōng

孙悟空
Monkey King

jìng

净

jìng

净

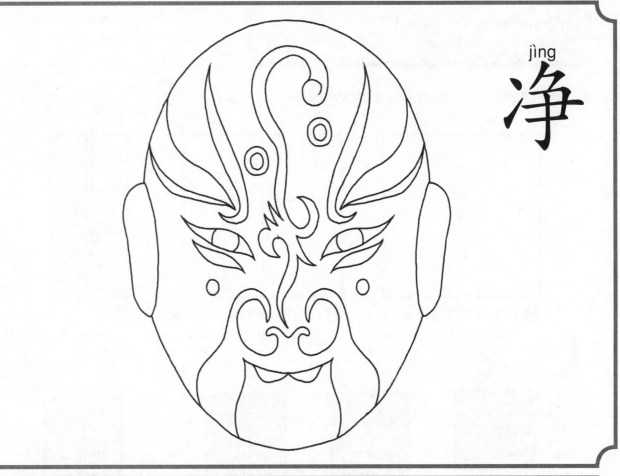

jìng

净

Origami Fun: Pinwheel
趣味折纸：风车

Follow these steps to make a pinwheel.

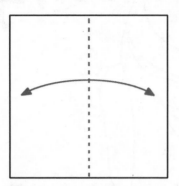

❶ Fold in half to make a crease and open again

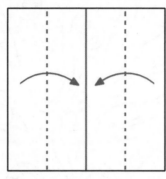

❷ Fold to meet the center line along the crease

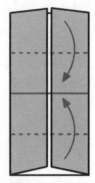

❸ Fold on the dotted lines towards the center

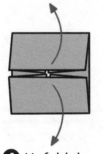

❹ Unfold these two folds

❺ Open the corners and fold forward on the dotted lines

❻ Open the ↑ and flatten

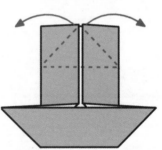

❼ Open the corner folds and flatten like figures 5 and 6

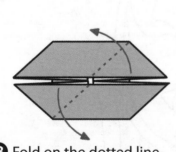

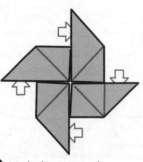

❽ Fold on the dotted line

❾ Lightly open the → part to make slight spaces

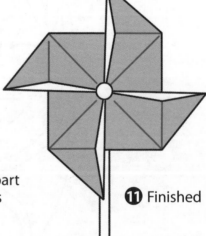

❿ Push a paper fastener or pin through the center and attach to a straw or disposable chopstick

⓫ Finished

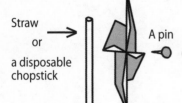

Straw or a disposable chopstick → A pin

fēng chē

风车 Pinwheel

Art Project: Tangram Fun
创意手工：七巧板

Cut out the seven pieces of the tangram and use them to create the following animals.

(qī qiǎo bǎn)
七巧板 Tangram

tù zi
兔子
rabbit

é
鹅
goose

sōng shǔ
松鼠
squirrel

gǒu
狗
dog

māo
猫
cat

yú
鱼
fish

niǎo
鸟
bird

è yú
鳄鱼
crocodile

名字：＿＿＿＿＿＿＿＿＿＿＿＿＿＿＿　＿＿＿＿月＿＿＿＿日

Art Project: Tangram Fun
创意手工：七巧板

zhè shì
这是＿＿＿＿＿＿＿＿＿＿＿＿。 (This is a ＿＿＿＿＿＿＿＿＿＿＿＿.)

tā shì wǒ de hǎo péng yǒu
它是我的好朋友。(It is my good friend.)

Reading: Chinese Calligraphy and Painting
读一读：中国书法和中国画

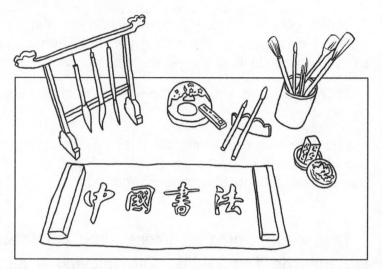

　　琴、棋、书、画是古代中国读书人必备的四种技艺。"书"和"画"离不开"文房四宝"，也就是笔、墨、纸、砚。

　　"书"就是书法，它不仅是书写文字而已，还是一种独特的表达思想的方式。我们可以从书法的风格来了解作者的性格和思想。

　　中国人一向认为好的画就像一首好的诗。所以我们常说"诗中有画，画中有诗。"以前很多人既是有名的画家，也是优秀的诗人和书法家。

　　中国画主要分为山水画、花鸟画和人物画三种。

　　书画作品上的题字和印章除了帮助我们辨识作者，了解作者的思想和感情之外，还可以当作书画作品的装饰，增加美感。

Qín, qí, shū, huà shì gǔ dài zhōng guó dú shū rén bì bèi de sì zhǒng jì yì. "Shū" hé "huà" lí bù kāi "wén fáng sì bǎo", yě jiù shì bǐ, mò, zhǐ, yàn.

"Shū" jiù shì shū fǎ, tā bù jǐn shì shū xiě wén zì ér yǐ, hái shì yì zhǒng dú tè de biǎo dá sī xiǎng de fāng shì. Wǒ men kě yǐ cóng shū fǎ de fēng gé lái liǎo jiě zuò zhě de xìng gé hé sī xiǎng.

Zhōng guó rén yí xiàng rèn wéi hǎo de huà jiù xiàng yì shǒu hǎo de shī. Suǒ yǐ wǒ men cháng shuō "Shī zhōng yǒu huà, huà zhōng yǒu shī." Yǐ qián hěn duō rén jì shì yǒu míng de huà jiā, yě shì yōu xiù de shī rén hé shū fǎ jiā.

Zhōng guó huà zhǔ yào fēn wei shān shuǐ huà, huā niǎo huà hé rén wù huà sān zhǒng.

Shū huà zuò pǐn shang de tí zì hé yìn zhāng chú le bāng zhù wǒ men biàn shí zuò zhě, liǎo jiě zuò zhě de sī xiǎng hé gǎn qíng zhī wài, hái kě yǐ dāng zuò shū huà zuò pǐn de zhuāng shì, zēng jiā měi gǎn.

In ancient China, scholars were expected to master the four skills: Qin (playing a musical instrument), Qi (playing chess), Shu (calligraphy), and Hua (painting). To become successful in the disciplines of calligraphy and painting, it was necessary for scholars to have "Wenfang Si Bao", which translates to "Four Treasures of the Study". These four treasures are Chinese writing brush, paper, inkstick and inkstone.

"Shu" refers to Chinese calligraphy, which is more than just a way of writing Chinese characters. It is a unique art form of expression and self discipline. The artist's personality, emotions, and way of thinking are all revealed in this special art form.

In China they say that a good painting is a good poem and vice versa. In other words, there is painting in poetry and poetry in painting. In ancient China many great artists were also great poets. The three major categories in Chinese painting are landscapes, flowers and birds, and figure portraits.

Most Chinese calligraphy and paintings include an inscription and seal by the artist which adds to the decorative beauty of the artwork.

Fill in the Blanks: Four Treasures of the Study
填空：文房四宝

Fill in the blanks using the words provided.

bù jǐn	zhǐ	xìng gé	bì bèi de	huà zhōng yǒu shī	bǐ
不仅	纸	性格	必备的	画中有诗	笔
sī xiǎng	rén wù huà	ér yǐ	dú tè de	chú le	zhī wài
思想	人物画	而已	独特的	除了	之外

1. 琴、棋、书、画是中国古代读书人＿＿＿＿＿＿四种技艺。

(qín、qí、shū、huà shì zhōng guó gǔ dài dú shū rén ＿＿ sì zhǒng jì yì。)

2. "文房四宝"就是＿＿＿＿、墨、＿＿＿＿、砚。

(wén fáng sì bǎo jiù shì ＿＿、mò、＿＿、yàn。)

3. 书法＿＿＿＿＿＿是书写文字＿＿＿＿＿＿，它还是一种

(shū fǎ ＿＿ shì shū xiě wén zì ＿＿，tā hái shì yì zhǒng)

＿＿＿＿＿＿表达思想的方式。

(＿＿ biǎo dá sī xiǎng de fāng shì。)

4. 我们可以从书法的风格来了解作者的＿＿＿＿＿＿和

(wǒ men kě yǐ cóng shū fǎ de fēng gé lái liǎo jiě zuò zhě de ＿＿ hé)

＿＿＿＿＿＿。

5. 所以我们常说"诗中有画，＿＿＿＿＿＿。"

(suǒ yǐ wǒ men cháng shuō shī zhōng yǒu huà，＿＿。)

6. 中国画主要分为山水画、花鸟画和＿＿＿＿＿＿三种。

(zhōng guó huà zhǔ yào fēn wéi shān shuǐ huà、huā niǎo huà hé ＿＿ sān zhǒng。)

7. 书画作品上的题字和印章＿＿＿＿＿＿帮助我们了解

(shū huà zuò pǐn shang de tí zì hé yìn zhāng ＿＿ bāng zhù wǒ men liǎo jiě)

作者的思想和感情＿＿＿＿＿＿，还可以当作书画作品

(zuò zhě de sī xiǎng hé gǎn qíng ＿＿，hái kě yǐ dāng zuò shū huà zuò pǐn)

的装饰，增加美感。

(de zhuāng shì，zēng jiā měi gǎn。)

（一）造句 Making sentences

不仅……而已，还……

1. 书法不仅是书写文字而已，它还是一种独特的表达思想的方式。

2. 马克不仅会说英语和西班牙语而已，他还会说中文。

3. ＿＿＿＿＿＿＿＿＿＿＿＿＿＿＿＿＿＿＿＿＿＿＿＿＿＿＿＿＿

＿＿＿＿＿＿＿＿＿＿＿＿＿＿＿＿＿＿＿＿＿＿＿＿＿＿＿＿＿＿＿

除了……之外，还……

1. 书画作品上的题字和印章除了帮助我们辨识作者之外，还可以当作书画作品的装饰，增加美感。

2. 学中文除了可以帮助我们认识中国人之外，还可以帮助我们了解中国文化。

3. ＿＿＿＿＿＿＿＿＿＿＿＿＿＿＿＿＿＿＿＿＿＿＿＿＿＿＿＿＿

＿＿＿＿＿＿＿＿＿＿＿＿＿＿＿＿＿＿＿＿＿＿＿＿＿＿＿＿＿＿＿

（二）简答题 (Write your answers in pinyin or characters.)

1. 什么是古代中国读书人必备的四种技艺？
   What are the four skills required of ancient Chinese scholars?

   ＿＿＿＿＿＿、＿＿＿＿＿＿、＿＿＿＿＿＿、＿＿＿＿＿＿。

2. 什么是"文房四宝"？ What are the "Four Treasures of the Study"?

   ＿＿＿＿＿＿、＿＿＿＿＿＿、＿＿＿＿＿＿、＿＿＿＿＿＿。

3. 中国画主要分为哪三种？
   What are the three major categories of Chinese painting?

   ＿＿＿＿＿＿、＿＿＿＿＿＿、＿＿＿＿＿＿。

4. 为什么中国书画作品上常有题字和印章？ Why are
   inscriptions and seals usually included in the artwork of Chinese calligraphy and painting?

   ＿＿＿＿＿＿＿＿＿＿＿＿＿＿＿＿＿＿＿＿＿＿＿＿＿＿＿＿＿＿

   ＿＿＿＿＿＿＿＿＿＿＿＿＿＿＿＿＿＿＿＿＿＿＿＿＿＿＿＿＿＿

Let's Talk: Nationalities and Countries
说一说：国籍与国家

Dialogue 1

(A) nǐ shì nǎ guó rén
你是哪国人？

(B) wǒ shì měi guó rén   nǐ ne
我是美国人？你呢？

(A) wǒ shì zhōng guó rén   dàn shì wǒ zhù zài měi guó
我是中国人。但是我住在美国。

(B) nà nǐ huì shuō zhōng wén ma
那你会说中文吗？

(A) dāng rán huì   wǒ huì shuō zhōng wén   yě huì shuō yīng wén
当然会！我会说中文，也会说英文。

(B) nǐ zhēn bàng
你真棒！

Dialogue 2

(A) zhōng guó zài nǎr
中国在哪儿？

(B) zhōng guó zài yà zhōu
中国在亚洲。

(A) mò xī gē zài nǎr
墨西哥在哪儿？

(B) mò xī gē zài zhōng nán měi zhōu
墨西哥在中南美洲。

(A) ào dà lì yà zài nǎr
澳大利亚在哪儿？

(B) ào dà lì yà zài
澳大利亚在

＿＿＿＿＿＿＿＿＿＿＿＿。

Dialogue 3

(A) nǐ qù guò zhōng guó ma
你去过中国吗？

(B) cóng lái méi yǒu   dàn shì wǒ hěn xiǎng qù
从来没有。但是我很想去。

(A) nǐ xiǎng qù zhōng guó de nǎ xiē dì fang
你想去中国的哪些地方？

(B) wǒ xiǎng qù
我想去＿＿＿＿＿＿＿＿＿、

hé
和＿＿＿＿＿＿＿。

名字：＿＿＿＿＿＿＿＿＿　＿＿月＿＿日

Let's Write!
写一写

zú 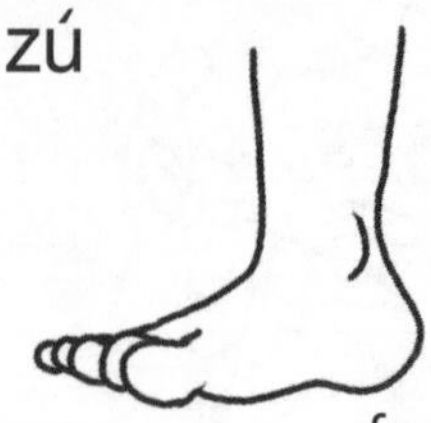 / foot	足	足		
shēn 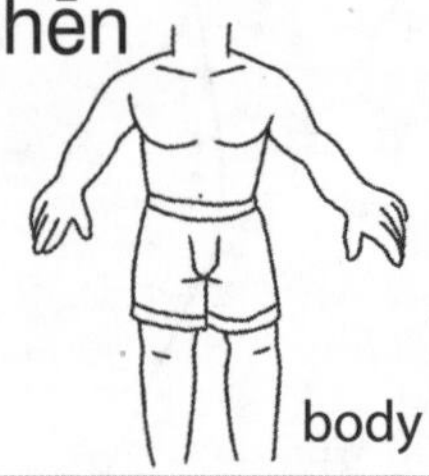 / body	身	身		
dòu 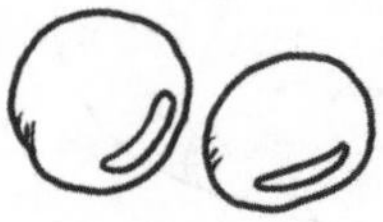 / beans	豆	豆		
cǎo  / grass	草	草		
chóng  / worm	虫	虫		
niǎo  / bird	鸟	鸟		

350

八月
August

shǔ 暑假
jiǎ

hǎi tān 海滩

August 八月

年 _____

xīng qī rì 星期日	xīng qī yī 星期一	xīng qī èr 星期二	xīng qī sān 星期三	xīng qī sì 星期四	xīng qī wǔ 星期五	xīng qī liù 星期六

What's Happening in August?
八月知多少？

jīn tiān shì   yuè   rì
1. 今天是_____月_____日。

míng tiān shì   yuè   rì
2. 明天是_____月_____日。

hòu tiān shì   yuè   rì
3. 后天是_____月_____日。

zuó tiān shì xīng qī
4. 昨天是星期_____。

qián tiān shì xīng qī
5. 前天是星期_____。

bā yuè yí gòng yǒu   tiān
6. 八月一共有_____天。

bā yuè zhōng tè bié de rì zi shì
7. 八月中特别的日子是_____。

bā yuè de tiān qì hěn
8. 八月的天气很_____。

bā yuè shí wǔ rì de yì xīng qī qián shì   yuè   rì
9. 八月十五日的一星期前是____月____日。

de shēng rì shì   yuè   rì
10. _____的生日是____月____日。
    (a person's name)

huá chuán 划船	yě cān 野餐	lù yíng 露营
hǎi tān 海滩	dǎ bàng qiú 打棒球	lǚ xíng 旅行 travel
qí chē 骑车	diào yú 钓鱼	chōng làng 冲浪

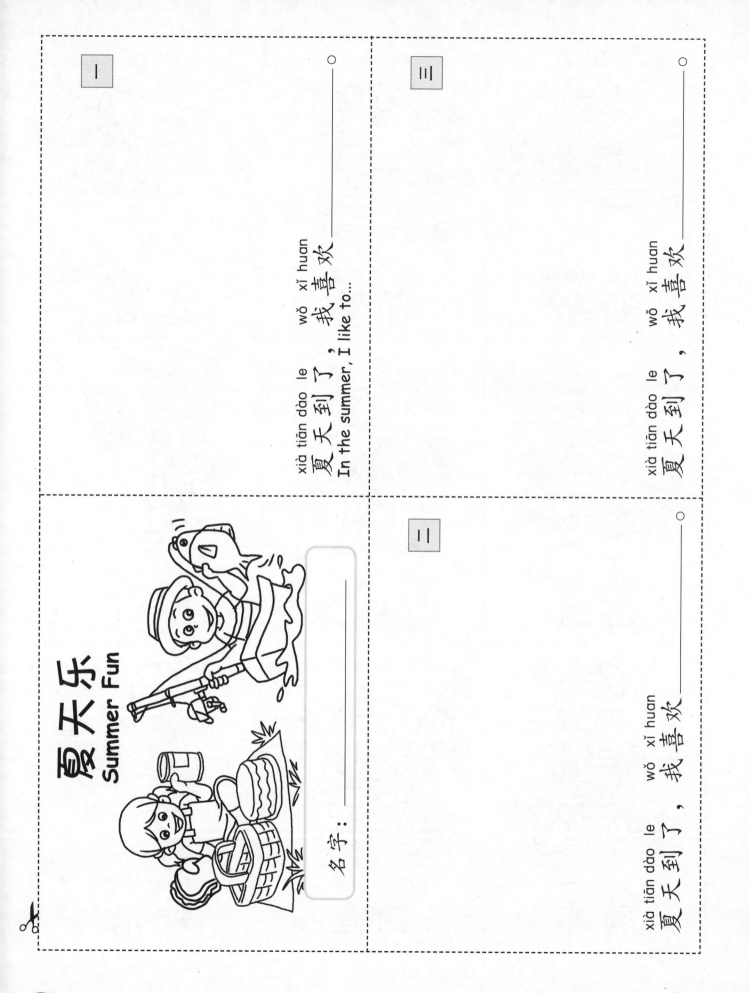

一

xià tiān dào le　　wǒ xǐ huan
夏天到了，我喜欢
In the summer, I like to...

三

xià tiān dào le　　wǒ xǐ huan
夏天到了，我喜欢

二

xià tiān dào le　　wǒ xǐ huan
夏天到了，我喜欢

夏天乐
Summer Fun

名字：

tài yáng 太阳	shā 沙	bèi ké 贝壳
hǎi ōu 海鸥	hǎi làng 海浪	jiù shēng yuán 救生员
chéng bǎo 城堡	kǎo ròu 烤肉	shài tài yáng 晒太阳

名字：＿＿＿＿＿＿＿＿＿＿＿＿＿＿＿＿＿＿ ＿＿＿＿月＿＿＿＿日

Read and Circle: At the Beach
读一读，圈一圈：在海滩

Circle the word that matches the picture on the left.

	hǎi ōu　　hǎi làng　　bèi ké 海鸥　　海浪　　贝壳
	chéng bǎo　　kǎo ròu　　tài yáng 城堡　　烤肉　　太阳
	hǎi làng　　jiù shēng yuán　　shài tài yáng 海浪　　救生员　　晒太阳
	hǎi làng　　hǎi ōu　　hǎi tān 海浪　　海鸥　　海滩
	tài yáng　　kǎo ròu　　bèi ké 太阳　　烤肉　　贝壳
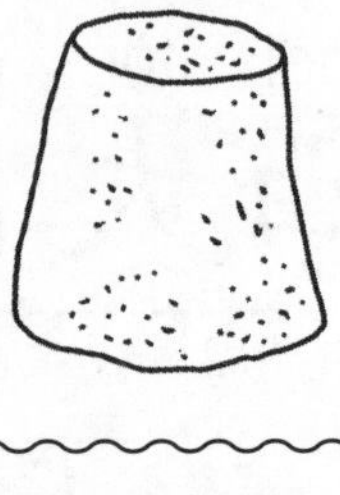	shā　　hǎi　　làng 沙　　海　　浪

tài yáng yǎn jìng 太 阳 眼 镜	máo jīn 毛 巾	hǎi tān sǎn 海 滩 伞
tuō xié 拖 鞋	fáng shài yóu 防 晒 油	yóu yǒng yī 游 泳 衣
shuǐ tǒng 水 桶	chōng làng bǎn 冲 浪 板	chǎn zi 铲 子

Read and Circle: Beach Words
读一读，圈一圈：海滩词语

Circle the word that matches the picture.

chǎn zi
铲 子

hǎi tān sǎn
海 滩 伞

chōng làng bǎn
冲 浪 板

hǎi làng
海 浪

máo jīn
毛 巾

tuō xié
拖 鞋

chéng bǎo
城 堡

bèi ké
贝 壳

tài yáng
太 阳

fáng shài yóu
防 晒 油

tài yáng yǎn jìng
太 阳 眼 镜

hǎi làng
海 浪

hǎi ōu
海 鸥

bèi ké
贝 壳

kǎo ròu
烤 肉

tuō xié
拖 鞋

shā
沙

shuǐ tǒng
水 桶

yóu yǒng yī
游 泳 衣

kǎo ròu
烤 肉

chéng bǎo
城 堡

bèi ké
贝 壳

jiù shēng yuán
救 生 员

chōng làng bǎn
冲 浪 板

Guess and Write: What Is That?
猜一猜，写一写：那是什么？

Use words from the word bank to fill in the blanks.

chōng làng bǎn	kǎo ròu	jiù shēng yuán
冲浪板	烤肉	救生员
shài tài yáng	yóu yǒng yī	hǎi tān
晒太阳	游泳衣	海滩
hǎi ōu	chǎn zi	tài yáng yǎn jìng
海鸥	铲子	太阳眼镜

1. The shore along the sea.

2. To cook outdoors.

3. A tool you need to build sandcastles.

4. Expose your body to the sun.

5. An object you wear to block the sunlight.

6. Use it for surfing.

7. A bird that lives by the sea.

8. A person who rescues swimmers in the ocean.

9. You wear it when you swim.

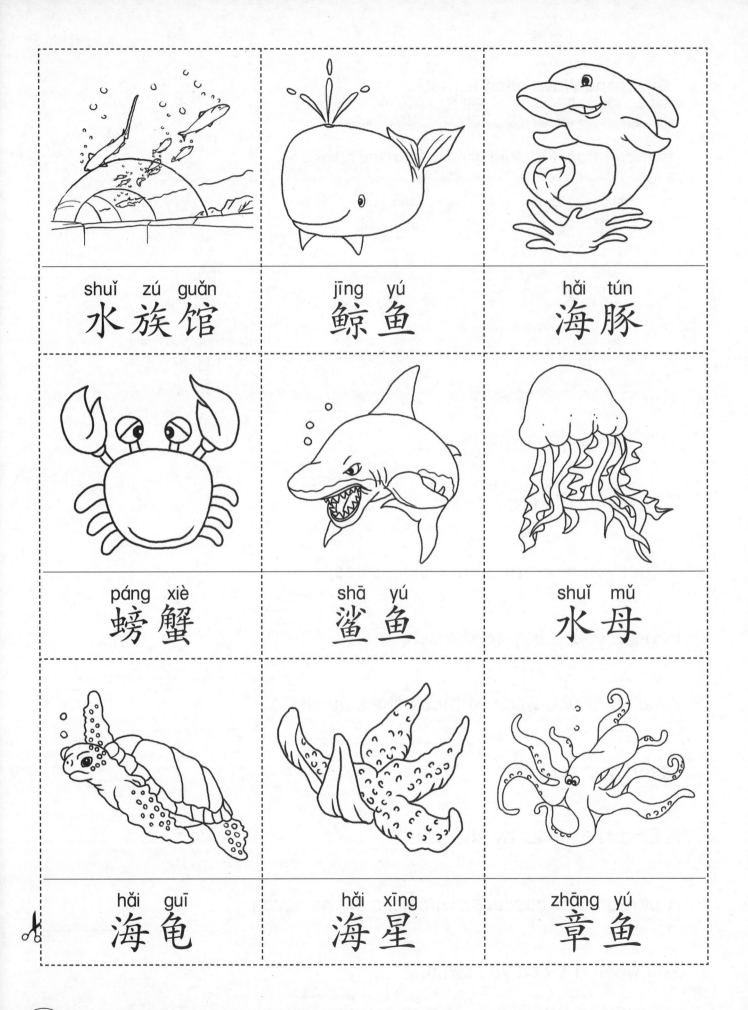

shuǐ zú guǎn 水族馆	jīng yú 鲸鱼	hǎi tún 海豚
páng xiè 螃蟹	shā yú 鲨鱼	shuǐ mǔ 水母
hǎi guī 海龟	hǎi xīng 海星	zhāng yú 章鱼

名字：_____   _____月_____日

Combine two of the single characters in the boxes to make up the names of different sea animals.

lóng	hǎi	yú	guī	jīng	zhāng
龙	海	鱼	龟	鲸	章
mǔ	xiā	shuǐ	xīng	tún	shā
母	虾	水	星	豚	鲨

Draw a picture of each sea animal and label them in the spaces provided.

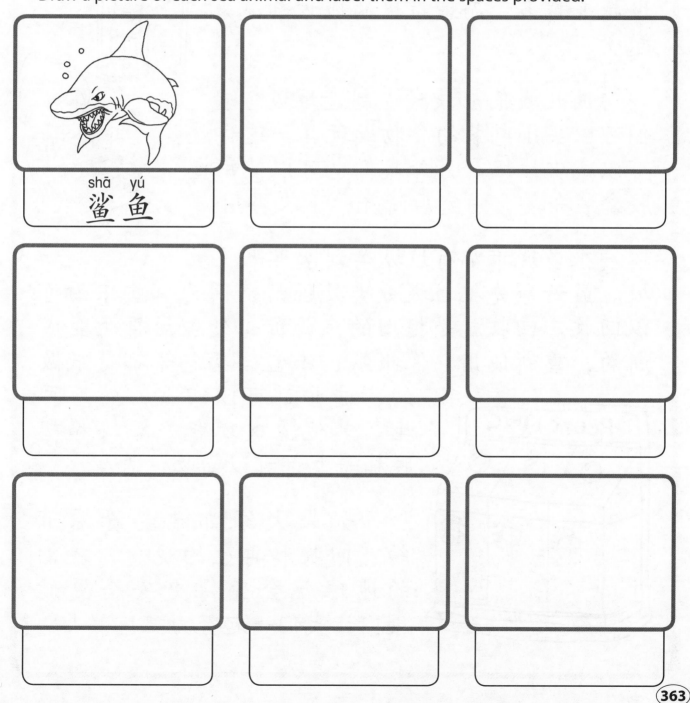

shā yú
鲨鱼

363

Reading: Reduce, Reuse, Recycle
读一读：资源的节约、再生和回收

　　我们每天制造很多垃圾。你知道这些垃圾都到哪里去了呢？它们都被丢到垃圾场埋起来。很多人不喜欢住在垃圾场附近。可是我们制造的垃圾越来越多，而埋垃圾的地方却越来越少。

　　因此我们应该减少制造垃圾。我们可以买小包装的食物或玩具，这样就可以减少垃圾。另外我们也可以使用塑胶盒装午餐，用完后清洗，下次再用。

　　很多城市都有垃圾车到家里来收垃圾。最好事先把垃圾分类处理好，因为有些东西可以回收。回收就是把旧的东西加工处理后再生变成新的，重新使用。像报纸、纸盒、杂志等都是纸做的，这些都可以回收，然后再生。其他像玻璃瓶、罐头和塑胶桶等也都可以回收、再生。

　　如果大家都学会资源节约、回收和再生的观念，我们的地球就会变得更安全更健康！让我们一起努力吧！

Wǒ men měi tiān zhì zào hěn duō lā jī. Nǐ zhī dào zhè xiē lā jī dōu dào nǎ li qù le ne? Tā men dōu bèi diū dào lā jī chǎng mái qǐ lai. Hěn duō rén bù xǐ huan zhù zài lā jī chǎng fù jìn. Kě shì wǒ men zhì zào de lā jī yuè lái yuè duō, ér mái lā jī de dì fang què yuè lái yuè shǎo.

Yīn cǐ wǒ men yīng gāi jiǎn shǎo zhì zào lā jī. Wǒ men kě yǐ mǎi xiǎo bāo zhuāng de shí wù huò wán jù, zhè yàng jiù kě yǐ jiǎn shǎo lā jī. Lìng wài wǒ men yě kě yǐ shǐ yòng sù jiāo hé zhuāng wǔ cān, yòng wán hòu qīng xǐ, xià cì zài yòng.

Hěn duō chéng shì dōu yǒu lā jī chē dào jiā li lái shōu lā jī. Zuì hǎo shì xiān bǎ lā jī fēn lèi chú lǐ hǎo, yīn wèi yǒu xiē dōng xi kě yǐ huí shōu. Huí shōu jiù shì bǎ jiù de dōng xi jiā gōng chǔ lǐ hòu zài shēng biàn chéng xīn de, chóng xīn shǐ yòng. Xiàng bào zhǐ, zhǐ zhāng, zá zhì děng dōu shì zhǐ zuò de, zhè xiē dōu kě yǐ huí shōu, rán hòu zài shēng. Qí tā xiàng bō li píng, guàn tou hé sù jiāo tǒng děng yě dōu kě yǐ huí shōu, zài shēng.

Rú guǒ dà jiā dōu xué huì zī yuán jié yuē, huí shōu hé zài shēng de guān niàn, wǒ men de dì qiú jiù huì biàn de gèng ān quán gèng jiàn kāng! Ràng wǒ men yì qǐ nǔ lì ba!

We produce garbage every day. Do you know where all of our garbage goes? It goes to landfills. A landfill is a place where garbage is dumped and buried. Most people do not want to live near landfills. But, as we produce more garbage, there are fewer places to bury it.

Therefore, we should find ways to reduce the amount of garbage we produce. We can buy foods and toys that come in smaller packages to reduce our garbage. We can also pack our lunch in plastic containers that can be washed and used again.

In many towns and cities, garbage trucks go to homes to pick up garbage. It is best to sort your garbage so that some of it can be recycled. Recycle means to make old things into new things that can be used again. Newspapers, boxes, magazines and many other things are made of paper that can be recycled and used again. Other items such as bottles, jars, cans, and plastic containers can also be recycled and reused.

If we all learn to reduce, reuse, and recycle, the earth will be a safer and healthier place to live. Let's work together to make this happen!

Circle: True or False?
圈一圈：对不对？

Read each sentence and circle the correct answer.

	duì　　bí duì

1. lí kāi fáng jiān shí guān dēng
离开房间时关灯。
Turn off the light when you leave the room.
对 / 不对

2. yòng zhǐ dài zhuāng wǔ cān hé shuǐ píng
用纸袋装午餐和水瓶。
Bring lunch in a paper bag and a new bottle of water every day.
对 / 不对

3. bái zhǐ liǎng miàn yìn shuā
白纸两面印刷。
Print on both sides of the paper.
对 / 不对

4. mǎi dà bāo zhuāng wán jù
买大包装玩具。
Buy toys in big packages.
对 / 不对

5. bǎ lā jī fēn lèi
把垃圾分类。
Sort out the garbage.
对 / 不对

6. huí shōu jiù yī hé xié zi
回收旧衣和鞋子
Recycle old clothes and shoes.
对 / 不对

7. zài hǎi tān shang luàn diū lā jī
在海滩上乱丢垃圾。
Throw garbage on the beach.
对 / 不对

8. yòng shuǐ píng jiā xīn shuǐ
用水瓶加新水。
Refill water in a reusable water bottle.
对 / 不对

9. wǔ cān shǐ yòng yí cì xìng cān jù
午餐使用一次性餐具。
Pack lunch with disposable plates and spoons.
对 / 不对

10. huí shōu bō li zhǐ bǎn guàn tou hé píng guàn
回收玻璃、纸板、罐头和瓶罐。
Recycle glass, cardboard, cans and jars.
对 / 不对

11. jìn kě néng zǒu lù shàng xué
尽可能走路上学。
Walk to school if you can.
对 / 不对

12. bǎ niú nǎi píng diū jìn lā jī tǒng
把牛奶瓶丢进垃圾桶。
Throw the milk container in the garbage can.
对 / 不对

　　早在哥伦布发现美洲新大陆约60年以前，中国明代的郑和已经完成七次到非洲和亚洲的海上探险航行。

　　郑和生在云南的回族家庭。他的祖父和父亲都曾去过麦加。郑和从小就喜欢听航海探险的故事，尤其是神秘的阿拉伯故事和马可波罗游记。

　　郑和十二岁时，就被明朝的军队抓去当太监。不久他被送到皇宫当侍卫，后来成为明成祖的大将，被尊称为"三宝太监"。因为他很聪明又有战功，明成祖很信任他，派他到国外推广外交，宣传中国文化。

　　从1405到1433的二十八年期间，郑和带领了一支庞大的"宝船"舰队向西洋航行七次，横越中国海、红海和印度洋，并在第四次航行时到达最远的非洲东岸。他的舰队包括了两百多艘船和两万八千个船员、士兵、技术员和翻译员等。郑和到访了三十个国家并且赠送了很多丝绸、茶叶、金银和瓷器等礼物。郑和也带了很多西方国家的香料、象牙、药品、珍珠和珍奇的动物回中国。

　　在那期间，外国很多国王、使节和商人纷纷来中国加强合作关系。此外，郑和七次下西洋也大大地推动了全世界的航海事业。郑和下西洋比哥伦布发现美洲早了87年，比麦哲伦航行到东南亚早了116年。

Zǎo zài Gē Lún Bù fā xiàn měi zhōu xīn dà lù yuē liù shí nián yǐ qián, zhōng guó míng dài de Zhèng Hé yǐ jīng wán chéng qī cì dào fēi zhōu hé yà zhōu de hǎi shang tàn xiǎn háng xíng.

Zhèng Hé shēng zài yún nán de huí zú jiā tíng. Tā de zǔ fù hé fù qīn dōu céng qù guò mài jiā. Zhèng Hé cóng xiǎo jiù xǐ huan tīng háng hǎi tàn xiǎn de gù shi, yóu qí shì shén mì de ā lā bó gù shi hé Mǎ Kě Bō Luó yóu jì.

Zhèng Hé shí èr suì shí, jiù bèi míng cháo de jūn duì zhuā qù dāng tài jiàn. Bù jiǔ tā bèi sòng dào huáng gōng dāng shì wèi, hòu lái chéng wéi Míng Chéng Zǔ de dà jiàng, bèi zūn chēng wéi "sān bǎo tài jiàn". Yīn wèi tā hěn cōng míng yòu yǒu zhàn gōng, Míng Chéng Zǔ hěn xìn rèn tā, pài tā dào guó wài tuī guǎng wài jiāo, xuān chuán zhōng guó wén huà.

Cóng yī sì líng wǔ dào yī sì sān sān de èr shí bā nián qī jiān, Zhèng Hé dài lǐng le yì zhī páng dà de "bǎo chuán" jiàn duì xiàng xī yáng háng xíng qī cì, héng yuè zhōng guó hǎi, hóng hǎi hé yìn dù yáng, bìng zài dì sì cì háng xíng shí dào dá zuì yuǎn de fēi zhōu dōng àn. Tā de jiàn duì bāo kuò le liǎng bǎi duō sōu chuán hé liǎng wàn bā qiān gè chuán yuán, shì bīng, jì shù yuán hé fān yì yuán děng. Zhèng Hé dào fǎng le sān shí gè guó jiā bìng qiě zèng sòng le hěn duō sī chóu, chá yè, jīn yín hé cí qì děng lǐ wù. Zhèng Hé yě dài le hěn duō xī fāng guó jiā de xiāng liào, xiàng yá, yào pǐn, zhēn zhū hé zhēn qí de dòng wù huí zhōng guó.

Zài nà qī jiān, wài guó hěn duō guó wáng, shǐ jié hé shāng rén fēn fēn lái zhōng guó jiā qiáng hé zuò guān xi. Cǐ wài, Zhèng Hé qī cì xià xī yáng yě dà dà de tuī dòng le quán shì jiè de háng hǎi shì yè. Zhèng Hé xià xī yáng bǐ Gē Lún Bù fā xiàn měi zhōu zǎo le bā shí qī nián, bǐ Mài Zhé Lún háng xíng dào dōng nán yà zǎo le yì bǎi yī shí liù nián.

About 60 years before Columbus discovered America, a Chinese explorer named Zheng He led seven voyages to explore Africa and Asia.

Zheng He was born in Yunnan province, China. He came from a Muslim family. Both his grandfather and father had made journeys to Mecca and Zheng He was fascinated by the tales of far away lands that he heard during his childhood. He loved to listen to mysterious Arabian stories and the adventures of Marco Polo.

When Zheng He was 12 years old, he was captured in an army attack. He was sent to work in the Imperial Court and eventually became an important advisor to Emperor Cheng Zu. He became known as "San Bao", which means "Three Jewels". Because of his high intelligence and achievements during battles, he won the trust of Emperor Cheng Zu and was chosen to lead diplomatic missions to the West.

For 28 years, from 1405 to 1433, Zheng He led a massive "Treasure Fleet" and traveled to the West seven times. On these voyages he crossed the China Sea, the Red Sea, the Indian Ocean, and even reached the east coast of Africa during his 4th voyage. His fleet consisted of more than 200 ships that carried 2,800 crewmen which included sailors, soldiers, engineers, and interpreters. Zheng He visited more than 30 countries and presented gifts of tea, silk, gold, silver, and porcelain from China. In return he received spices, ivory, medicines, pearls and rare animals to take back to China.

Zheng He's voyages were a great contribution to the progress of navigation in his time. During the time of his voyages many kings, ambassadors and businessmen traveled to China. It is noteworthy that his first voyage was completed 87 years before Columbus sailed to America and 116 years before Magellan's voyage to Southeast Asia.

Quiz: Zheng He
考考你：郑和

Answer the following questions.

zhèng hé xià xī yáng yí gòng jǐ cì

1. 郑和下西洋一共几次？
How many voyages did Zheng He make?

_____

zhèng hé wèi shén me yào xià xī yáng

2. 郑和为什么要下西洋？
Why did Zheng He make these voyages?

_____

zhèng hé zuì yuǎn dào dá shén me dì fang?   shì dì jǐ cì háng xíng dào dá de

3. 郑和最远到达什么地方？是第几次航行到达的？
Where is the farthest place that Zheng He visited? During which voyage did he visit this place?

_____

zhèng hé cóng zhōng guó dài shén me wù pǐn zuò wéi lǐ wù

4. 郑和从中国带什么物品作为礼物？
What gifts did Zheng He bring from China to the West?

_____

zhèng hé cóng wài guó dài huí shén me wù pǐn

5. 郑和从外国带回什么物品？
What did Zheng He bring back to China from his voyages?

_____

zhèng hé xià xī yáng duì shì jiè yǒu shén me gòng xiàn

6. 郑和下西洋对世界有什么贡献？
What was the most important contribution of Zheng He's voyages to the world?

_____

_____

Let's Talk!
说一说

Dialogue 1

nǐ xǐ huan qù hǎi tān ma
Ⓐ 你喜欢去海滩吗？
(Do you like to go to the beach?)

xǐ huan a
Ⓑ 喜欢啊！

nǐ hé shéi qù hǎi tān
Ⓐ 你和谁去海滩？

yǒu shí hou hé bà ba mā ma　　yǒu shí hou hé péng you
Ⓑ 有时候和爸爸妈妈，有时候和朋友。

nǐ men qù hǎi tān zuò xiē shén me
Ⓐ 你们去海滩做些什么？

wǒ men qù yóu yǒng　huá shuǐ huò shài tài yáng
Ⓑ 我们去游泳、滑水或晒太阳。

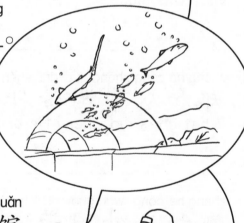

Dialogue 2

zhè gè shǔ jià nǐ yào qù nǎ li
Ⓐ 这个暑假你要去哪里？

wǒ bà ba mā ma yào dài wǒ qù shuǐ zú guǎn
Ⓑ 我爸爸妈妈要带我去水族馆。

qù shuǐ zú guǎn yào zuò shén me
Ⓐ 去水族馆要做什么？

wǒ men yào qù kàn shā yú hé hǎi tún
Ⓑ 我们要去看鲨鱼和海豚。

wǒ shǔ jià nǎr dōu bú qù　zhǐ huì dào péng you jiā kǎo ròu
Ⓐ 我暑假哪儿都不去，只会到朋友家烤肉。

nà yě bú cuò ya
Ⓑ 那也不错呀！

Let's Write!
写一写

jīn gold	金	金		
mén door	门	门		
bèi shellfish	贝	贝		
yán word	言	言		
shí food	食	食		
zhōu boat	舟	舟		

APPENDICES

❶ Answer Key for Word Search and Crossword Puzzles
字谜答案

1) Word Search: Zodiac Animals ❶
   找一找：生肖 一

(See p. 89)

2) Word Search: Zodiac Animals ❷
   找一找：生肖 二

1. 牛 : 6个   4. 龙 : 12个
2. 山羊 : 3个   5. 老虎 : 3个
3. 马 : 5个   6. 兔子 : 2个

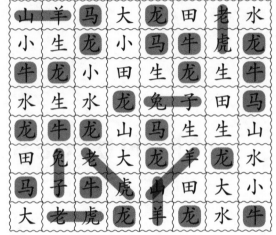

(See p. 90)

3) Word Search: Chinese New Year
   找一找：农历新年

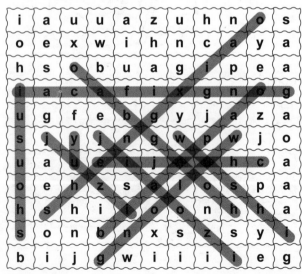

(See p. 99)

1) Word Search: Adjectives
   找一找：人物形容词

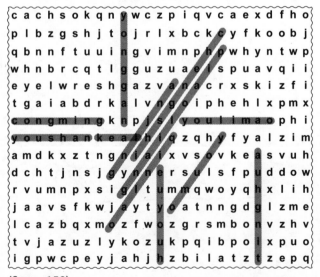

(See p. 159)

2) Crossword Challenge: Adjectives
填字谜：人物形容词

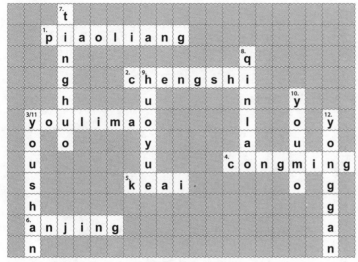

(See p. 160)

3) Word Search: Daily Activities
找一找：日常活动

(See p. 173)

March 三月

---

1) Word Search: Countries around the World
找一找：世界各国

1. měi guó/United States
2. zhōng guó/China
3. yì dà lì/Italy
4. fǎ guó/France
5. é luó sī/Russia
6. rì běn/Japan
7. dé guó/Germany
8. jiā ná dà/Canada
9. hán guó/South Korea
10. yīng guó/United Kingdom
11. mò xī gē/Mexico
12. ào dà lì yà/Australia

(See p. 188)

2) Crossword Puzzle: Landforms
填字谜：地形

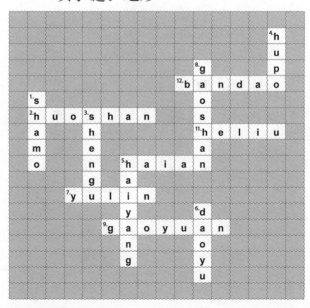

(See p. 193)

3) Word Search: My Community
找一找：我的社区

a	s	u	a	i	y	c	y	u	u	i	g	u	n	
g	o	n	g	a	n	j	u	g	a	g	g	a	z	
g	n	a	h	c	i	h	s	i	j	o	a	h	c	
h	a	n	a	g	x	d	u	j	y	w	u	a	e	
t	u	s	h	u	g	u	a	n	x	y	y	y	y	
x	y	g	n	y	n	g	e	n	x	h	h	i	u	
x	u	g	o	a	x	o	t	a	x	n	a	n	o	
g	n	j	u	g	h	i	a	y	h	u	u	y	u	
j	i	a	g	j	z	x	s	x	a	a	h	h	a	
j	y	n	n	a	g	y	g	n	o	g	o	n	u	
x	n	s	a	a	w	i	g	f	n	j	g	n	u	
a	a	g	c	a	u	n	y	y	u	n	i	n	n	
c	i	i	g	i	o	n	i	o	o	u	c	f	h	
c	d	o	u	j	g	n	a	f	o	a	i	x	a	

1. School
2. Police station
3. Hospital
4. Post Office
5. Movie Theater
6. Fire Station
7. Library
8. Park
9. Supermarket
10. Shopping mall
11. Bank
12. Restaurant

(See p. 202)

4) Word Search: Community Helpers
找一找：社会人士

						¹·j								
³·s						i						²·x		
h		⁴·k		n		n		⁵·y				i		
o		e		g		c		a				a		
u		x		c				y				o		
⁶·y	o	u	c	h	a	i						f		
i		e		a								a		
		j						⁷·c				n		
⁸·x	i	a	o	z	h	a	n	g						
								u				y		
								s				u		
		⁹·h	u	s	h	i						a		
¹⁰·l	a	o	s	h	i							n		

(See p. 203)

April 四月

1) Tang Poem: Qingming
唐诗：清明

清	**明**	**雨**	纷
行	人	断	魂
酒	家	何	处
遥	指	杏	村

清	明	雨
人	断	魂
问	酒	家
杏	花	村

雨	纷
断	魂
酒	家
杏	村

雨
魂
酒
村

（人） ：行人；牧童
（地） ：路上；酒家；杏花村
（时间）：清明

(See p. 250)

2) Crossword Puzzle: Chinese Inventions
填字谜：中国的发明

				¹·I	C	E	C	R	E	A	M	
	²·M	A	T	C	H	E	S					
				³·P	O	R	C	E	L	A	I	N
			⁴·P	A	P	E	R					
⁵·C	O	M	P	A	S	S						
	⁶·P	R	I	N	T	I	N	G				
			⁷·R	I	C	E						
	⁸·A	B	A	C	U	S						
			⁹·K	I	T	E						
¹⁰·S	U	N	G	L	A	S	S	E	S			

(See p. 256)

3) Word Search: Chinese Inventions
找一找：中国的发明

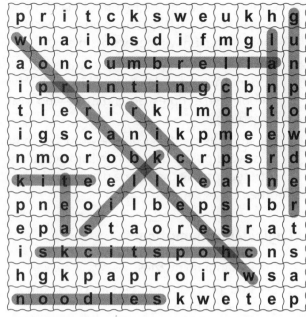

(See p. 257)

May 五月

1) Word Search: Chinese Food
找一找：中国菜

(See p. 280)

July 七月

1) Word Search: Independence Day
找一找：美国独立日

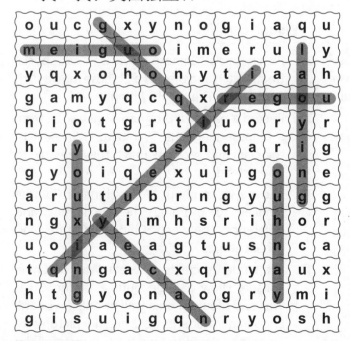

(See p. 335)

❷ 100 Ideas To Celebrate Foreign Language Month

Verbal/Linguistic

1. Let students send home a newsletter about recent topics covered in Chinese class.

2. Let students listen to a local Chinese radio station in class.

3. Request that a Chinese greeting be used as part of the school's daily announcements.

4. Make a homework assignment involving students teaching their family members a list of Chinese words or phrases.

5. Let students research on a topic related to China and make an oral presentation to the class.

6. Record a self-introduction by each student on audio tape or videotape.

7. Let students make up a skit in Chinese and perform it in front of the class.

8. Let students write a school lunch menu using Chinese characters.

9. Let students retell a popular children's story using simple phrases in Chinese.

10. Let students learn to use an online English–Chinese dictionary.

11. Let students make a bilingual picture word book.

12. Let students write an essay or journal in Chinese.

13. Let students practice writing Chinese characters with a Chinese calligraphy brush and rice paper. Make a Chinese character quilt with students' work.

14. Let students host or participate in an essay contest.

15. Let students host or participate in a poster contest.

16. Let students make up designs for different types of greeting cards in Chinese. Students can "order" copies to be printed from cards made by their classmates.

17. Let students host a Chinese poetry contest.

18. Let students participate in activities sponsored by foreign language organizations such as NYSALT.

19. Choose one day in the month of March to be "Speak Mandarin Day". Encourage students to speak Mandarin whenever possible.

20. Introduce a Chinese tongue twister to all students who are learning Chinese in the school. Hold a contest among those who wish to participate.

21. Let students create a Chinese word search or crossword puzzle using a familiar vocabulary list. Students can then share puzzles with each other.

Logical/Mathematical

22. Create tangram puzzles.

23. Let students count numbers and play number games in Chinese.

24. Make projects with numbers in Chinese.

25. Let students do math calculations with numbers in Chinese.

26. Let students find out the width and height of the Great Wall of China.

27. Let students figure out the zodiac animal signs of famous people by using their birth years.

28. Let students collect data to make a chart or pie graph on a topic taught in a Chinese lesson.

Visual/Spatial

29. Plan a special "Chinese Movie Day" as a special treat. Watch and discuss a Chinese movie such as Mulan or The Monkey King.

30. Record a part of a program or newscast from a Chinese language TV network. Show it to the class and see how much they are able to understand.

31. Show a video about life in China or Chinese families to examine the similarities and differences between Chinese culture and other cultures.

32. Let students create a Great Wall of China collage. Draw a large outline of the Great Wall and mount it on a wall or bulletin board. Encourage students to bring in pictures of anything related to Chinese culture to fill the wall and make a class collage.

33. Let students design a travel brochure about a city in China that includes colorful pictures of famous sites.

34. Let students paint a Chinese landscape painting with a calligraphy brush. Display students' work in a prominent place in the school.

35. Let students make and display labels for objects in the classroom.

36. Let students observe panda behaviors on websites that offer live panda cam views of pandas in zoos in the United States.

Bodily/Kinesthetic

37. Demonstrate how to cook an easy Chinese dish or how to make tea.

38. Let students plan a field trip to Chinatown, a local Chinese restaurant, or a museum that features some aspect of Chinese history or culture.

39. Let students build a model of the Great Wall of China using recycled materials such as cardboard boxes.

40. Invite a professional or find a parent volunteer to do a demonstration related to a Chinese cultural art.

41. Collaborate with the gym department to introduce popular Chinese games like table tennis, Chinese jump rope, Chinese yoyo and the shuttlecock.

42. Make a Chinese shuttlecock and host a Chinese shuttlecock contest.

43. Teach a lesson on how to use chopsticks and have a contest.

44. Introduce a traditional Chinese group game such as "The hawk catching the young chicks".

45. Teach a lesson on the ancient Chinese art of paper folding and make a display of students' work.

46. Teach a lesson on the ancient Chinese art of paper cutting and make a display of students' work.

Musical/Rhythmic

47. Plan a Chinese Song Showcase in which each class sings a different children's song or Chinese folk song in Chinese.

48. Invite a musician who knows how to play a Chinese instrument to do a demonstration for the class.

49. Teach a Chinese folk dance that children can perform in class.

50. Let students create a rhyme or rap song using any previously learned vocabulary words and phrases.

51. Play a favorite CD or tape of Chinese music as students enter and exit the classroom.

52. Let students listen to Chinese background music while they work on art projects in class.

53. Invite students to sing a Chinese song over the intercom once a week in March.

54. Encourage students to sing the Chinese version of "Happy Birthday to you" for people who celebrate their birthday in March.

55. Let students practice singing familiar English songs that are translated in Chinese in both languages.

56. Let students make up a Chinese song using previously learned vocabulary words and phrases and the tune to a familiar song.

57. Let students practice counting numbers to the beat of an instrumental Chinese song.

58. Let students make up body movements that reflect the meaning of a Chinese song to go along with a new song.

59. Choose a segment of the Beijing Olympic DVD that highlights Chinese song and dance to show and discuss.

Interpersonal

60. Let students promote your Chinese language program by contributing to the school, district or town newsletter.

61. Invite guest speakers with a Chinese background to discuss their experiences related to learning Chinese and Chinese culture.

62. Let students sample different types of Chinese food.

63. Invite parents to a Chinese lesson to make a specific project with their children.

64. Let students interview teachers, staff and family members who have visited China.

65. Let students collect recipes to compile a Chinese cookbook.

66. Schedule a group of advanced level students to teach a lesson to beginner level students.

67. Display students' work throughout the school.

68. Display students' work in the local library.

69. Host a class or school-wide Chinese trivia contest/jeopardy game.

70. Ask a trivia question related to China after the morning announcements each day in March.

71. Serve Chinese food at lunch for some days in March.

72. Let students create an e-mail communication using Chinese language.

73. Let students set up a pen pal exchange with other students who are learning Chinese or with students in China.

74. Inform students about any appropriate Chinese Cultural Arts performances that are open to the public in the school's vicinity.

75. Make a display of books and videos about Chinese in the school or public library.

76. Host a party for local exchange students with Chinese food and music.

77. Organize an exchange student program.

78. Make a collection for a cause related to China such as "Pennies for Pandas" to the World Wildlife Fund.

79. Organize a Chinese talent show for students to participate by telling a story, singing, dancing or acting out a simple skit in Chinese.

80. Set up a video conference with students in another school who are learning Chinese or with a class in China.

Intrapersonal

81. Let students participate in a poster contest with Chinese themes.

82. Allow students to brainstorm about ways to celebrate Foreign Language Month and support their efforts to implement their ideas.

83. Introduce a current topic in China's current events and encourage students to express their opinions and feelings about it in a discussion or in a written assignment.

84. Let students look at pictures of children who live in China and compare their physical surroundings with children who live in our country.

85. Let students create a self-portrait with traditional Chinese clothing.

86. Make a puppet and make up a little puppet show for the class.

87. Designate one day in March as "Chinese Lucky Color Day" and ask students to wear red, yellow or gold.

88. Let students learn about some famous Chinese people and how they achieved success.

89. Let students explore online Chinese resources that interest them.

90. Let students play online Chinese games.

91. Let students learn about the many inventions from ancient China and discuss their impact and importance.

92. Let students read and discuss books with Chinese themes.

93. Let students create a slogan, banner or poster about learning Chinese and explain it to the class.

94. Let students design and make a kite. If possible, take the class outdoors to fly it.

95. Let students learn about a typical day in the life of a student in China and compare it with a typical day in a student's life here.

Naturalist

96. Let students make a 3-dimensional map of China.

97. Let students explore the climate phenomenon of different regions in China. Make a weather report about the weather in some of China's major cities.

98. Let students make a list of animals that are indigenous to China and choose one to research.

99. Let students learn about the history of problems associated with China's Yellow and Yangtze Rivers and the Three Gorges Dam that was built to alleviate those problems.

100. Let students learn about some typical designs prevalent in Chinese structures like pagodas, temples and bridges and make drawings or models of them.

庆祝外语月100条

1. 让学生把一份报道近期中文教学内容的校讯带回家。

2. 让学生在班上收听当地中文电台。

3. 要求学校以中文传达一部分的每日公告。

4. 布置家庭作业，让学生教导家人一些中文词汇。

5. 让学生研究一个关于中国的课题，然后以口述方式呈现给班上同学。

6. 用录音带或录影带录下每位学生的自我介绍。

7. 让学生准备一出短剧，表演给同学看。

8. 让学生用汉字写出一份学校午餐菜单。

9. 让学生利用简单的中文词语复述一个家喻户晓的儿童故事。

10. 让学生学习使用一个网上的英汉词典。

11. 让学生制作一个绘画文字本。

12. 让学生用中文书写一篇文章或日记。

13. 让学生用毛笔和宣纸练习书写汉字，再把学生的作品做成一张汉字百衲被。

14. 让学生主持或参加一个作文比赛。

15. 让学生主持或参加一个海报设计比赛。

16. 让学生以中文设计不同的贺卡。学生可以"订购"同学们所做的贺卡复本。

17. 让学生主持一场中文诗歌比赛。

18. 让学生参加由外语机构如NYSALT所赞助的活动。

19. 将三月里的某一天定为"中文日"。鼓励学生多说中文。

20. 向在学校里学习中文的学生介绍中文绕口令。

21. 让学生利用一个熟悉的词汇表设计中文字谜，然后和同学一起玩。

逻辑、数理方面

22. 制作七巧板谜题。

23. 让学生用中文数数字以及玩数字游戏。

24. 让学生用中文数字布置专题作业。

25. 让学生用中文数字算数。

26. 让学生找出万里长城的长度和宽度。

27. 让学生利用名人出生年份找出他们所属的生肖。

28. 让学生为中文课里所教的某个主题收集数据，做成图表。

视像、艺术方面

29. 筹备一个特别的"中文电影日"。观赏并讨论一部中文电影，如《花木兰》或《西游记》。

30. 录下一个中文电视台的部分节目或新闻报道，然后在班上播放，看学生能够了解多少。

31. 播放关于中国的生活或华人家庭生活的短片，探讨中华文化与其他文化的异同。

32. 让学生制作一张长城拼贴图。画出长城的轮廓，然后将它贴在墙上或布告栏上。鼓励学生带关于中华文化的任何东西，贴在墙上，做成班级贴拼图。

33. 让学生设计一个旅游小册子，介绍中国的某个城市。册子里要附上当地名胜地的彩照。

34. 让学生用毛笔画一幅中国山水画。将学生的作品展示在校园显眼处。

35. 让学生为班里的物件制作中文标签。

36. 让学生在互联网上观赏生活在美国动物园里的熊猫的视频。

实践操作方面

37. 示范如何烹煮一道简单的中国菜或如何泡茶。

38. 让学生到唐人街、当地中餐馆或展示中国历史或文化的博物馆做实地考察。

39. 让学生利用循环材料如纸箱制作长城模型。

40. 邀请一位专家或自愿家长来进行关于中华文化艺术的示范。

41. 和学校体操部合作，引介受欢迎的中国游戏，如乒乓、跳绳、溜溜球和毽子。

42. 制作一只毽子，然后举行一场踢毽子比赛。

43. 教导如何使用筷子，然后举行一场比赛。

44. 介绍一个传统的中国群体游戏，如老鹰捉小鸡。

45. 教导古代中国折纸艺术，然后展示学生作品。

46. 教导古代中国剪纸艺术，然后展示学生作品。

音乐、舞蹈方面

47. 举行一个中文歌曲音乐会，让各班以中文献唱一首儿歌或中国民谣。

48. 邀请一位懂得如何制作中国乐器的音乐家为学生做示范。

49. 教导一支中国民间舞蹈，让学生以小组形式呈献给班上同学。

50. 让学生利用之前学过的任何字词，创作一首韵文或说唱歌曲。

51. 在学生进出班时，播放一张中文音乐光盘或卡带。

52. 当学生在班上制作手工时，播放中文音乐。

53. 邀请学生在三月里每星期一次对着对讲机唱一首中文歌曲。

54. 鼓励学生为在三月过生日的朋友唱中文版的《生日快乐》。

55. 让学生练习以中英文演唱熟悉的、翻译成中文的英语歌曲。

56. 让学生利用之前所学的字词以及熟悉的歌曲旋律来创作一首中文歌曲。

57. 让学生跟着一首中文歌曲的节奏，练习数数字。

58. 让学生设计能够表达某一首中文歌曲含义的肢体动作，以配合那首歌曲。

59. 从北京奥运会的影碟中节选出一段关于中文歌曲和舞蹈的内容，播放给学生看，然后一起讨论。

人际互动方面

60. 让学生投稿校刊、区刊或镇刊以推广你的中文计划。

61. 邀请拥有中文背景的嘉宾来分享他们学习中文以及中华文化的经验。

62. 让学生品尝不同种类的中国菜。

63. 邀请家长参加一堂中文课，和他们的孩子一起做手工。

64. 让学生访问曾到过中国的教师、职员以及家人。

65. 让学生收集食谱以汇编成一本中文烹饪书。

66. 让一群高年级学生为低年级学生上一堂课。

67. 在校园各处展示学生作品。

68. 在当地图书馆展示学生作品。

69. 举办一个班级或全校中文问答比赛。

70. 在三月每天早上的晨报后，问一道和中国有关的小问题。

71. 在三月的某些日子为学生提供中式午餐。

72. 让学生利用中文写电子邮件。

73. 让学生和其他正在学中文或在中国的学生通信。

74. 通知学生有关学校附近、开放给公众的任何适合的中文文化艺术表演的信息。

75. 在学校或公共图书馆里展示中文书籍以及视频。

76. 为本地的交换生举办一个派对，提供中式食品和中文音乐。

77. 举办一个学生交流活动。

78. 为某个和中国有关的志工项目筹款，例如给世界自然基金会的"保护熊猫小额基金"。

79. 为学生举办一个才艺秀，让他们以中文讲故事、唱歌、跳舞或表演短剧。

80. 和其他学校正在学习中文的学生，或和在中国学校的一班学生开视频会议。

挑战自我方面

81. 让学生参加一个具有中文主题的海报设计比赛。

82. 让学生想出庆祝外语月的方式，并协助他们落实计划。

83. 提出一个和中国有关的时事课题，鼓励学生通过讨论或书写的方式表达看法和意见。

84. 让学生为自己画一幅穿着传统中国服装的个人塑像图。

85. 制作一个木偶并为学生准备一场小型的木偶戏。

86. 将三月其中一天定为"中国吉祥颜色日"，让学生在那天穿红色、黄色或金色的衣服上学。

87. 让学生看看生活在中国的孩子的照片，比较两地孩子的生活环境。

88. 让学生阅读一些著名华人成功的奋斗史。

89. 让学生搜索一些能够引发他们学习兴趣的网上中文资源。

90. 让学生玩中文网络游戏。

91. 让学生认识中国古代的发明，讨论它们对后世的影响及重要性。

92. 让学生阅读并讨论具有中文主题的书籍。

93. 让学生制作一个有关学习中文的标语、横幅或海报，然后解释给同学听。

94. 让学生设计并制作一只风筝。可能的话，带全班到户外放风筝。

95. 让学生认识中国学生的日常作息，并将之与本地学生的作比较。

自然地理方面

96. 让学生制作一张立体的中国地图。

97. 让学生查一查中国不同地方的气候。准备一份关于中国一些主要城市的气象报告。

98. 让学生列出生长在中国的动物。选择其中一个进行研究。

99. 让学生了解中国黄河与长江一直以来所带来的问题，以及为解决这些问题而建造的长江三峡大坝。

100. 让学生认识中国建筑物中的一些典型设计，如宝塔、寺庙和桥梁，然后根据设计作画或制作模型。

中文奖状

CHINESE LANGUAGE

Certificate of Achievement

gōng xǐ

恭喜！ Congratulations!

Awarded to

_____

Student's Name

For Achievement of Participation in
the Study of Chinese Language and Culture

_____

Signature of Principal

_____

Signature of Chinese Teacher

_____

Issue Date

语言：Communication

听：

说：

读：

写：

语法：

文化：Cultures

本课主题 Topic

其他学科贯连：Connections

英语或其他外语：

数学：

自然科学：

音乐：

美术：

体育：

比较：Comparisons

_____ VS._____

同：

异：

社区应用：Communities

名字：———

mouth	ear	man	ox	big	up	water	sun
heart	eye	woman	sheep	small/little	down	fire	moon
son	hand	field	horse	middle	person	wood	mountain

名字：

gold	foot	big river	you	winter	left	we, us, they	sky
door	body	jade	I, me	wind	right	name	rice
shellfish	beans	stone	he, him	rain	east	word	soil

N
W ← E
S

word	grass	river	spring	fish	west	flower	morning
food	worm	clothing	summer	friend	south	country	more
boat	bird	knife	autumn	friend	north	bamboo	some

Use these reward coupons as an incentive for students to demonstrate good behavior and/or performance. Students who accumulate 100 points can trade them in for a free homework pass or some other appropriate prize. (It is recommended to print this page on color paper.)

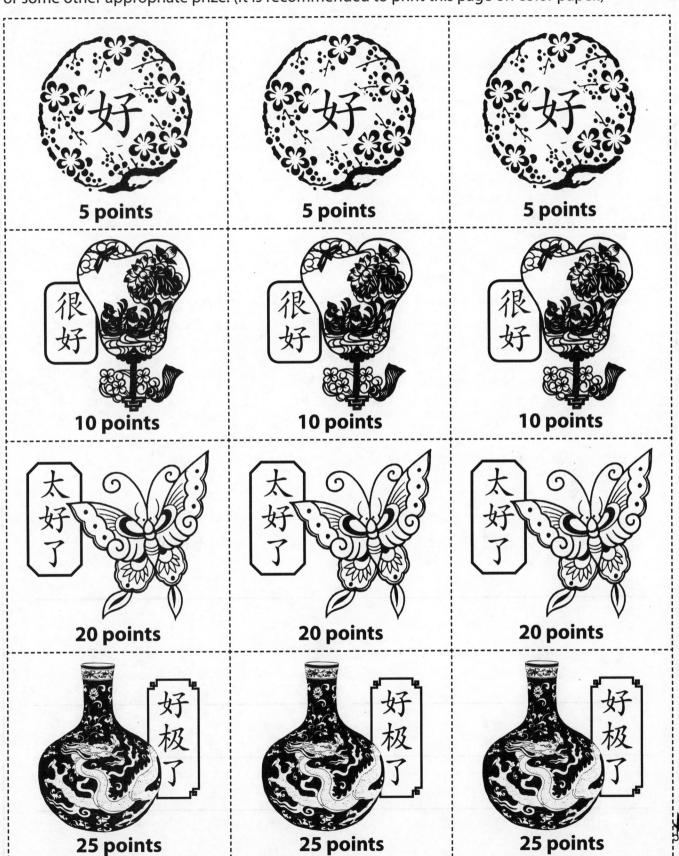

5 points	**5 points**	**5 points**
10 points	**10 points**	**10 points**
20 points	**20 points**	**20 points**
25 points	**25 points**	**25 points**

名字：＿＿＿＿＿＿＿＿＿＿＿＿＿＿＿　＿＿＿月＿＿＿日

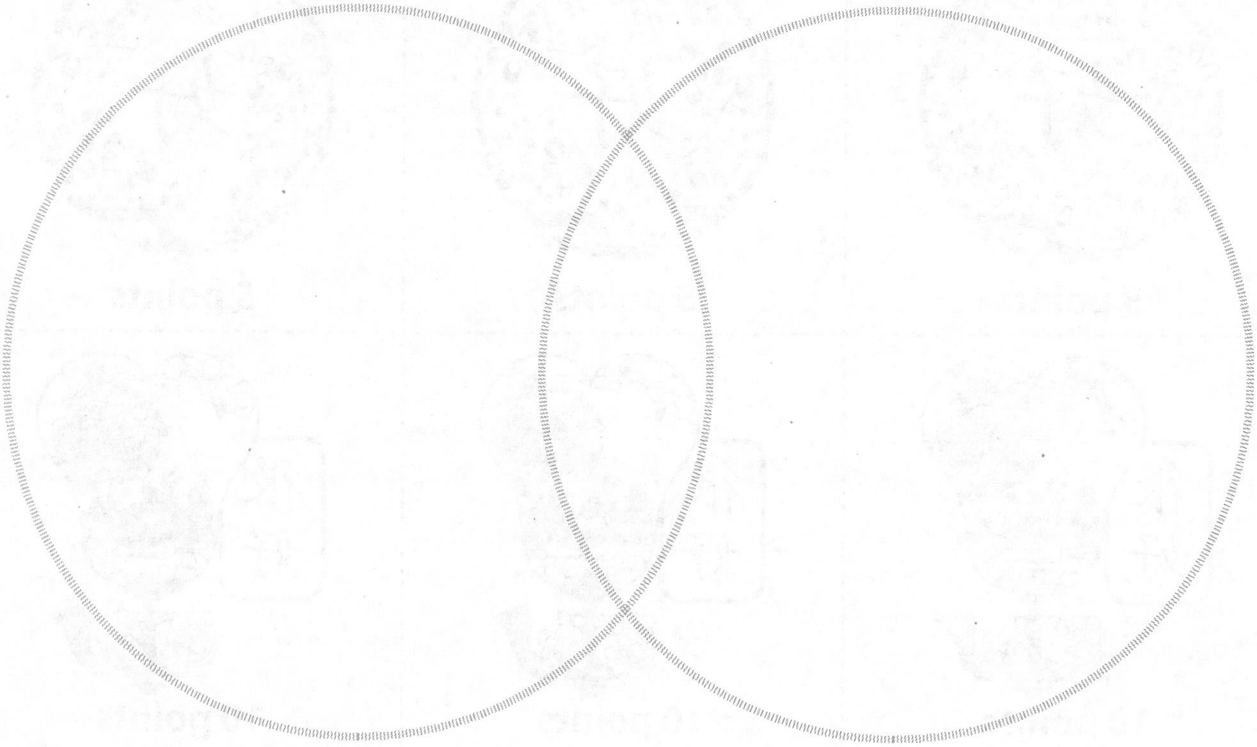

（相同）　　　　　　　　　　　　　　（不相同）

_____　　_____

_____　　_____

_____　　_____

_____　　_____

名字：_____

_____月 _____日

名字：＿＿＿＿＿＿

月＿＿日

作文题目

FREE

BINGO 宾果游戏卡

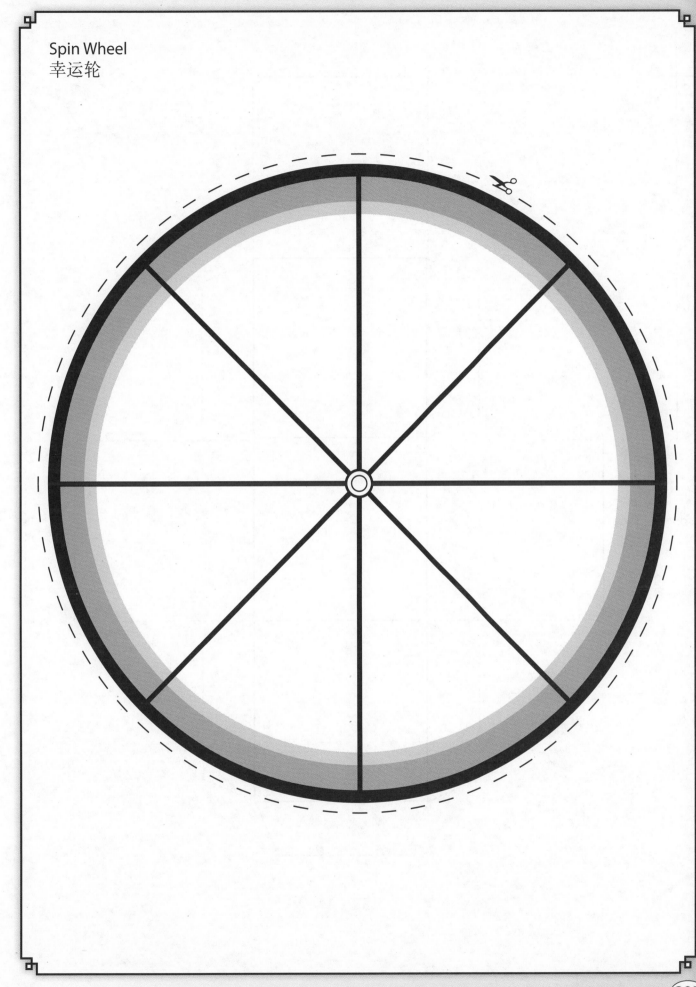

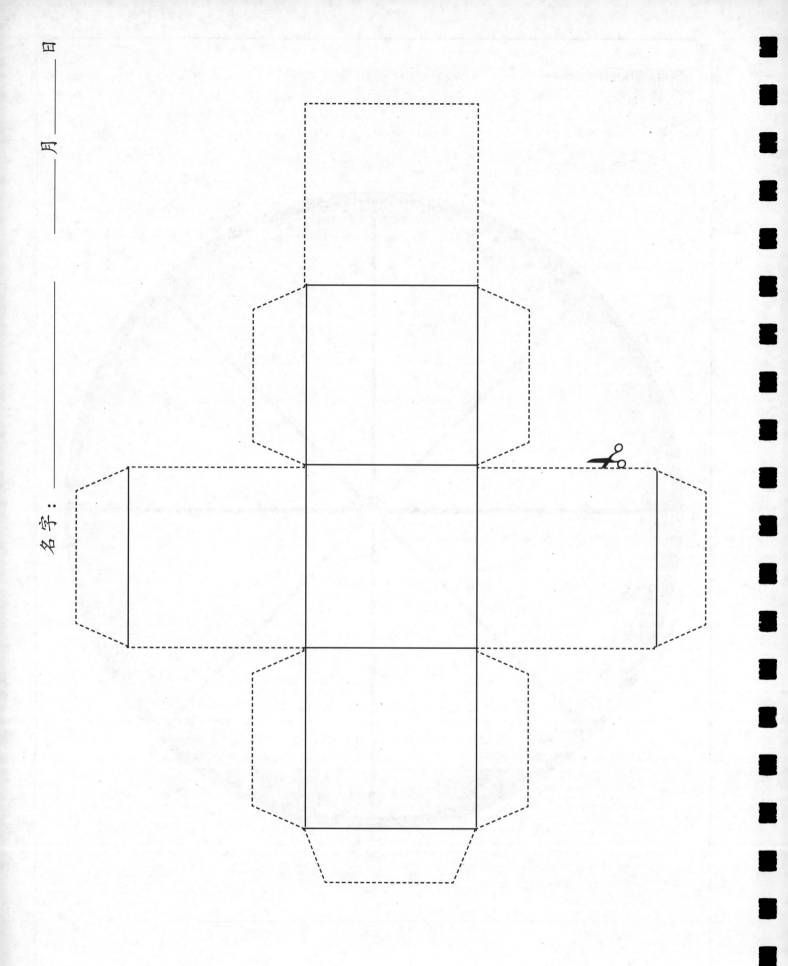

名字：

měi guó
美 国
United States of America (U.S.A.)

zhōng guó
中国
China

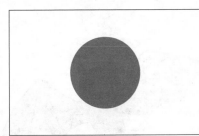

rì běn
日本
Japan

yīng guó
英国
England (United Kingdom)

fǎ guó
法国
France

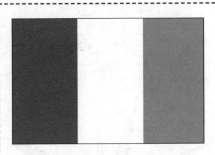

yì dà lì
意 大 利
Italy

jiā ná dà
加 拿 大
Canada

mò xī gē
墨 西 哥
Mexico

ào dà lì yà
澳 大 利 亚
Australia

dé guó
德国
Germany

é guó
俄国
Russia

hán guó
韩国
Korea

hēi sè
黑色

bái sè
白色

hóng sè
红色

lǜ sè
绿色

huáng sè
黄色

lán sè
蓝色

zōng sè
棕色

chéng sè
橙色

zǐ sè
紫色

Note: In certain areas, "棕色 *(zōng sè)*" is also known as "咖啡色 *(kā fēi sè)*", and "橙色 *(chéng sè)*" is also known as "橘子色 *(jú zi sè)*".

Project Samples
作品展示

January 一月

1) Zodiac Animal Projects
十二生肖手工艺

(See p. 5)

(See p. 5)

(See p. 5)

(See p. 5)

(See p. 5)

2) Chinese Zodiac Lantern
生肖灯笼

(See pp. 5, 91)

3) Zodiac Animal Necklace, Headband, of Banner
生肖项链、头环和条幅 (See p. 6)

4) Chinese New Year Couplets
对联 (See pp. 9, 111)

5) Paper-cut Fish
新年挂饰 (See pp. 9, 112)

6) Happy New Year Fish
"年年有余" 挂饰 (See pp. 10, 114)

7) Dragon Puppet
龙头纸偶 (See pp. 9, 113)

(See pp. 9, 113)

8) Lucky Words Paper Cuts
吉祥字剪纸 (See pp. 10, 115)

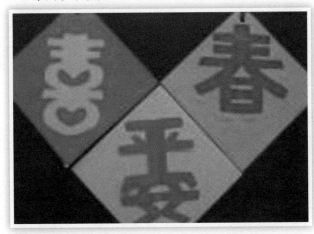

(See pp. 10, 115)

9) Red Envelope
红包 (See pp. 10, 116)

10) Firecrackers
鞭炮 (See pp. 10, 117)

(See pp. 10, 117)

(See pp. 10, 117)

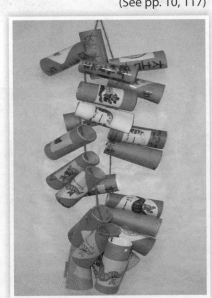

11) Chinese Lantern Paper Cut
灯笼剪纸 (See pp. 13, 125)

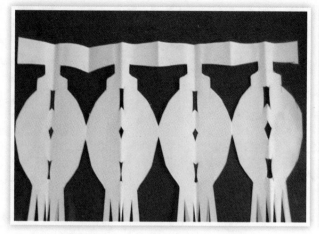

(See pp. 13, 125)

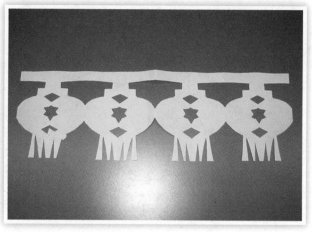

12) Chinese New Year Lantern
新年灯笼 (See pp. 13, 126)

February 二月

1) Banner Design for "100"
百日旗 (See pp. 16, 136)

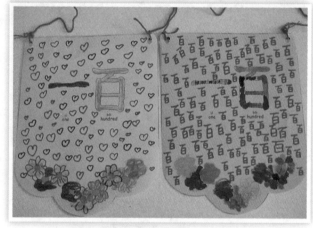

2) My Little Heart for You
我的心送给你 (See pp. 18, 143)

3) The Clock on the Great Wall
长城上的大钟 (See pp. 21, 162)

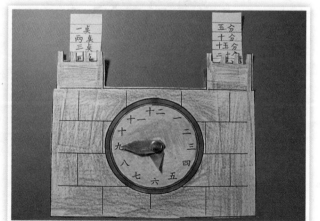

March 三月

1) Landform Model
   地形模型
   (See p. 28)

2) Chinatown Community
   唐人街社区模型
   (See p. 31)

(See p. 31)

3) Paper Cuts
   剪纸
   (See pp. 35, 215)

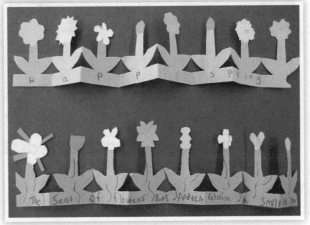

(See pp. 35, 215)

May 五月

1) Mother's Day Card
   母亲节卡片
   (See pp. 50, 283)

June 六月

1) Father's Day Shirt Card
父亲节卡片   (See pp. 55, 311)   (See pp. 55, 311)

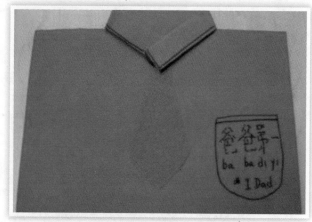 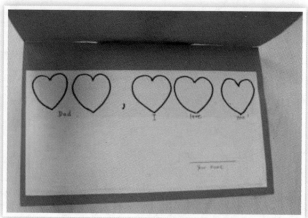

2) Dragon Boat
龙舟   (See pp. 58, 326)   (See pp. 58, 326)

July 七月

1) Peking Opera Face-Painting
京剧脸谱制作   (See pp. 61, 339)   (See pp. 61, 341)

 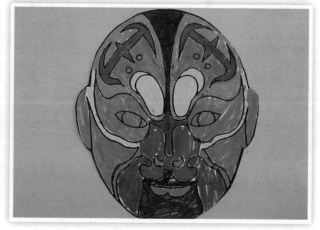

(See pp. 61, 340)   (See pp. 61, 341)

2) Origami Fun
    趣味折纸   (See pp. 62, 342)

3) Tangram Fun
    七巧板   (See pp. 62, 343)   (See pp. 62, 343)

   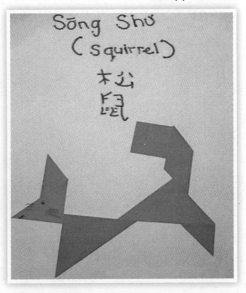

About the Authors

Marisa Fang 林宛芊

Originally from Taiwan, lead author Marisa Fang graduated from Fu Jen University, majoring in Spanish. She then received her M.S. degree in New York and taught ESL for four years before becoming a Chinese teacher. She is also Board Treasurer of the Chinese Language Teachers' Association of Greater New York, co-author of *Chinese Treasure Chest Volumes 1 and 2* (Cengage Learning, 2008, 2010), *Chinese 123 – I Sing Along* (2009), *Flying with Chinese* (2007 - Now), and *Chinese Culture for Children* (2004, 2005).

Helen Jung 马慕贞

Helen Jung has over 20 years of teaching experience in both Hong Kong and New York. She received her M.A. degree from SUNY at Stony Brook. Her professional interest lies in creating game-like activities that can stimulate students' learning in a fun way. She is the co-author of *Chinese Treasure Chest Volumes 1 and 2* (Cengage Learning, 2008, 2010), *Chinese 123 – I Sing Along* (2009) and *Chinese Culture for Children* (2004, 2005).

Rosemary Firestein 傅爱玫

Rosemary began studying Chinese as an undergraduate student at Temple University, and spent two years as an exchange student at Nankai University in Tianjin, China. She then received her M.Ed. degree in Foreign Language Education from Temple University's Graduate School. Rosemary taught ESL and Chinese in the Philadelphia public schools for 13 years. She is the co-author of *Chinese Treasure Chest Volumes 1 and 2* (Cengage Learning, 2008, 2010).

(From left: Rosemary Firestein, Marisa Fang, Helen Jung)

The three authors are currently teaching Chinese as a Foreign Language to American students in Plainview-Old Bethpage Central School District, Long Island, New York.

Word Search: Chinese Food
找一找：中国菜

Find the Chinese characters for the Chinese food items in the box below the puzzle.

糖	花	甜	芥	冰	芝	豆	鸡	北	酸	排	糖
京	醋	蓝	花	腐	蛋	排	糖	芥	蓝	牛	肉
豆	北	排	生	芥	牛	京	豆	蛋	腐	骨	蓝
牛	蛋	干	骨	芝	花	鸡	玉	排	芝	北	肉
冰	花	鸡	北	米	冰	米	芝	蛋	糖	京	芥
腐	汤	豆	芝	麻	汤	圆	生	鸡	干	汤	芝
骨	蛋	辣	生	糖	牛	蓝	排	汤	淇	麻	北
北	淇	京	酸	蛋	骨	北	鸡	芥	鸡	婆	酸
豆	鸭	豆	腐	干	京	腐	点	冰	糖	豆	牛
鸡	京	芝	酸	蛋	肉	甜	豆	花	淇	腐	排
汤	北	芥	骨	牛	糖	鸡	冰	酸	干	淋	京
酸	肉	汽	水	汤	腐	芥	芝	蓝	骨	蛋	鸡

1. 糖醋排骨   tāng cù pái gǔ

2. 豆腐干   dòu fu gān

3. 玉米汤   yù mǐ tāng

4. 麻婆豆腐   má pó dòu fu

5. 芥蓝牛肉   gài lán niú ròu

6. 甜点   tián diǎn

7. 北京鸭   běi jīng yā

8. 酸辣汤   suān là tāng

9. 汽水   qì shuǐ

10. 芝麻汤圆   zhī ma tāng yuán

11. 花生   huā shēng

12. 冰淇淋   bīng qí lín

13. 芝麻鸡   zhī ma jī

14. 蛋花汤   dàn huā tāng

名字：_____ _____月_____日

Song: Rainbow Sister
儿歌：虹彩妹妹

名字：_____　____月____日

Pick and Put: What's in the Refrigerator?
排一排，放一放：冰箱里有什么？

Organize the food items in the refrigerator.

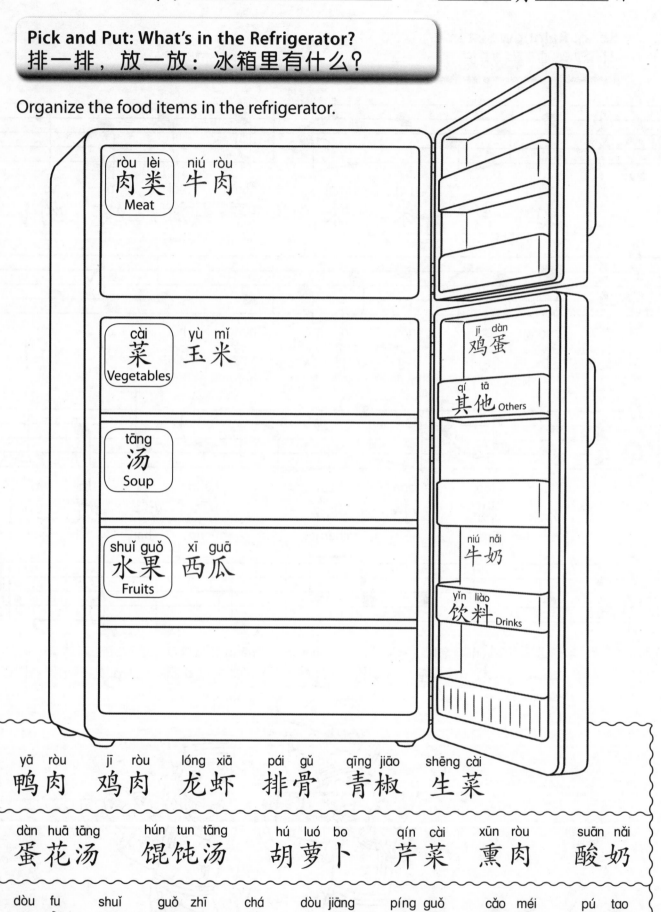

ròu lèi	niú ròu
肉类	牛肉
Meat	

cài	yù mǐ
菜	玉米
Vegetables	

| tāng |
| 汤 |
| Soup |

shuǐ guǒ	xī guā
水果	西瓜
Fruits	

jī dàn
鸡蛋

qí tā
其他 Others

niú nǎi
牛奶

yǐn liào
饮料 Drinks

| yā ròu | jī ròu | lóng xiā | pái gǔ | qīng jiāo | shēng cài |
| 鸭肉 | 鸡肉 | 龙虾 | 排骨 | 青椒 | 生菜 |

| dàn huā tāng | hún tun tāng | hú luó bo | qín cài | xūn ròu | suān nǎi |
| 蛋花汤 | 馄饨汤 | 胡萝卜 | 芹菜 | 熏肉 | 酸奶 |

| dòu fu | shuǐ guǒ zhī | chá | dòu jiāng | píng guǒ | cǎo méi | pú tao |
| 豆腐 | 水果汁 | 茶 | 豆浆 | 苹果 | 草莓 | 葡萄 |

Art Project: Mother's Day Card
创意手工：母亲节卡片

Follow the steps below to make this paper cut. Then paste the paper cut onto a card as a front page design. Write your special message to your mother inside the hearts.

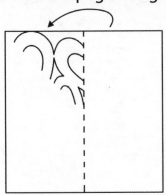

1. Fold the square paper in half.

2. Fold again in half to form a small square.

3. Fold again in half to form a triangle.

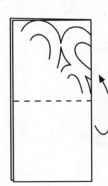

4. Cut out the shape accordingly.

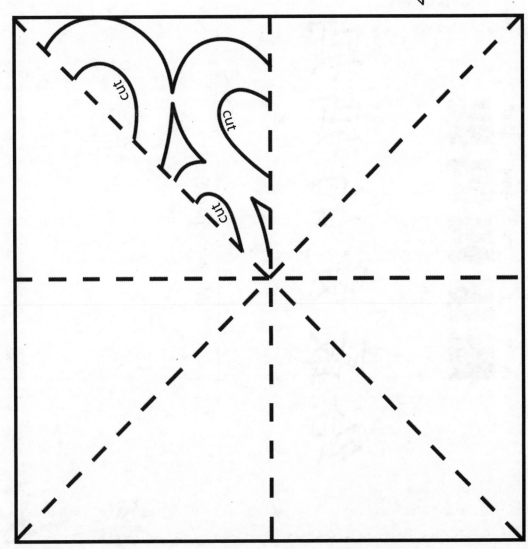

Note: See p. 399 for a sample.

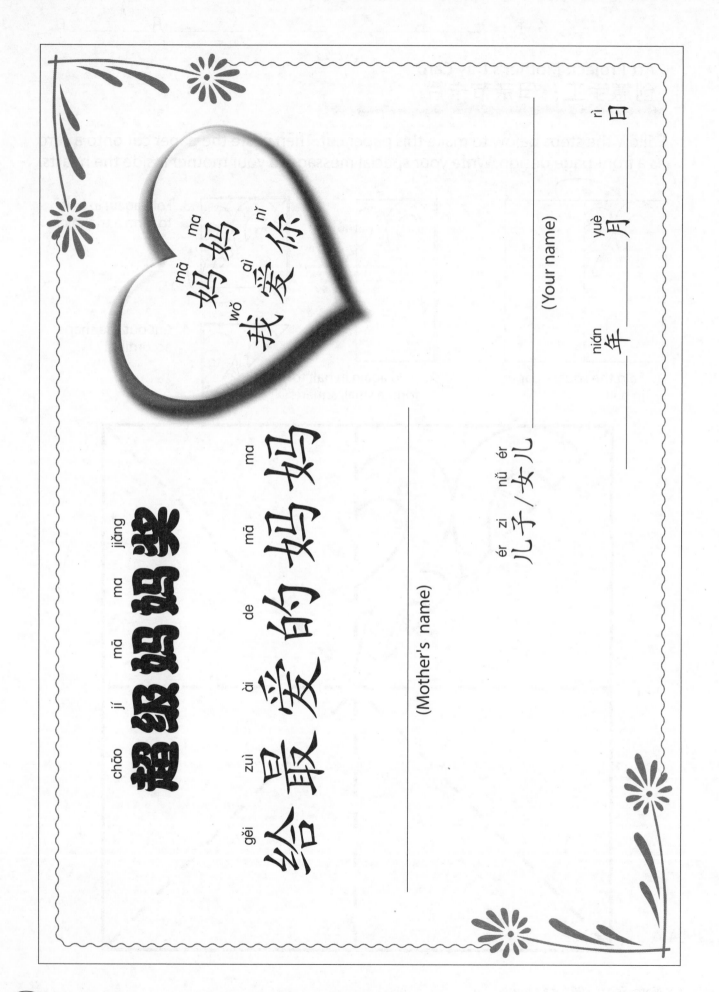

mā ma
妈妈
wǒ ài nǐ
我 爱 你

chāo jí mā ma jiǎng
超级妈妈奖

de mā ma
的 妈妈

gěi zuì ài
给 最 爱

_____
(Mother's name)

ér zi nǚ ér
儿子/女儿

nián yuè rì
年____ 月____ 日____

(Your name)